"It is often remarked, but seldom demonstrated, that Methodists learn their theology through hymns. S T Kimbrough, Jr., has given us the gift of a close reading of Charles Wesley as both a theologian and a practitioner of music, as what Kimbrough calls a 'lyrical theologian.' Kimbrough sees Wesley's work as both catechetical and formative in the life of the church that sings his hymns. By giving a theological ordering to the hymns and sacred poetry, Kimbrough has greatly enhanced Methodism's reception of its greatest hymnodist. This book will be a standard for all who study and practice Charles Wesley's lyrical theology."

 —M. Douglas Meeks
 Cal Turner Chancellor Professor of Theology and Wesleyan Studies
 Vanderbilt University Divinity School

"S T Kimbrough, Jr., rescues the poetic eloquence and relevance of Charles Wesley for contemporary theological readers . . . This book will make his lyrics immediately accessible to everyone and help deepen Methodist theological and spiritual formation for seminarians, clergy persons as well as laity. After five hundred years, it is time, albeit rather belatedly, to balance his significance with his brother, John Wesley's importance, for the spiritual movement that they both helped ground and develop, with his vivid biblical imagination and inspiring sound."

 —Young-Ho Chun
 Professor of Systematic Theology
 Saint Paul School of Theology

"By a skillful combination of literary analysis, doctrinal exposition, and historical information S T Kimbrough, Jr., has identified a genre of 'lyrical theology' that finds a prime embodiment in the sacred poetry of Charles Wesley. The Wesleyan hymns in particular have for long shaped the theological memory of the Methodist movement, and their classic expression of the Christian faith as well as their fervent encouragement of the Christian life suit them also for ecumenical service."

 —Geoffrey Wainwright
 Robert Earl Cushman Professor of Christian Theology
 Duke Divinity School

The Lyrical Theology of Charles Wesley

The Lyrical Theology of Charles Wesley

A READER

S T Kimbrough, Jr.

CASCADE *Books* · Eugene, Oregon

THE LYRICAL THEOLOGY OF CHARLES WESLEY
A Reader

Cascade Books
An Imprint of Wipf and Stock Publishers
199 W. 8th Ave., Suite 3
Eugene, OR 97401

www.wipfandstock.com

ISBN 13: 978-1-60608-653-7

Cataloging-in-Publication data:

Kimbrough, S. T., 1936–

The lyrical theology of Charles Wesley : a reader / S T Kimbrough, Jr.

xx + 340 p. ; 23 cm. — Includes bibliographical references and indexes.

ISBN 13: 978-1-60608-653-7

1. Wesley, Charles, 1707–1788. 2. English poetry—History and criticism—18th
century. I. Author.

BX8495.W4 K56 2011

Manufactured in the U.S.A.

This volume is dedicated to
Steven Forris Kimbrough (1958–2010),
my son, faithful brother and father, gifted poet, and best friend.

"O for the touch of a vanished hand,
And the sound of a voice that is still!"

ALFRED LORD TENNYSON

Contents

1. . The numbers in parenthesis indicate the numbers of the poetical selections, pages 111–275.

Contents

Contents

Preface

One of the difficulties in studying the theology of Wesleyan hymns and sacred poems is that since it is couched in a literary and liturgical art form, it does not fit into the usual intellectual paths defined over the last two centuries for the study of theology, which tends to be a prose endeavor. Charles Wesley composed a number of thematic collections of hymns, such as those based on the Christian year, e.g., *Hymns for the Nativity of our Lord, Hymns for our Lord's Resurrection, Hymns for Ascension-Day, Hymns for Whitsunday*, but his lyrics on a plethora of theological themes, such as sanctification, perfection, holiness, etc., are scattered throughout his over 9,000 hymns and poems from a writing and publishing career that spanned almost fifty years. One of the primary purposes of this volume is to bring together a collection of hymns and sacred poems representative of Charles Wesley's theological thinking. The texts are organized within a theological outline in order to make the study of his theological ideas and concepts more readily accessible, though many of them could be placed in diverse theological categories. By no means should one consider the placement of any text of Wesley in a specific category as the only option, since he frequently addressed many themes and issues within a single text.

The theological outline[1] used for the organization of Wesley's poetry is in five sections: (1) The Glory of the Triune God, (2) The Grace of Jesus Christ, (3) The Power of the Holy Spirit, (4) The Community of Faith, and (5) A New Heaven and a New Earth.

In the first two chapters of this volume I have sought to define lyrical theology and Charles Wesley as a lyrical theologian. It is hoped that this will assist in establishing a new approach to the theology of hymns, which

---

1. It follows generally the theological outline of *The United Methodist Hymnal* (1989), but with amplifications and additions.

is often relegated to the arena of hymnology, but not taken that seriously. It is here maintained that Charles Wesley's poetry not only represents a doxological lyrical theology, but also a theology of deep reflection, sometimes not intended for congregational singing.

In chapter 3 Wesley is set in his own context of the eighteenth century. A number of aspects of his own identity, which greatly assist one in reading his poetry more effectively, are addressed: biblical interpreter, commitment to Christ and the church, ecclesial theologian, sacramental evangelist, catholic vision, advocate of the poor. After examining briefly the historical and theological contexts of the eighteenth century within which Charles Wesley is found, the chapter concludes with an exploration of three aspects of Charles Wesley's lyrical theology whose understanding is vital for the reading and interpreting of his poetic corpus: lyrical theology as doxology, lyrical theology as a reflective process, and historically oriented lyrical theology.

The fourth chapter, "Literary and Ecclesial Sources Used in Charles Wesley's Poetry," explores some of the literary influences on Wesley which are evidenced in his verse, e.g., Shakespeare, Milton, Dryden, Prior, Young, as well as Greek and Latin poets. Wesley draws on their structure, rhyme, language, metaphors, imagery, and content. One also encounters an array of ecclesial sources in Wesley's poetry. Knowledge of them is essential to the comprehension of his lyrics. Of particular interest are the Thirty-Nine Articles of Religion, the Book of Common Prayer, the Holy Scriptures, and the Early Fathers of the Church.

Chapter 5, "The Wesleyan Poetical Sources Used in this Volume," provides the reader with a brief description of the historical and theological contexts surrounding each original Charles Wesley source from which the poems in this volume are taken.

The selection of poems follows chapter 5. Generally the hymns and poems have been included in their entirety, since contemporary hymnbooks often omit certain stanzas. For example, the eleven stanzas of "Christ the Lord is risen today" appear here, even though most hymnbooks include only four, five, or six stanzas. It is important to read the entire poem in order to grasp the fullness of what Wesley is saying through his lyrics. In a few instances selected parts of lengthy poems have been included. Where a text has been edited, the original text is indicated in a footnote. Where Wesley is reflecting on a biblical text, it is cited in a footnote in the Authorized or King James Version, since this is the text Wesley was using.

Where Wesley gave titles to his hymns and poems, they are included. Where he did not, first lines or other lines have been added as titles for explanatory purposes. The sources for the poems are noted in the footnotes.

It is not the intent in this volume to provide an extended discussion of or commentary on the content of the poems included here, but rather to aid readers of Wesley's poetry, as far as possible, to become authentic interpreters of his lyrical theology. While Wesley unquestionably addressed many theological ideas, they are couched in the language of poetry. Poetical language is multi-faceted and, just as one sees many different colors when one turns a diamond in the light, so it is with theology expressed in poetry. That does not mean, however, that one may simply see and hear in Wesley's poetry what one wishes. There are times his position is unequivocally clear. There are other times when his theology is nuanced by the Holy Scriptures, time, events, literature, political and ecclesial currents, heated theological debates of his own time, and the turn of a phrase. Many aspects of his faith interpretation are influenced by context, language, and the social location of knowledge. So often the language of poetry allows the Mystery to be a mystery, something with which Charles Wesley seems to be more comfortable than his brother John.

It is hoped that the background provided here for reading Wesley's poetry will enable new understanding of his texts and appropriate, meaningful interpretation of his lyrical theology that is faithful to his time and relevant to the present.

S T Kimbrough, Jr.
Research Fellow
Center for Studies in the Wesleyan Tradition
The Divinity School
Duke University
Durham, NC

Acknowledgments

Deep appreciation is expressed to two theological institutions for the opportunity to teach courses on the theme of this book, "lyrical theology"—as a Bell Scholar at The Theological School of Drew University and as a Distinguished Guest scholar in residence at Wesley Theological Seminary in Washington DC. Both experiences helped shape the form and content of this volume. Gratitude is also expressed to Randy Maddox of The Divinity School of Duke University for his helpful comments regarding the approach to this subject and to Charles A. Green for assistance in technical matters and copyediting.

Abbreviations

Short Titles and Abbreviations for Poetry/Hymn Publications by John and Charles Wesley

Ascension Hymns (1746)	*Hymns for Ascension-Day*, 1746	[#121][2]
Collection (1780)	*A Collection of Hymns for the Use of the People Called Methodists*	[#408]
CPH (1737)	*A Collection of Psalms and Hymns*, 1737	[#8]
CPH (1738)	*A Collection of Psalms and Hymns*, 1738	[#9]
CPH (1741)	*A Collection of Psalms and Hymns*, 1741	[#44]
CPH (1743)	*A Collection of Psalms and Hymns*, (2nd ed. of 1741, 1743)	[#44]
Earthquake Hymns (1750)	*Hymns occasioned by the Earthquake* (Pt. I, 1750; Pts. I & II, joint reprint, 1756)	[#181]
	(Pt. II, 1750)	[#182]
Family Hymns (1767)	*Hymns for the Use of Families*, 1767	[#299]
Fast Day Hymns (1782)	*Hymns for the Nation in 1782* and *Hymns for the National Fast, Feb. 8, 1782* (in two parts)	[#422, 423]
Festival Hymns (1746)	*Hymns on the Great Festivals, and other occasions*, 1746	[#124]
Funeral Hymns (1746)	*Funeral Hymns*, 1746	[#115]
Funeral Hymns (1759)	*Funeral Hymns*, 1759 (enlargement of #115)	[#232]
Gloria Patri (1746)	*Gloria Patri, &c., or Hymns on the Trinity*, 1746	[#126]
HLS (1745)	*Hymns on the Lord's Supper*, 1745	[#98]
HSP (1739)	*Hymns and Sacred Poems*, 1739	[#13]
HSP (1740)	*Hymns and Sacred Poems*, 1740	[#40]
HSP (1742)	*Hymns and Sacred Poems*, 1742	[#54]
HSP (1749)	*Hymns and Sacred Poems*, 1749	[#171]

2. The numbers in this column reference the bibliographic work of Baker, *Representative Verse of Charles Wesley*, 379–94.

Abbreviations

Hymns for Children (1763)	*Hymns for Children,* 1763	[#258]
	Hymns for the Year 1756	[#214]
HTTP (1744)	*Hymns for Times of Trouble and Persecution,* 1744	[#83]
HGEL (1741)	*Hymns on God's Everlasting Love,* 1741	[#46]
HGEL (1742)	*Hymns on God's Everlasting Love,* 2nd Series, [1742]	[#47]
Hymns for the Invasion (1759)	*Hymns on the Expected Invasion,* 1759	[#233]
Intercession Hymns (1758)	*Hymns of Intercession for All Mankind,* 1758	[#225]
Intercession Hymns (1759)	*Hymns of Intercession for the Kingdom of England,* 1759	[#231]
MSP (1744)	*A Collection of Moral and Sacred Poems,* 1744	[#78]
Nativity Hymns (1745)	*Hymns for the Nativity of our Lord,* 1745	[#112]
New Year's Day Hymns (1750)	*Hymns for New Year's Day,* 1750, [1749]	[#176]
Pentecost Hymns (1746)	*Hymns of Petition and Thanksgiving for the Promise of the Father,* 1746	[#122]
Redemption Hymns (1747)	*Hymns for those that seek and those that have Redemption in the Blood of Jesus Christ,* 1747	[#140]
Resurrection Hymns (1746)	*Hymns for our Lord's Resurrection,* 1746	[#116]
Scripture Hymns (1762)	*Short Hymns on Select Passages of the Holy Scriptures,* 1762	[#249]
Select Hymns (1761)	*Select Hymns: With Tunes Annext,* 1761	[#244]
Select Hymns (1765)	*Select Hymns, etc.* (2nd edn. of 1761, enlarged), 1765	[#244]
Thanksgiving Hymns (1746)	*Hymns for the Public Thanksgiving-Day, October 9, 1746*	[#125]
Thanksgiving Hymns (1759)	*Hymns to be used on the Thanksgiving-Day, Nov. 29, 1759*	[#237]
Trinity Hymns (1767)	*Hymns on the Trinity,* 1767	[#302]

Other Abbreviations

AV/KJV	King James Version of the Bible (1611); Authorized Version of the Church of England
BCP	Book of Common Prayer
CW Journal	S T Kimbrough, Jr., and Kenneth G. C. Newport, editors. *The Manuscript Journal of the Rev. Charles Wesley, M.A.,* 2 vols. Nashville: Abingdon, 2007.

Poet. Works	George Osborn, editor. *The Poetical Works of John and Charles Wesley*, 13 vols. London: Wesleyan-Methodist Conference Office, 1868–1872.
PWHS	*Proceedings of the Wesley Historical Society*. Ilford: Robert Odcombe Associates, date as appropriate. Previous publishers: Ashworth Nuttall, Alfred A. Taberer.
PCWS	*Proceedings of The Charles Wesley Society*. Madison, NJ: The Charles Wesley Society, date as appropriate.
Rep. Verse	Frank Baker, editor. *Representative Verse of Charles Wesley*. London: Epworth, 1962.
Unpub. Poetry	S T Kimbrough, Jr., and Oliver A. Beckerlegge, editors. *The Unpublished Poetry of Charles Wesley*, 3 vols. Nashville: Abingdon/Kingswood, 1988, 1990, 1992.

Technical Matters

1. The poems that appear in the section, "Poetical Selections," are quoted from the first editions or printings in which they appeared. Generally original spelling and punctuation have been preserved. The capitalization of proper nouns has not been retained.

2. Though Charles Wesley's style of headings for poems was quite varied, each poem has been given a title.

   - If a hymn has a specific number, e.g., Hymn 21, that is indicated in the footnotes.

   - Sometimes Wesley simply gives a poem a number. This is indicated in the footnotes by "No." followed by the designated number.

   - The poems quoted from *Scripture Hymns* (1762) are usually preceded in the original source by sequential numbers and verses of Scripture. The volume and page number, along with the Scripture reference and text, are given in the footnotes. Some poems from other sources also include headings with Scripture references, and most of these are retained.

   - Many titles are Wesley's own; however, some titles have been added for explanatory purposes. If the heading or title at the beginning of a poem appears in the edition of the poem quoted, this is indicated by the words "original title" in the footnote and original capitalizations of words are retained. When a title has been added to a poem by use of its first line or other line/phrase of the poem, only the first word and proper names are capitalized.

- Each poem title is preceded by a chronological reference number for this volume.

3. Original sources and locations of the poems are indicated in the footnotes.

4. Occasionally Wesley changed the wording in a later edition of the poem for clarity or to correct an error in diction or meter. Where important, this is noted.

5. The entire texts of the poems, i.e., all stanzas, are included here, except where otherwise indicated.

6. Generally Wesley's spellings are retained; however, verb forms in the past tense are spelled in full, e.g. finish'd = finished. Some archaic spellings have been modernized, e.g. burthen = burden, antient = ancient, shew = show, quire = choir. Capitalization is retained for proper and place names.

7. All roman numerals have been converted to arabic numerals.

8. The abbreviations of the titles of original sources are utilized as they appear in the list of sources above.

9. For full bibliographic information of works cited in the footnotes see the bibliography at the conclusion of the volume.

10. In the section titled "Poetical Selections" there are many poems by Charles Wesley based on biblical passages that he often included immediately before his poetry. He usually quoted biblical texts from the Authorized or King James Version of the Bible, though he sometimes made his own translations from Hebrew and Greek. He had a great affection for the Coverdale Version of the Psalter that appeared in the Book of Common Prayer and sometimes quoted from it. In "Poetical Selections" the quoted texts are from the AV/KJV unless otherwise indicated, since it greatly influenced his use of imagery, style, metaphors, phraseology, etc.

I

Lyrical Theology

1

Lyrical Theology[1]

The term *lyrical theology* requires considerable definition if it is to be used with clarity and integrity. Obviously the noun *theology* is itself problematic in terms of what it means to speak of a "God word" or a "word about God." Nonetheless, its constant usage, though in diverse ways, in the arenas of church and theological science makes it a familiar term used with confidence and regularity. It acquires many adjectival modifiers: *systematic* theology, *pastoral* theology, *biblical* theology, etc. Here we speak, however, of a *lyrical* theology.

The word "lyric," which derives from a song accompanied by the lyre, applied to poetry may designate a text of songlike rhythm characterized by emotional and sensual expression, as well as subjectivity. Sonnets, odes, hymns, and elegies may be lyric poetry. In other words, a lyric poem expresses emotion through verse, which possesses a songlike quality.

Lyrical theology designates a theology couched in poetry, song, and liturgy, characterized by rhythm and expressive of emotion and sentiment. One may speak of lyrical prose, and much of our understanding of what theology means and is, is bound to the prose page. Certainly the content and boundaries of continental theology, of which North Americans in particular are often the well-meaning but wrong-headed inheritors, is ensconced in the world of prose.

1. The author expresses deep appreciation to Dubuque Theological Seminary of Dubuque, Iowa, and to United Theological Seminary of Dayton, Ohio, for lecture opportunities, which provided the impetus for the precipitation of the ideas expressed in this chapter, originally published in the *Journal of Theology* [Dayton, OH] (1994) 18–43, and which has been in part adapted for this volume.

Theology of Song

Lyrical theology, then, is a "sung" theology, or at least a theology expressed in poetry and song. This means that the mode of expressing what we so often are accustomed to hear and see in prose comes to fruition in a different world of language. Of course, the diverse definitions of "poetry" which saturate the world of literature are as varied as its distinguished authors. T. S. Eliot views poetry as an experiential, structured organic unit, which combines numerous resources of language.[2] For Hart Crane poetry requires saturation with words in order for appropriate patterns to be distilled at the proper moment. Henry Vaughan claims:

> O! 'tis an easy thing
>   To write and sing;
> But to write true, unfeigned verse
> Is very hard! O God, despise
> These weights, and give my spirit leave
> To act as well as to conceive.[3]

Foreboding indeed is the task of poets, for they are mortals *and* artists; their verse issues from a mysterious inner effervescence of soul and spirit, as well as from the conscious exercise of technical discipline. They bring together life and language; they wed method and meaning. Vital to the understanding of their creative process, however, is the realization that no matter what gives birth to the poem—be it emotion, sense, character, scene, event, insight, idea—it is not born nor developed in a vacuum. It has a context in the world, a social location.

When we imagine a world without poetry and poets, it is a deeply unsatisfying image. To poetry and poets we owe the pleasure of sensation, the awakening of the senses, exhilaration, ecstasy, the voice of conscience, the awareness of morality, truth, and justice. In their words, metaphors, similes, figures of speech, and imagery we see our own lives pass before our eyes. As Tanner says in Shaw's *Man and Superman,* "The Artist's work is to show us ourselves as we really are. Our minds are nothing but this

---

2. See Eliot, *Selected Essays,* especially the chapters "Tradition and the Individual Talent," "The Function of Criticism," "A Dialogue on Dramatic Poetry"; and also his *Essays Ancient and Modern.*

3. Drew, *Poetry,* 19.

knowledge of ourselves and he who adds a jot to such knowledge creates new mind."[4]

What of the distinction between poetry and prose, especially when we discuss theology? Will it serve us well? Will it help us with Henry Vaughan "to act as well as to conceive?" No doubt most of what is written in poetry could be reduced to prose, especially whatever "message" is found therein, but poetry is not measured by its claims or assertions about life, rather by the way it perceives, illuminates, and creates moods and intensity.

Finally, I turn to Yeats for a description of poetry which is essential to a discussion of lyrical theology: "It is blood, imagination, intellect running together. . . . It bids us touch and taste and hear and see the world, and shrink from all that is of the brain only, from all that is not a fountain jetting from the entire hopes, memories and sensations of the body."[5] In other words, poetry engages, vitalizes, and animates mind and body.

Poetry, however, is not merely printed or written word. It is a symphony of sounds, rhythmical patterns, metaphorical language, and imagery. And words we sometimes hear daily take on different meaning or come to mean more in the context of poetical language and song than they do in normal usage.

Unquestionably books are filled with the pros and cons of what constitutes the best kind of poetical expression—rhymed or free verse, for example. Even great poets differ on the qualities of poetry, which should constantly characterize it. Here are but a few examples. On the sounds of poetry Alexander Pope says, "The sounds must seem an echo of the sense."[6] Robert Frost claims that the imagery of poetry often says one thing and means another.[7] Coleridge comments on the words of poetry: "The best words in their best order."[8]

---

4. Shaw, *Man and Superman*, 16.

5. Yeats, *Autobiography*; see also *Discoveries* and *The Cutting of an Agate*.

6. Drew, *Poetry*, 19.

7. Frost, "Constant Symbol," and "Figure a Poem Makes."

8. Coleridge, *Biographia Literaria*, 183.

Biblical Poetry

Given such comments about poetry, one asks—How do they apply to sacred poetry, biblical poetry? What of the Psalms as poetry—Do the sounds echo the sense? Does the imagery of the Psalms say one thing and mean another? Do the Psalms indeed provide the best words in their best order? Is the design of the Psalms "performance in words"? We may have "yes/no/but" answers to all of these questions, because of our perspective on the Psalms as sacred poetry, as the Word of God, as a Word and as words from God somehow communicated to us through the Holy Spirit. Nevertheless, we cannot expect that the human creativity expressed in poetic art has been nullified by divine intervention, since this art is so blatantly evident in the Psalms.

Let us ask a more basic question. Why does theology embody lyric song? It is because there is a need for the lyric in a fallen world, and human need is the author of lyricism. What is the world's song? It is as diverse as the need. It is not only a song of anguish and death, but one of jubilation and celebration. But some cry out in the midst of suffering and destruction for silence:

> By the rivers of Babylon,
>> there we sat down and wept,
>> when we remembered Zion.
> On the willows there
>> we hung up our lyres.
> For there our captors
>> required of us songs,
>> and our tormentors, mirth, saying,
> "Sing us one of the songs of Zion!"
> How shall we sing the Lord's song
>> in a foreign land? (Ps 137:1–4 RSV)

There are those who cry out in the midst of suffering in our time—can there be a song, can there be poetry after the Holocaust?

Qoheleth resounds, "There is nothing new under the sun" (Ecc 1:9). Yet, the Psalmist pleads, "Sing a new song to the Lord" (Ps 96:1). There are old songs, new songs, and old songs sung in new fashion! There is silence! And songs are a response to a fallen history. Note the verb tense in the line of the worldwide-known Civil Rights anthem "We shall overcome." The "overcoming" is in the future; it is incomplete in this world. Like so many of the biblical Psalms, this song tells the story of the human predicament in a fallen world. A song emerges from misery, pain, and joy. Hence, the art of poetry provides a paradigm of life and death, which spans the spectrum of human emotions. An old song dies, a new song is born. Hence, lyrical theology is a dynamic ongoing creative process, and its songs exist inside and outside of time. They can transcend time!

An African-American woman stood before the Texas state legislature to testify in the face of massive budget cuts in the arts a few years ago and said in essence: Give me a pair of shoes and they are gone in a year; give me a bag of groceries and they are gone in a week; give me a song and I have it for life! The song of the human soul indeed can transcend time and space and has incredible staying power to sustain.

The Psalms

Where do we turn for the songs of lyrical theology? First of all, we turn to the songbook of Scripture, the Psalms. There are other songs of the Hebrew Scriptures, but this is the largest single collection, which has continued to have an impact on Jewish and Christian traditions and worship, as well as world literature. It is fair to say that not all of them qualify technically as "lyrical," if one adheres to a strict definition of "lyric," e.g., the historical Psalms, but since by *lyrical theology* we generally mean "a sung theology," we shall not quibble over such definition.

What of the language of the Psalms? Interestingly it is precisely the poetry that is often not translated in the translation process. Even when we speak of the Psalms as the "Word of God," we must reckon with the human words and artistic form in which they come to us. When we read a Hebrew psalm with a distinct verbal sequence, embedded in rhythm and organized by a literary structure such as parallelism, we know we are in the presence of poetry. This is a characteristic of the Psalms, which is vital to their singing and reading. It identifies two parallel lines of verse, in which the second functions in different ways: it may express the idea of the first line in a different manner, it may express a contrasting idea, or further develop the idea. These three types of parallelism are commonly known as *synonymous, antithetical,* and *synthetical,* for example:

synonymous: The earth is the Lord's and the fullness thereof,
        the world and they that dwell there. (Ps 24:1 KJV)

antithetical: For the Lord knows the way of the righteous,
        but the way of the ungodly shall perish. (Ps 1:6 KJV)

synthetic: God sits in the heavens and laughs;
        the Lord holds them in derision. (Ps 2:4 own
        translation)

In addition to parallelism one finds stresses primarily of 3:3 and 3:2 within the lines of Hebrew poetry but never in the sense of Greek or Roman poetry with poets' careful observance of iambs and hexameters. While meter, such as may be designated meter, grows out of the parallel structure of Hebrew poetry, most translations pay little attention to it.

Alliteration, assonance, and word play are also characteristic of Hebrew poetry. Alliteration has to do with the repetition of the initial sound of a word or syllable in one or more closely following words or syllables. An English translation of Ps 122:6,

> Pray for the peace of Jerusalem!
> "May they prosper who love you!"

does not adequately express the musical cadence of *sh* and *l* in the Hebrew text:

> *sha^{a}lu sh^{e}lom y^{e}rushālāyim*
> *yishlayu oh^{a}vayik*

Assonance has to do with the resemblance or correspondence of sounds in accented vowels and is especially characteristic of Hebrew poetry where pronominal suffixes and verbs recur. Notice the inadequacy of the translation of Ps 23:2 to capture the assonance of the Hebrew poetry:

> The Lord makes me lie down in green pastures,
> leads me beside still waters.

The Hebrew reads:

> *binōth deshe' yarbbitsēni*
> *'al-mē m^{e}nuḥōth y^{e}naḥ^{a}lēni*

There are, of course, other characteristics of Hebrew poetry, but here we only wish to illustrate that the language is not merely a dead language on the printed page, rather one of sounds. It is created out of sounds and formed for vocalism and singing.

While parallelism is perhaps the characteristic of Hebrew poetry one can grasp best in English translation, because some translations do at least delineate parallel lines, it is extremely important for lyrical theology to be acquainted with the dynamic movement from one verse to another in Hebrew poetry. Robert Alter in *The Art of Biblical Poetry* speaks of the "impulse of intensification" as "the motor force in thousands of lines of biblical poetry."[9] Hence, he describes how one often moves from a rather standard term to a more literary one in the next line, e.g., from *qol* (voice) to *'unrah* (speech) or from *shema'an* (hear) to *ha'zena* (give ear, listen).

There is sometimes a cascading effect wrought in the Psalms by the doubling of words and intensification of dynamic meaning from line to line. For example, Ps 88:10–12:

> Do you work wonders for the dead?
>> Do the shades rise up to praise you?
> Is your steadfast love declared in the grave,
>> or your faithfulness in Abaddon?
> Are your wonders known in the darkness,
>> or your saving help in the land of forgetfulness?

There is, however, what one might call free verse in the Psalms, which makes no use of parallelism at all. Psalm 137, which has already been cited, is a primary example of a psalm that avoids parallelism throughout. In the Psalms we find parallelism that intensifies and specifies; we find dynamic reverse movement as well as forward movement, and there is also static parallelism.

It is most interesting that among the literatures of the ancient Near East biblical poetry tends to avoid narrative. The writers of the Hebrew Psalms utilize poetry for songs of celebration, lament, prophecy, oracle, reflection, liturgy, didactic argument, but rarely to tell a story. Nor do the Hebrew poets feel the need to examine nature and objects as contemporary poets do; rather they let them speak for themselves.

---

9. Alter, *Art of Biblical Poetry*, 135.

Why Biblical Poetry?

Aside from the former assertion that there is a need for a song or lyric in a fallen world, why is there poetry in the Bible? Why does one find there this mode of lyrical expression? Unquestionably some of the Psalms were indeed songs, but what makes them really different from the rest of the Bible? What difference does it make to what they say that it is expressed in poetry? After all, poetry must function via connections of sounds, rhythms, words, images, themes, ideas, specific literary structures (parallelism), and sentence structure. Miraculously this complex process in the poetry of the Psalms elucidates hidden meanings, even contradictory meanings, which are often not as readily conveyed in other forms of writing and speech. Poetical language coagulates and distills the thought, ideas, events, and emotions of the moment and enables the interrelation and future communication of them. Through poetry Israel articulated a broad spectrum of human emotions, needs, and intellect in a fallen world, from a monotheistic worldview, and in an encapsulated language of succinct verbal structures, which at times seem quite oversimplified.

Here it is important to note that lyrical theology does not require narrative theology. It assumes it. This becomes extremely clear, when one reads Psalm 8 over against Genesis 1 and 2. Psalm 8 captures the moment—the instant of perceiving the world that surrounds the psalmist. As Alter claims, "Ps. 8 is a luminous instance of how poetic structure was made to yield a picture of the world that eloquently integrated underlying elements of Israelite belief."[10] More than the narrative of Genesis 1 and 2, however, it is the short lyric poem, Psalm 8, which has the tremendous potential to evoke a sense of awe about creation, yes, even to experience creation dynamically—to feel who one is—in a way almost impossible through narrative. Psalm 8 translates the impulse of creation into the human heart. Here we have part of the genius of lyrical theology.

Notice the dynamic power of the movement between the lines of Psalm 8. Four elements characterize its parallelism.

(1) *Specification*: the majesty of God, 8:1–2,

> O Lord, our Lord,
> how majestic is your name in all the earth!

10. Ibid., 117.

> Your glory is chanted above the heavens
> > by the mouth of babes and infants;
> you have set up a defense against your foes
> > to still the enemy and the avenger.

(2) *Focusing*: the observance of creation and the value of human beings, 8:3–4,

> When I look at your heavens, the work of your fingers,
> > the moon and the stars which you have established;
> what are human beings that you are mindful of them,
> > and mortals, that you care for them?

(3) *Heightening*: the description of the place of human beings in creation, 8:5,

> Yet you have made them little less than God,
> > and crowned them with glory and honor.

(4) *Sequentiality*: the order of human dominion in creation, 8:6–8,

> You have given them dominion over the works of your hands;
> > you have put all things under their feet,
> all sheep and oxen,
> > and also the beasts of the field,
> the birds of the air, and the fish of the sea,
> > whatever passes along the paths of the seas.
> O Lord, our Lord,
> > how majestic is your name in all the earth!

Does Poetry Matter?

Having described what we mean by *lyrical theology,* located its large corpus in Holy Scripture, and addressed some aspects of biblical poetry integral to both the understanding and practice of lyrical theology, it is important to ask: Does the poetry matter? By all means, for it is the "auditory imagination" that enables fallen language to be redemptive. By "auditory imagination," I mean what T. S. Eliot describes as "the feeling for syllable and rhythm, penetrating far below the conscious level of thought and feeling, invigorating every word; sinking to the most primitive and forgotten, returning to the origin and bringing something back, seeking the beginning and the end."[11]

Language comes to us from the past, a social context, and human experience, which are as evil as ours. We are claimed by words which are not our own even when they seem elusive, obscure, confused, and weary. But this language is not dead. Bodies have given it birth, minds have thought it, hands have written, eyes have read it, tongues and lips have spoken it, bodies have responded to it. Therefore, the Christian view of Incarnation is vital to the language of lyrical theology, for the Word and words of Scripture become incarnate in the flesh. The word becomes flesh in human experience—in the flesh-experience of word. It is a human body experience. Just as the writer of a psalm attained a temporary oneness with language, so the incarnational experience of vocalizing the Psalms involves receiving though the words the breath of life breathed into them by divine Spirit. This incarnational experience is at the same time a resurrection experience, for "The best writing offers a glimpse, insofar as we are capable of imagining it, of the resurrection of the body and of more than the body."[12] This most certainly applies to the Psalms and to lyrical theology. Lyrical theology does not allow us to think of the Scriptures merely as God's Word which nullifies human experience in order to reveal itself. The words incarnate themselves in human bodies—minds and hearts, heads and hands, lips and mouth, diaphragm and pharynx. There is an incarnational power of biblical language we cannot know and experience until we engage the Psalms in singing, chanting, and oral reading. What Wordsworth says at the end of Book 5 of *The Prelude* applies here to the Psalms.

> Visionary power
> Attends the motions of the viewless winds,
> Embodied in the mystery of the words:
> There, darkness makes abode, and all the host
> Of shadowy things work endless changes,—there,
> As in a mansion like their proper home,
> Even forms and substance are circumfused
> By that transparent veil with light divine,
> And, through the turnings intricate of verse,

11. Eliot, *Selected Essays*, 164.

12. Edwards, *Towards a Christian Poetics*, 136.

> Present themselves as objects recognized,
> In flashes, and with glory not their own.[13]

The language of lyrical theology, i.e., poetry/verse both with and without music or other form of lyrical setting or presentation, can usually express in fewer words more truth than volumes of theological rhetoric.

The Primary Aspects of Lyrical Theology

What then are the primary aspects of lyrical theology to be gleaned from the Psalms? We shall address them remembering that the Psalms are liturgy; they are for worship, private—yes, but more particularly, corporate. They are for the community, which they engage in a vocation of doxology and praise. It is precisely this vocation that shapes the community of the faithful and its view of reality. It is this vocation that allows polarities and conflicts to be held in creative tension. It is the lyricism of doxology and praise that guards against over-ambition and definition. This vocation enables the community of the faithful to sing about what it often cannot talk about.

(1) *Lyrical theology is world-making.* Walter Brueggemann has addressed this subject pertaining to the Psalms rather thoroughly in his volume *Israel's Praise.* What he has to say is vital for lyrical theology, since it is grounded in worship and liturgy. The Psalms were created for use in the Temple of Jerusalem and became integral to Israel's worship and self-understanding. However, imagine the dichotomies to be held in tension by these powerful texts. As just stated, the Psalms were created for the Temple of Jerusalem. Jerusalem was the city of God, once ruled by David. But this city would be lost to the hands of other nations. Even so, God was still proclaimed the God of all nations. The songs of God's people, however, could no longer be sung in the Temple of Jerusalem, and the people of God became the dispossessed of the earth. How could a balanced view be held amid such paradoxes and dichotomies? Only in the language of poetry in which a vast repertory of conflicting images and ideas may be held in tension could Israel find the instrument of expressing such polarities and diverse meaning. In transcending time and space the psalmists succeed in juxtaposing the brevity of human existence with the eternity

---

13. Lines 595–605 of Book 5 of *The Prelude.* Online: http://www.bartleby.com/145/ww291.html.

of God so as to provide, as Alter says, "a certain access through contrast to the inconceivable timelessness of God."[14]

Brueggemann asserts: "In liturgy, world-making is indeed effected. The making of this world would be impossible without this dramatic enactment of liturgy. Implicit in this argument, then, is the provisional claim that social reality (and here we dare say religious reality) is a dramatic reality always to be enacted again. The claim of reality makes no sense unless its dramatic character is understood."[15]

The importance of "auditory imagination," which enables fallen language to be redemptive, has been noted above. Ricoeur maintains that behind what we conceive to be real there is imagination.[16] Hence, the "auditory imagination" of Israel—words, sound, language—functions to form reality. Therefore, in the celebration of liturgy, in the recital of the Psalms, those who speak and those who hear are involved in a world-making process. "In the moment of speech and imagination the person awakes, embraces, and experiences a new world."[17]

In the vocation of doxology and praise the act of liturgy does not create God, but it does create a new world. And if, in fact, in our own time clergy are not engaged through worship and liturgy in the social construction of reality, creating a new world, they are faithless to the ministerial office. A faithful community is formed by doxology and praise, by self-examination and reflection.

Psalm after psalm reveals that the world in which Israel exists is different from the world God wills. Israel calls the community to inquire:

> Why do the nations conspire
>   and the people plot in vain? (2:1)

> Why do the wicked renounce God,
>   and say in their hearts, "You will not call to account"? (10:13)

> How long must I bear pain in my soul,
>   and have sorrow in my heart all the day? (13:2)

---

14. Alter, *Art of Biblical Poetry*, 125.

15. Brueggemann, *Israel's Praise*, 11.

16. Ricoeur, *Essays in Biblical Imagination*.

17. Ibid., 22.

> O Lord, who shall dwell in your tent?
>> Who shall dwell in your holy hill? (15:1)

> For who is God except the Lord?
>> And who is a rock besides our God? (18:31)

> O why am I so burdened,
>> and why am I so troubled? (42:11)

Israel calls the faithful to create a world different from their own.

> Do not be afraid when some become rich,
>> when the wealth of their houses increases,
> for when they die they will carry nothing away;
>> their wealth will not go with them. (49:16–17)

In the liturgy of the Psalms the community of faith is called to a new social reality in which justice prevails, the dispossessed and oppressed are nurtured and loved, and love and peace reign.

The vocation of doxology and praise, the vocation of lyrical theology, may well be one of remembering and recital but never without enactment. It is the poetry of the Psalms that provides the world-shaping and world-making liturgy for the community of faith. It offers a world more viable than the one in which Israel lived and in which we live.

We may assert as did Israel that God is at the helm of history and that God is in control, but one swift glance at Israel's history and our own world reveals that God does not literally rule in the daily life of that ancient history and in ours. This is the reason why doxology and praise cannot stop—this is why the singing will and must continue.

Hence, lyrical theology is a theology of hope, which creates an alternative world. Its song evokes commitment and an actualization of the world the poets of Israel set before the community. It focuses on human need, personal and corporate, the poor, the marginalized, the oppressed, and dares to create out of this social reality, a new social possibility. Lyrical theology, therefore, can prevent the church from getting out of touch with its enabling memory.

(2) *Lyrical theology is a theology of sound.* Its words, rhythm, and stylistic characteristics are made for the ear, lips, body, and senses. Lyrical theology is therefore an experience. This is in part why it can be world-making, for it elicits response. Sentence structure, parallelism, rhetoric,

15

etc., become a song on the lips, in the heart, in one's life. Hence, the Psalms are the heartbeat of life, worship, and service.

Here it becomes clearer that lyrical theology does not make theology a mere object of consciousness. It engages the forces that shape worship and life.

Lyric and music are our response to remake a fallen world. That we should be the sound-boards of that theology should not surprise us, since we live as hearers between the sound of Adam's, Eve's, God's, and the Serpent's words in Eden and the sound of Paradise in John's vision on Patmos. Creation itself is filled with sound and is in part brought into being by sound—God's Word, speech. Pentecost is accompanied by "a sound . . . from heaven like the rush of a mighty wind" (Acts 2:2 RSV). The return of Christ will come with "a cry of command, the sound of the trumpet of God" (1 Thess 4:16 RSV). And in Psalm 65 the pastures, hills, meadows, and valleys "shout and sing together for joy" (Ps 65:12–13 RSV).

The Psalms perceive what is at the heart of lyrical theology—human need for words, action, gesture, movement, light, color, music, sound, and silence. Page after page of the Psalms illustrates that a lyrical theology allows for celebration and baring of the human soul without manipulation of the subject addressed, a grave pitfall of theological science in general.

(3) *Lyrical theology, the Book of Psalms in particular, has the ability to appropriate itself to us where we are.* It is not bound by time and space. It may move through time without linear chronology. St. Augustine poignantly makes this point in his own response to the Psalms:

> I am about to repeat a Psalm that I know. Before I begin, my expectation is extended over the whole; but when I have begun, how much soever of it I shall separate off into the past, is extended along my memory; thus the life of this action of mine is divided between my memory as to what I have repeated and expectation as to what I am about to repeat; but "consideration" is present with me, that through it what was future, may be conveyed over, so as to become past. Which the more it is done again and again, so much the more the expectation being shortened, is the memory enlarged; till the whole expectation be at length exhausted, when that whole action being ended, shall have passed into memory. And this which takes place in the whole Psalm, the same takes place in each several portion of it, and each several syllable; the same holds in that longer action, whereof this Psalm may be a

part; the same holds in the whole of life, whereof all [our] actions, whereof all [our] lives are part.[18]

Some years ago it was my destiny to arrive at the steps of the Duke University Chapel just as a woman had leaped to her death from the chapel's tower. This tragedy transpired immediately prior to the beginning of a worship service in the chapel. All who entered were devastated and bound by silence. I recall my inner dilemma over what I would do as the director of music that day. That aspect of my anxiety subsided as the worship leader announced that the complete liturgy would consist only of the Psalms. For over thirty minutes all who had come to worship heard and spoke only Psalms. The way in which the words appropriated themselves to me, and others in those moments, is literally indescribable. Such words as:

> The Lord is my shepherd,
>   I shall not want. (Ps 23:1)

> God is our refuge and strength,
>   a very present help in trouble. (Ps 46:1)

> Out of the depths have I cried to you, O God. (Ps 130:1)

This may well be a passive appropriation of the Psalms, but it is nonetheless powerful, for it sustains the human spirit, gives strength where there is weakness, and is psychologically and physiologically stabilizing.

The Psalms, however, also appropriate themselves to us actively and dynamically. They engage us in social realities.

Psalm 146:5–9 immediately engages the human desire for happiness.

> Happy are those whose help is in the God of Jacob,
>   whose hope is in the Lord, their God,
>   . . .
> who keeps faith forever;
>   who executes justice for the oppressed;
>   who gives food to the hungry.
> The Lord sets the prisoners free;
>   the Lord opens the eyes of the blind;

---

18. *Confessions*, 11.38 (Pusey, 274–75).

> the Lord lifts up those who are bowed down;
> > the Lord loves the righteous.
> The Lord watches over aliens,
> > and upholds the widow and the orphan;
> > but the Lord brings the way of the wicked to ruin.

The happy ones are those whose help is in the God of Jacob. One can have hope because the God of creation is faithful, executes justice for the oppressed, feeds the hungry, sets prisoners free, gives sight to the blind, lifts up the bowed down, loves the righteous, watches over aliens, upholds the widow and orphan, and brings the way of evil to ruin. This is but a description of the society God wills, and obedient servants are those who seek to make it a reality. Creating this world, the world God wills, is praise to the Lord. It is a doxology of song and service.

In singing the Psalms God's words become our words, God's will for the world becomes our will:

> The Lord says, "Now I will arise,
> > because the poor are plundered,
> > because the needy groan;
> > I will place them in safety for which they long." (Ps 12:5)

If as Ps 33:5 claims,

> The Lord loves justice and righteousness,
> > the earth is full of the steadfast love of the Lord,

we too must love justice and righteousness.

(4) *Lyrical theology does not seek to impart information to be turned into articles of orthodox belief.* It does not dissect belief. It celebrates, complains, rejoices, agonizes, weeps, and rages, bringing the full spectrum of human emotion unashamedly and without timidity before God. The Psalms illustrate such theology from beginning to end. Within them lyrical theology functions as a verbal art. It is a world of imperatives.

> Answer me when I call. (4:1)
> Be angry, but do not sin. (4:4)
> Commune . . . on your beds, . . . be silent. (4:4)
> Offer right sacrifices. (4:5)
> Lead me, Lord. (5:8)
> Turn, . . . save my life. (6:4)
> Depart from me, all you workers of evil. (6:7c)

Break the arm of the wicked and evildoers. (10:15)
Prove me, O Lord, and try me;
    test my heart and mind. (26:2)
Wait for the Lord. (27:14)
Be a rock of refuge for me. (31:2c)
Love the Lord. (31:23)
Rejoice in the Lord. (33:1a)
Praise the Lord. (33:2a)
Do not be angry because of the wicked,
    do not be envious of wrongdoers! (37:1)
Refrain from anger, and forsake wrath!
    Do not be angry; it only leads to evil. (37:8)
Hope in God. (42:5c)
Be still and know that I am God. (46:10a)
Hear this, all peoples! (49:1a)
Create in me a clean heart, O God. (51:10a)
Cast your burden on the Lord. (55:22)
Hide me from the secret plots of the wicked. (64:2a)
Sing to the Lord a new song. (33:3)

The Psalms direct our thoughts, voices, and actions to God, others, and all creation without requiring that we have closely reasoned each word and guarded all affirmation about God, ourselves, faith, community, and the world. They allow us to go out as Abram, not knowing where we are going with confidence that God is there in the midst of the darkness. We can hold the dichotomies and polarities of the world in tension and cry out with Jehoshophat: "We do not know what to do, but our eyes are on you" (2 Chron 20:12 NRSV). In one moment we plead in the words of a Psalm, "Be angry and sin not" and in another moment in words from another Psalm, "Do not be angry; it only leads to evil."

Hence, lyrical theology helps us in faith to hold the paradoxes and inconsistencies of life in balance without subjecting them to theological logic and without translating theological affirmations into canons of belief. In so doing lyrical theology transforms our thoughts and actions, and it reorients our lives.

(5) *Lyrical theology emanates from a life of prayer.* If we want to learn how to pray, we must, sing, chant, say, and pray the Psalms. They are the language of prayer, a language that is both personal and corporate, private and social, a language which is divine and human.

If we pray the Psalms, we shall verbalize in the complaint passages not only our own failings but those of society. Even when we pray the words of a royal psalm, as though we were royalty, we will discover what it is like to ignore the deepest concerns and needs of the masses. Why must one plead that God will give the king justice to deal with the righteous and the poor? Because there have been so many rulers who have exploited the needy and the oppressed. The Psalmist reminds us of how readily one forgets to execute justice. Hence, even in our own small domains, even in the words intended for a king, we may learn to have pity on the weak and needy, to deliver the needy when they call, to save the lives of the needy, and to redeem them from oppression and violence (see Psalm 72).

We may be imbued with humility, penitence, love, forgiveness, and justice as we pray the Psalms, which communicate these character traits and more. It is possible to pray the Psalms until we personify them, until we are the answer to the prayers of ages past and become the answer to our own prayers. It is possible to be arrogant and become humble; it is possible to be hard-hearted and to become penitent and of a contrite heart. This is the miracle of lyrical theology, of the Psalms, of transformation. We can become what we think, say, sing, and chant. It is the miracle of which Jean-Paul Sartre speaks when he says that human beings may become what they are not. It is also the miracle of which St. Paul speaks when he declares that all things become new.

(6) *Lyrical theology evokes a life of service.* When we sing "serve the Lord with gladness" in Psalm 100, we cannot engage in a spiritual thumbsucking exercise and thus fulfill the breadth of the mandate of the Psalms for a life of service. We must also sing Psalm 101!

> I will sing of loyalty and justice. (101:1a)
>
> . . .
>
> I will walk with integrity of heart. (101:2c)

We must become the source of unity when we sing:

> Behold, how good and pleasant it is,
>   when kindred live together in unity. (133:1)

We must sing Psalm 10 and emulate a God who would do justice to the orphan and the oppressed. We must sing Psalm 11 and be vulnerable to be judged:

> The Lord . . . examines all mortals,
> hates the lover of violence,
>> and loves righteous deeds. (11:4–5b, 7b)

The Psalms demand transformation! They affirm that we cannot love violence and serve God.

Lyrical theology affirms that the vocation of doxology and praise is one of service to God, others, and creation. We must sing Psalm 104 and become a part of God's renewal of the face of the earth (104:30b). In fact, we can only sing with integrity Ps 104:33,

> I will sing to the Lord as long as I live!
> I will sing praise continually;

if we are willing to be personifications of renewing service not only to God and others, but to the earth also. Lyrical theology's evocation of a life of service embodies an ecological imperative too!

(7) *Lyrical theology mandates proclamation.* There is evangelism in the Psalms. There is a call to transformation and conversion, as already noted; however, the vocation of doxology and praise is not merely a vocative one in which we pray the Psalms to God personally and corporately for the sake of our spiritual nurture and that of the community of faith. The Psalms call us to proclamation—to tell what God has done and to make that known from generation to generation!

> I will tell of all of your wonderful works. (9:1)

> Tell God's deeds among the people! (9:11)

> Then my tongue shall tell of your righteousness
> and of your praise all the day long. (35:28)

> Sing to the Lord, bless God's name;
> proclaim God's salvation from day to day. (96:2)

If we do not fulfill the mandate of proclamation, if we do not sing Jerusalem's song, we must also pray with the Psalmist:

> Let my tongue stick to the roof of my mouth,
> if I do not remember you. (137:6ab)

There may be times when we ask with Israel in Babylon,

> How shall we sing the Lord's song
>> in a foreign land? (137:4)

When we do, in our silence our tongues may stick to the roof of our mouths and we will no longer be able to sing. Yes, the vocation of doxology and praise demands that we "tell to all generations what God has done."

> One generation shall laud your works to another,
>> and shall declare your mighty acts. (145:4)
>
> . . .
>
> They shall celebrate the memory of your great goodness,
>> and shall sing aloud of your righteousness. (145:7)
>
> My mouth will speak the praise of the Lord;
>> let all flesh bless God's holy name forever and ever. (145:21)

Conclusion

Where then does lyrical theology lead us in attempting to understand and actualize a word of God, a word about God, in the contemporary church and world? What is there to be *said* theologically which has not already been *said*? That is precisely the point—theology, as mundane as it sounds, is a world of words—lyrical theology is more than words, for it involves sound—the sounds of human speech, yes, but more—music! *It is an experience!* Lyrical theology is the experience of word and music, and the sound thereof, which mediate the knowing of God, more directly and effectively than the words themselves are capable of doing.

2

Lyrical Theology: Theology in Hymns[1]

Some years ago I wrote an article for *Theology Today* entitled "Hymns are Theology,"[2] in which I made the case for a more serious consideration of this genre of sacred literature as theology. In that article I maintained, "The hymns of the church *are* theology. They are theological statements: the church's lyrical, theological commentaries on Scripture, liturgy, faith, action, and hosts of other subjects which call the reader and singer to faith, life, and Christian practice."[3]

In the years since the appearance of that article, I have written about this subject in the previous chapter using the phrase *lyrical theology* to describe the genre of theological literature, commonly known as hymns. Clearly theological science is thought of and practiced primarily as a prose discipline. While there may be some theologians who write in a lyrical style, the qualities and characteristics of poetry are generally not considered part of the matrix of theological expression: rhyme, meter, rhythm, diction, assonance, alliteration, or technically descriptive terms for poetical rhetoric, such as epanadiplosis,[4] antistrophe,[5] epizeuxis,[6] and epistrophe.[7]

1. Much of the material in this chapter appeared under the same title in *Theology Today* 63 (2006) 22–37. Used by permission.
2. Kimbrough, "Hymns Are Theology," 59–68.
3. Ibid., 59.
4. This is the beginning and end of a clause or line with the same word.
5. This is the repetition of a phrase in the reverse order.
6. This is the immediate repetition of a word or phrase within the same sentence.
7. This is the repetition of a word or words at the end of lines or phrases.

In his excellent volume, *The Faith We Sing*, published in 1983, Paul Schilling averred: "Christian theology is the thoughtful enquiry into the meaning of the faith called forth by God's self-disclosing activity, especially in Jesus Christ. It seeks through critical examination to discover the truths implied in the history and experience of the Christian community and to interpret them in the most intelligible and persuasive manner."[8] He also maintained, however, that "any exploration of the meaning of God for any aspect of our experience is theological."[9] Thus he clearly expressed a broader view of theology than one that is merely prose-oriented, for one may explore the meaning of God through poetry and hymns/songs.

In recent years there have been some important explorations of hymns as theology, which have greatly advanced the discussion. While *Singing the Faith,* a series of essays by diverse authors edited by Charles Robertson and published by Canterbury Press in 1990, does not address specifically hymns as theology, the various essays illuminate the viewpoint that liturgy is not merely a context for the life of hymns, nor are hymns merely an embellishment of liturgy.

Teresa Berger's *Theology in Hymns?*[10] is a superb study of the Wesleys' *A Collection of Hymns for the Use of the People Called Methodists* (1780). She sees Wesleyan hymnody primarily within the context of doxological theology and brings the fullness of continental theological science to bear on hymnody. Interestingly this work is a doctoral dissertation, which was written about the hymns and hymn writing of the Anglican priests, John and Charles Wesley, for the Roman Catholic faculty of the University of Münster in Germany.

In the last chapter of Brian Wren's *Praying Twice*, an excellent study of congregational song, the author asks—How do hymns do theology? He is convinced that hymn lyrics are "vehicles of theology."[11] Later in the chapter he maintains:

> expressing a theological concept in verse entails moving from concept to metaphor, from elaboration to epigram, and from balanced prose to the energy of rhyme and rhythm, any or all of which make substantive, and not merely stylistic, alterations to what is

8. Schilling, *Faith We Sing,* 30.

9. Ibid.

10. Berger, *Theology in Hymns?* 147ff.

11. Wren, *Praying Twice,* 351.

being expressed. . . . Moreover, because a hymn has a limited word length and time frame, a poet must be selective, highlighting some themes and omitting others. For these reasons, it is unlikely that a hymn lyric can "carry" theological concepts without also interpreting them, and thus in its own way doing theology.[12]

Wren understands that hymns cannot do systematic theology, but they can offer a digestion of theological concepts, language, metaphors, and viewpoints. He maintains that "one way in which a hymn can do theology is to state, pithily and vividly, theological viewpoints whose claims are argued elsewhere, or to frame praise, thanksgiving, longing, lament, trust, commitment, and other God-centered responses based on such viewpoints."[13]

Thomas G. Long's *Beyond the Worship Wars: Building Vital and Faithful Worship* addresses the most common context in which hymns function theologically, namely, worship. He claims that "Full-length hymns and shorter choruses are employed to gather the people, to reinforce the reading of Scripture and the preaching, to generate a sense of mystery throughout, to cultivate congregational participation, to express thanksgiving and joy, to surround the offerings of the people, and to send the congregation into the world to service."[14] This is no doubt in part the reason for the frequent averment of some musicians and theologians that congregations receive their theology more often from the hymns they sing than from the sermons they hear.

Most considerations of lyrical theology (or hymns as theology) tend to address the functionality of hymns in the context of worship, the significance, content, and context of the text, the appropriateness of text and music, the appropriateness for the liturgy or worship service of which they are a part, and diverse styles ("traditional" and "contemporary" hymns, gospel hymns, psalms, chants, ritual songs, praise songs, choruses, etc.). One finds serious and helpful discussions regarding the role of hymns and shorter song forms within liturgical renewal, the charismatic and Pentecostal movements, the Church Growth movement, mainline church worship (its decline and/or renewal), evangelical churches, Roman Catholicism, and Orthodox churches.

12. Ibid.
13. Ibid., 369.
14. Long, *Beyond the Worship Wars*, 61.

While the functionality, content, context, style, liturgical appropriateness, the effectiveness and ineffectiveness of "traditional" hymns and "contemporary" praise and worship songs are being explored quite carefully,[15] as well as the effect of all these realities on the theological memory of the church, few discussions treat the questions: What is the spirituality behind the hymns or songs which gave them birth? Out of what spiritual ethos did they emerge? A response to these questions is essential if one is to grasp the theological import and impact of hymns.

The Spirituality Behind the Song

The Spiritual Ethos Behind the Psalms

Unquestionably, some are willing to jettison the songs birthed in the church over two thousand years, as though one may set aside the Holy Spirit's witness in song through the centuries as having no bearing at all on the church or community of faith in the twenty-first century. Churches and individuals who share this view participate in an ecclesiological reductionism that all but obliterates God's effective historical witness through the church for some two thousand years. This reduces the theological expression of the church in its song through the ages to insignificance, to nothingness.

The issue, however, is not one of antiquarianism versus contemporaneity. The church's song was not created out of a spiritual vacuum. It was born in adversity, suffering, persecution, sinfulness, apostasy, pilgrimage, celebration, joy, jubilation, worship of God, etc. Hence, it is not surprising to find in the Book of Psalms, the epitome of lyrical theology in the Hebrew Bible, an expression of the fullness of human emotion—sorrow, joy, anxiety, conflict, resolve, alienation, reconciliation, despair, hope, determination, resignation, etc. The Psalms emerged from a people who had experienced violence and war, love and hate, alienation and persecution, oppression and slavery, bondage and deliverance, promise and fulfillment. They emerged from a people who both remembered and forgot to worship the God of their deliverance and salvation.

15. See Hustad, *Jubilate II*; Wren, *Praying Twice;* Dawn, *Reaching Out without Dumbing Down.*

Some Psalms rehearse God's deeds among the people as the matrix of connectedness from one generation to another; others recount the sins of the people of Israel and God's covenant faithfulness; some are communal expressions of despair and hope; and others are very personal accounts of encounter with God. Psalms are the voice of petition, repentance, and reconciliation. They are cries of anger and rage, and they bring the full spectrum of human response to God in worship and praise. Central to the language of the Psalms are the following themes: God's covenants with Noah and with Abraham, God's deliverance of the Hebrews from slavery in Egypt, the forty years of wandering in the wilderness and the ultimate deliverance into the land of promise (Canaan), and the establishment of holy places of worship (Tabernacle and Temple). Through a complex maze of human experience God's chosen people come to know the tension of alienation and belonging, and that somehow God is at the helm of history. Even so there were times they felt they had no songs to sing: "On the willows there we hung up our harps, for there our captors asked us for songs, and our tormenters asked for mirth, saying, 'Sing us one of the songs of Zion!'" (Ps 137:2–3 PPW/NRSV)

Though God's people were often wayward, there were among them seers and prophets, persons of wisdom, who reminded them with constancy that they can articulate all of this experience in song and incorporate it into their worship and praise of God. This is why, if one wishes to learn to pray, one should sing and pray the Psalms. Why? Because they are born out of everyday human experience, out of the conflicts of life which are as common today as they were in biblical times, and a worshiping community need not be afraid to bring all of this experience as an offering to God.

The spirituality behind the song is a benchmark for the theology of hymns in worship or wherever they are used. The songs of Scripture emerge from the life, soil, and toil of the people. God's people did not sing the Psalms in a vacuum. They sang them with a connectedness to the past, present, and future.

The Psalms are songs of drama. One senses the continuity of the story of the people as it moves to various climaxes in their life. The songwriter and the singers are actors in the drama, but the drama, the story, is the central focus and not themselves. Here we discover a vital question for lyrical theology in twenty-first-century worship. Are the singers today actors in the drama of God's history and is God's drama of salvation at the heart of the experience of making music to God's glory?

When we worship God today, we do not sing merely for our own gratification. Just as "An encounter with God is not something that human beings control or arrange,"[16] the singing of hymns and spiritual songs should not be a manipulative process for the self-edification of worshipers.

If we take the songbook of the Bible seriously, namely, the Book of Psalms, we must ask of hymns/songs we sing in worship today: What do we know about the spiritual ethos out of which the hymns/songs emerge? Do they connect us to the past, present, and future of God's salvation history? Do they enable us to be actors in God's drama of salvation? We can test every hymn/song with these questions.

The Spiritual Ethos Behind Hymns

One of the most prolific hymn writers of the last three hundred years was Charles Wesley, an Anglican poet-priest of the eighteenth century. Many of his hymns have been sustained in standard English-language hymnbooks for over two hundred years, and scores of them have been translated into numerous languages. While he is purported to have written 6,500 hymns, in fact he wrote some 9,000 hymns, sacred poems, and secular poems. Many of his sacred lyrics became hymns sung by communities of faith. How was it possible for someone in the eighteenth century to be that prolific without a computer or other electronic aids? Did he just set out to write a hymn each day no matter what transpired? If so, would that not make the whole process quite mechanical and perfunctory?

Wesley was an artist and had learned the high art of poetry from studying the Latin classical poets, such as Virgil (Publius Vergillus Maro), Ovid (Publius Ovidius Naso), Juvenal (Decimus Junius Juvenalis), by reading the best English poets of his time and his immediate past, and, of course, he grew up in the home of a poet, his father Samuel. Two of his brothers, Samuel and John, as well as his sister Mehetabel, were also excellent poets. But why does he burst on the scene of *sacred* poetry in 1738? And why, if he could have been a successful secular poet as his unpublished poetry reveals, did he choose to be a sacred poet and publish

16. Long, *Beyond the Worship Wars*, 21.

none of his secular verse?[17] Charles Wesley's vision of human existence and creation was radically transformed on May 21, 1738 (Pentecost Day) by his experience of Christ as God's revelation of redemptive love for himself and for all humankind. Therefore, he decided to use his poetic art as the best possible expression of God's incarnate love so that others might sing of it and be redeemed and nurtured by it.

When we observe his daily discipline, we discover the spiritual ethos that gives his poetry birth. There are regular spiritual practices that are integral to his daily life and are the source of the language and heartbeat of his poetical expression. In fact, these are the imperatives for his writing, and from which his lyrical theology emerges.

(1) *The daily reading of the Holy Scriptures.* This daily discipline coupled with his lifelong study of the original texts in Hebrew and Greek, as well as in Latin, meant that he absorbed the metaphors, imagery, language, and experiences of the Scriptures, made them his own, and at times translated them into "contemporary" verse for his own day. In the following poem based on the *Sh^ema Y'israel* (Deut 6:4–7), he describes how he integrated the reading of the Holy Scriptures into daily life.

> 3. When quiet in my house I sit,
>   Thy book be my companion still,
> My joy thy sayings to repeat,
>   Talk o'er the records of thy will,
> And search the oracles divine,
> Till every heart-felt word is mine.
>
> 4. O might the gracious words divine
>   Subject of all my converse be,
> So would the Lord his follower join,
>   And walk, and talk himself with me,
> So would my heart his presence prove,
> And burn with everlasting love.
>
> 5. Oft as I lay me down to rest,
>   O may the reconciling word
> Sweetly compose my weary breast,
>   While on the bosom of my Lord
> I sink in blissful dreams away,
> And visions of eternal day.

17. See his secular verse in volumes 1 and 3 of *Unpub. Poetry.*

6. Rising to sing my Saviour's praise,
   Thee may I publish all day long,
   And let thy precious word of grace
      Flow from my heart, and fill my tongue,
   Fill all my life with purest love,
   And join me to thy church above.[18]

The spiritual ethos out of which Charles Wesley's lyrical theology grows is one that feeds upon God's Word "Till every heartfelt word is mine."

(2) *Daily prayer and regular praying of the Psalms.* While in the colony of Georgia he wrote in his Journal: "After spending an hour at the camp in singing such psalms as suited the occasion, I went to bed in the hut . . ." (March 25, 1736).[19] And on April 11 of the same year he recorded in his Journal, "What words could more support our confidence than the following, out of the psalms for the day?"[20] (The text he cites is Ps 56:1–5 KJV/AV, "Be merciful unto me, O God; for man goeth about to devour me. . . . Nevertheless, though I am sometimes afraid, yet put I my trust in Thee. . . ."[21] etc.)

Many of his hymns are earnest prayers to God. Here are four lines each from two hymns, "Love divine, all loves excelling" and "Spirit of faith, come down," which are Wesley's own prayers, but when sung by the community of faith, they become its corporate pleas.

Breathe, O breathe, thy loving Spirit
   Into every troubled breast;
Let us all in thee inherit,
   Let us find the second rest.[22]
         * * * *
   Spirit of faith, come down,
   Reveal the things of God
And make to us the Godhead known
   And witness with the blood.[23]

18. *Scripture Hymns* (1762), 1:91–93. Four stanzas of a six-stanza hymn are quoted here.

19. Kimbrough and Newport, *CW Journal*, 1:13.

20. Ibid., 1:20.

21. BCP Psalter, abbreviated here.

22. *Redemption Hymns* (1747) 11, Hymn 9.

23. *Pentecost Hymns* (1746) 30, Hymn 27.

Wesley's life of daily prayer and regular praying of the Psalms evoked poetry of prayer for worship and praise, much of which is still timely. The spiritual ethos that birthed his lyrical theology emerged from lifelong faithfulness to the prayers and sacraments of the church. Hence, we come to the importance of the Eucharist.

(3) *Charles Wesley considered daily Eucharist, and if not daily at least weekly, an imperative.* He reflects on the saints of old as examples of those who practiced "Constant Communion."[24]

> 1. Happy the saints of former days
>   Who first continued in the Word,
> A simple lowly loving race,
>   True followers of their Lamb-like Lord.
>
> 2. In holy fellowship they lived,
>   Nor would from the commandment move,
> But every joyful day received
>   The tokens of expiring love.
>
> 3. Not then above their Master wise,
>   They simply in his paths remained,
> And called to mind his sacrifice
>   With steadfast faith and love unfeigned.
>
> 4. From house to house they broke the bread
>   Impregnated with Life divine,
> And drank the Spirit of their Head
>   Transmitted in the sacred wine.
>
> 5. With Jesu's constant presence blest,
>   While duteous to his dying word,
> They kept the Eucharistic feast,
>   And supped in Eden with their Lord.

But later in the poem he asks:

> 10. Where is the pure primeval flame,
>   Which in their faithful bosom glowed?
> Where are the followers of the Lamb,
>   The dying witnesses for God?

24. *HLS* (1745) 139–41, Hymn 166.

11. Why is the faithful seed decreased,
    The life of God extinct and dead?
    The daily sacrifice is ceased,
    And charity to heaven is fled.

And finally he pleads for the restoration of the daily practice:

16. O wouldst thou to thy church return!
    For which the faithful remnant sighs,
    For which the drooping nations mourn,
    Restore the daily sacrifice.

17. Return, and with thy servants sit,
    Lord, of the sacramental feast,
    And satiate us with heavenly meat,
    And make the *World* thy happy guest.

One of Charles Wesley's most significant contributions to lyrical theology is a volume dedicated solely to the subject of its title: *Hymns on the Lord's Supper* (1745). His poetry there and elsewhere is imbued with the language of the liturgy, BCP, and the Holy Scriptures.

(4) *Fasting was a weekly practice of Charles Wesley.* Each Friday he and his brother John practiced this ancient tradition of denial and personal cleansing. It is a spiritual discipline through which Charles sought Christ.

With fasting and prayer
  My Savior I seek,
And listen to hear
  The Comforter speak;

In searching and hearing
  The life-giving Word
I wait thy appearing,
  I look for my Lord.[25]

(5) *Regular service to, with, and among the poor.* This was for Charles Wesley the personification of Christ's love, with which he yearned to be filled, and the culmination of the disciplines of daily Bible reading, prayer,

25. Stanza 2 of a four-stanza Eucharistic hymn which appears in *A Short View of the Difference between the Moravian Brethren, Lately in England; And the Reverend Mr. John and Charles Wesley* (1745). There are two other printings, Dublin, 1747, and Bristol, 1748 (second edition), which include the hymn.

regular fasting, and Eucharist. In each of those disciplines he sought the Savior, and where better to seek Christ and await his appearing and than among the poor? Thus he writes:

> The poor as Jesus' bosom-friends,
>   The poor he makes his latest care,
> To all his successors commends,
>   And wills us on our hands to bear:
> The poor our dearest care we make,
>   Aspiring to superior bliss,
> And cherish for their Saviour's sake,
>   And love them with a love like his.[26]

Love and care of the poor is the highest of callings for followers of Christ.

The poor vicariously take Christ's place in the world; hence, when one responds to them, one responds to Christ. Wesley understands Matt 26:11 KJV/AV, "Ye have the poor always with you," in this manner:

> Yes, the poor supply thy place,
>   Still deputed, Lord, by thee,
> Daily exercise our grace,
>   Prove our growing charity;
> What to them with right intent
>   Truly, faithfully is given,
> We have to our Saviour lent,
>   Laid up for ourselves in heaven.[27]

The spiritual discipline of service to, with, and among the poor puts Wesley in contact with the heartbeat of the pain and suffering, hopelessness, and oppression that millions endure each day. This is why he can compose lyrical theology encompassing the poor with such sensitivity.

Having only looked at the spiritual ethos out of which the poetry of the biblical Psalms, the hymn book of the synagogue and the church, and the hymns of Charles Wesley emerge, how can this myopic view serve the understanding of theology in hymns in the twenty-first-century church? Furthermore, how can it assist us in reading the lyrical theology of Charles Wesley and grasping its relevance in our time?

26. MS Acts, 421; *Unpub. Poetry*, 2:404.
27. MS Matthew, 319; *Unpub. Poetry*, 2:46.

Towards Lyrical Theology

It is important to raise this question in a volume devoted to the lyrical theology of Charles Wesley, for there are many today who feel that he is from another time with outdated language and modes of expression. He is not contemporary, some might say.

We are confronted today with the so-called "worship wars" of "contemporary" vs. "traditional," "blended" worship vs. either of the two just mentioned, mega-churches vs. churches of small membership (and largely mainstream and traditional), archaic language vs. contemporary vernacular. We wonder whether to sing hymns, choruses, rounds/canons, refrains, gospel songs/hymns, chants, ritual songs, Spirit songs, our songs or other people's songs.

How shall we know what to sing? How shall we make judgments about the many ways in which the theology of a hymn/song may be conveyed and influenced? There are often many layers of theological meaning conveyed through a hymn/song. In conclusion, I shall explore a few of these, though the discussion by no means is exhaustive.

First of all, insofar as possible, one must consider the author's intent as regards the theology transmitted through the hymn. In and of itself, however, the theological meaning may vary, depending on the text and the context in which it is read or sung. For example, when one sings the following lines of Isaac Watts, it is in part clear what he wishes to convey, but it is clear that singers' interpretations also have a strong impact on the theological understanding, when Watts's words become their words.

> When I survey the wondrous cross
>   on which the Prince of glory died,
> My richest gain I count but loss,
>   And pour contempt on all my pride.

In the first two lines Watts emphasizes the importance of the sacrifice of Jesus Christ on the cross. The statement has a Christocentric emphasis, for the death of Christ on the cross becomes the focus of one's full attention. No matter who sings the hymn, this is a constant emphasis. However, when one comes to the next two lines, the theological understanding conveyed is influenced by one's own life situation and context. Watts probably has in mind the spirit of Paul's comments in Phil 3:7 KJV/AV, "But what things were gain to me, those I counted loss for Christ." Thus one might say that in the light of Christ's sacrifice any human gain is loss and all pride is contemptible. Nevertheless, in lines three and four there is an example of how the singer's response becomes vital in the theological understanding. What is "richest gain" and "loss" to one person may not be to another. Here within four lines one encounters a multi-layered theology involving the intent of the author and the response of the singer.

Second, culture, ethnicity, language, life experience, and events play strong roles in the contextualization of the theological meaning of hymns. For example, African Americans, who sing the following stanzas of the well-known hymn by Charles Wesley, "Jesus, Lover of my soul," will have theological understanding quite different from those who have no history of enslavement.

> Jesus, Lover of my soul,
>   Let me to thy bosom fly,
> While the nearer waters roll,
>   While the tempest still is high.
> Hide me, O my Savior, hide,
>   Till the storm of life is past;
> Safe into the haven guide;
>   O receive my soul at last.
>
> Other refuge have I none,
>   Hangs my helpless soul on thee;
> Leave, ah! leave me not alone,
>   Still support and comfort me.
> All my trust on thee is stayed,
>   All my help from thee I bring;
> Cover my defenseless head
>   With the shadow of thy wing.[28]

The metaphors and images in this hymn are readily accessible to African Americans: "the tempest still is nigh," "the storm of life," "helpless soul," "support," "comfort," and "defenseless head." They see those words and images through different eyes and sing them with different theological understanding.

In a similar manner one must go back to the context of the eighteenth century in which Charles Wesley wrote this hymn to understand what these words meant to those who heard them at that time. How would a

28. *HSP* (1740) 67–68.

prisoner going to the gallows have heard these words? What would they have meant to a slave who had been bought out of slavery and was being returned to Africa? How would they have resounded in a debtors' prison?

The distinguished Ghanaian theologian, Mercy Amba Oduyoye, has commented on the vast differences that words, imagery, terms, and phraseology have from language to language and how this can impact the theological meaning of a hymn. In her mother tongue, the Akan language of Ghana, for example, "the bowels" are the seat of human emotions, not "the heart." Thus to sing "rule in all our hearts alone" or "O let his love our hearts constrain" or "enter every trembling heart" is essentially meaningless in that language and culture. Wesley's line "To me, to all thy bowels move"[29] from stanza nine of his poem "Wrestling Jacob" has been deboweled in most modern hymn books and changed to "To me, to all thy mercies move." It is precisely Wesley's original wording, however, with which Akan-speaking Ghanaian Christians would identify.

Theological meaning may have a core and central focus applicable to all, but how it is grasped and interpreted through images, figures of speech, metaphors, similes, etc., varies greatly from culture to culture.

Third, the lyrical theology conveyed through a hymn/song may be determined in some measure by the liturgical or worship context. When hymns/songs are sung by the worshiping community in diverse worship contexts, they may take on different layers of meaning which may or may not be a part of the original intent of the author or may not be obvious from the words themselves.

If one sings a hymn/song in an evangelical free church, in a Pentecostal/charismatic, seeker service of worship, or in the daily offices or Eucharistic service of a confessional church, it may convey very different theological layers of meaning to the worshipers. For example, consider the Watts hymn mentioned above, "When I survey the wondrous cross." I have attended an evangelistic service in which this hymn was used as the hymn of invitation to encourage the uncommitted present to submit their lives to Christ. Clearly the focus was on the impact of the imagery of Christ on the cross as a sacrifice for the sinner and its power to convict one of the need of the Savior.

29. *HSP* (1742) 117.

I have also been present in an Episcopal church when this hymn was used as the hymn of preparation for the Eucharist or was sung at the Communion. In this liturgical context the focus was on Christ's sacrifice in the context of the Eucharist. But one experienced the text and its theology quite differently, namely, it is at the table of Christ that the vision of Calvary becomes truly clear. It is there that one has a true vision of God and of self, as one partakes of the body and blood that were broken and shed for all and which send one out to serve.

Singing the same hymns at different cycles of the Christian year may also be somewhat like turning a diamond in the light and seeing the different reflections and refractions of the light. One sees things differently in light of the context of the Christian year.

Fourth, the editing of hymn/song texts can change or shift the meaning of the theology they convey. For example, the hymn "Christ the Lord is risen today" is usually reserved for Easter Day and the tune most generally associated with it is entitled EASTER HYMN. In many hymnals there are only four stanzas of the original eleven, and these four often conclude with original stanza five:

> Soar we now where Christ has led,
> Following our exalted Head;
> Made like him, like him we rise,
> Ours the cross, the grave, the skies.[30]

How often I recall singing this hymn at Easter sunrise services as a child and a youth. Somehow it always left me with a thrilling sense of soaring to resurrection with Christ: "ours the cross, the grave, the skies." How appropriate for Easter! But little did I know as a youngster that the edited version of the original eleven-stanza hymn radically changed its theology.

The original concluding two stanzas of the hymn make very clear that it is appropriate for any Sunday, the day of every week on which Christians celebrate the resurrection of Christ. Stanzas ten and eleven bring one back to earth from soaring in the skies to everyday life.

> Hail the Lord of earth and heaven!
> Praise to thee by both be given:
> Thee we greet triumphant now;
> Hail the Resurrection, thou!

30. *HSP* (1739) 210.

> King of glory, soul of bliss,
> Everlasting life is this,
> Thee to know, thy power to prove,
> Thus to sing, and thus to love![31]

Wesley defines the Christian life as "thee to know, thy power to prove, / thus to sing, and thus to love." What a remarkable definition of eternal life in the present! As is often the case, Wesley uses a cascade of verbs to describe the reality of eternal life now: *know, prove, sing, love.*

Fifth, music and rhythm play distinct roles in the theology conveyed through hymns/songs. Pablo Sosa of Argentina remarks, "*it is rhythm which gives meaning to sound.* Supposing you could imagine a sound, which was sustained forever, unchanged, with no rhythmic suggestions at all, it would make no sense. It is rhythm, through variations in intensity, color, etc., which gives sound those qualities that we define as 'calm,' 'anxiety,' 'balance,' 'disruption,' and so on."[32] This is not surprising, given the movement and pulse of God's creative process as recorded in the book of Genesis that all of life and cultures seem to be imbued with rhythm.

Many rhythms are, however, unfamiliar. Is one not running a risk with a congregation to introduce rhythms it does not know or may feel uncomfortable trying to master? The following comments by George Mulrain of Trinidad and Tobago indicate that the answer is "Yes," but it is a risk that can enrich our theological understanding.

> There is something profoundly theological about making use of both local and foreign rhythms in worship. It matters not that the members of a congregation are not proficient in all the rhythms of the world. The fact is that in the worship of God we ought to express our solidarity with other persons who are equally the children of God, made in the divine image and likeness. Consequently, when a congregation in Africa sings a song from Latin America, it could be a reminder to those attending worship that they must be concerned with the struggles that constitute aspects of the life of the people of Latin America. When a congregation in the United States sings a worship song from India, it could serve to highlight that God is revered not only in Christianity, but in other faiths as well. Although the hymns and songs we sing may come from hundreds or thousands of miles away, we are still inextricably bound

31. Ibid., 211.

32. Unpublished paper, "Rhythm: A Global Perspective."

to those who birthed them as children of God. The testimony we give is not to a parochial God who is bound by geographical and cultural limitations, but rather it is a testimony to the universal deity, the God of all nations.[33]

What of the music itself—melodic line, harmonization, rhythmic pattern, etc.? Can we risk the unfamiliar here as well? If we truly believe the affirmation of Holy Scripture that God is the God of all peoples, indeed of all creation, then we must take the risk. This truth must be affirmed in our worship and witness. Dare we join voices with Cambodian Christians who usually do only monodic singing (no harmony) and often accompany their singing with a one-string violin, or with Christians who sing the Psalms to melodies learned at a mosque? Dare we sing a new setting of a very familiar hymn text by someone from another culture?

We may discover that familiar texts can be given new life and meaning through new musical settings from other cultures, and that familiar musical settings may or may not have communicated the fullness of the theological meaning in a text. For example, the use of Thomas Campbell's tune SAGINA for Charles Wesley's beloved text "And can it be that I should gain / an interest in the Savior's blood" is sacrosanct for many. Yet in reality Campbell's camp-meeting style, marshal-like tune turns one of Wesley's most introspective texts (the opening stanza is but one deep, reflective, personal question of self-examination) into an upbeat hymn of affirmation. Campbell's melody does not let the singers ask themselves the questions Wesley is raising. It transforms Wesley's question marks into exclamation points. Ludmila Garbuzova, a Russian pastor, has composed a new setting for this text with ascending and descending lines and with introspective pauses appropriate to Wesley's lyrics, which Russians sing with much rubato and deep reflection. Dare one risk its use?

Our global neighbors can help us discover anew the laments, the *kyrie eleison,* the *agnus dei,* the cries of the soul, which are often absent from thirty minutes of praise singing in one style. The shorter forms of many global songs can imbue worship music, even the hymns of Charles Wesley, with a fresh wind of the Spirit and a breadth of theological nurture for all.

33. Unpublished paper, "The Theological Understanding of Rhythm and Music."

Conclusion

Lyrical theology is ever emerging, but it does not emerge *from* a vacuum, nor *in* a vacuum. There is a spiritual ethos and a cultural context out of which every Christian hymn/song is born. As the church addresses what it shall sing in the present and future, it must be attentive to the spirituality that gives birth to song. The Wesleyan hymns and poems in this volume provide the opportunity to recapture the spiritual ethos and, perhaps to some extent, the cultural context out of which the hymns emerged.

In the next chapter we shall turn to the question of how to read the lyrical theology of Charles Wesley. We shall address some of the histori-cal, contextual, and theological background of his life and work, which can assist in determining whether his extensive repertory of hymns and poems can still connect the church with God's saving history. It is hoped that one will then be prepared to read the poetry in the latter part of this volume with a view toward asking afresh the following questions: Do Wesley's hymns and poems still summon us to a deepened spirituality in our journey with God in Christ, who calls the believing community to faithful discipline, worship, and service? Do they celebrate and dramatize God's story? Do they assist us to be absorbed by the gospel narrative? Do they witness to the perpetuity of God's covenant and the enduring presence of the Holy Spirit? Are Wesley's hymns and poems viable for twenty-first-century Christians?

Sixth, one must move beyond the familiar to the theological challenges of other cultures and voices. While I grew up singing songs from other cultures, most of them were English translations of European hymn texts with melodies from central Europe. Though I think my parents, who were extremely well-trained musicians, would have embraced the statement by Donald Hustad, "the art of aboriginals demonstrates God's grace and glorifies God as surely (if not as well) as that of Bach, who dedicated all his works *soli Dei Gloria*, 'to God's glory alone,'"[34] the resources simply were not available in *The Methodist Hymnal* (1939) of our church. The literature today, however, is vast and we have the opportunity as never before to enrich the witness, worship, and nurture of Christians through global song.[35] A positive sign is that many mainline church hymnals have

34. Hustad, *Jubilate II*, 6.

35. Some recent publications of importance are as follows: Bell, *Many and Great: Songs of the World Church*, Vol. 1, and *Sent by the Lord: Songs of the World Church*, Vol.

begun to include the songs of other cultures beyond the bounds of Anglo-European traditions.

> Our understanding of believers in other cultures will be increased if we share their worship experiences, whether they are more or less sophisticated than ours, more or less cerebral, more or less emotional, more or less physical. Beyond this, in sharing music that is different from our own, whether it be in a cathedral with Britten's *Festival Te Deum,* in a rural Alabama church with "shape note" music, or in a Thailand mountain village singing to the accompaniment of an *angklung,* we may expect to get a new glimpse of God and Christian truth.[36]

Brian Wren takes the emphasis on global song a step further in reference to the church's theology of mission when he observes: "While it is good to sing 'our own' hymns of global mission awareness, they should not be the main focus. For paleface congregations, singing about mission only from a white, Western perspective—however enlightened—is a kind of hymnological neocolonialism. Better by far to hear, welcome, and sing songs from our global neighbors themselves."[37]

2; Hesla, Preus, and Witt, *Global Songs—Local Voices: Songs of Faith and Liberation from Around the World;* Kimbrough and Young, *Global Praise 1* (1996, rev. 1999, 2000); *Global Praise 2: Songs for Worship and Witness* (2000), and *Global Praise 3: More Songs for Worship and Witness* (2004); Hawn, *Halle, Halle: We Sing the World Round;* Peacock and Weaver, *World Praise and World Praise 2: Songs and Hymns for a New Millennium;* Routley, *Cantate Domino: An Ecumenical Hymn Book;* Colvin, *Fill Us with Your Love and Other Hymns from Africa;* Matsikenyiri, *Africa Praise 1;* Loh, *Hymns from the Four Winds: A Collection of Asian American Hymns* and *Sound the Bamboo: CCA Hymnal 2000;* Lockward, *Tenemos Esperanza;* Hawn, *Gather into One: Praying and Singing Globally,* and *One Bread, One Body: Exploring Cultural Diversity in Worship;* Mulrain, Kimbrough, and Young. *Caribbean Praise;* Garbuzova, Kimbrough, and McGurty, *Russian Praise;* Hofstra, *Voices: Native American Hymns and Worship Resources;* Berthier, *Music from Taizé,* Vol. 1, and *Cantos de Taizé;* Lockward and Heckert, *For Everyone Born;* Deer and Young, *Singing the Sacred: Musical Gifts from Native American Communities;* Kimbrough, Young, and Lockward, *Put Your Arms Around the World: Global Songs and Activities for Children;* Martinez, *Mil Voces para Celebrar: Himnario Metodista; Libro de Liturgia y Cántico.*

36. Hustad, *Jubilate II,* 67.

37. Wren, *Praying Twice,* 288.

3

Charles Wesley's Lyrical Theology

Having established some of the parameters of lyrical theology and that Charles Wesley may be viewed and interpreted as a lyrical theologian, how are we to read his sacred poetry? This question is not raised in reference to established canons of literary interpretation of poetry, which have been discussed in many works on English literature. The question is posed primarily here in terms of the historical context within which Charles Wesley emerged as a sacred poet and the diverse theological problems facing eighteenth-century Christians in Great Britain. Both the historical and theological contexts are extremely significant in shaping Charles's poetical content, thought, and to some extent, his output, since many of his poems were motivated by and were responses to particular events and theological issues current in the eighteenth century.

While Charles Wesley's immediate ancestry was distinctively Christian, it is an interesting combination of conformity and nonconformity on both the maternal and paternal sides of the family. Even though he developed a passionate loyalty to the Church of England, its beliefs, liturgy, and practices, to some extent he held this heritage of conformity and non-conformity in tension throughout his life and ministry. Though perhaps somewhat unlike his brother John, he usually preferred to err on the side of loyalty to the Church of England with its beliefs and practices than on the side of non-conformity. Nevertheless, one will see in his poetry the evidence of an ongoing tension between conformity and non-conformity.

To understand Charles as a poet, it is important to review his familial poetical heritage, for it helped nurture his poetical gifts. His father,

Samuel, an Anglican priest, was an erudite classicist and poet, whose writing skills and excellence in the classics formed an important model for young Charles, who also excelled in Latin, Hebrew, and Greek. Samuel's first poetical publication was *Maggots: Or, Poems on Several Subjects, Never Before Handled* (1685), a series of rather immature poems on somewhat superficial subjects, e.g., "On the Grunting of a Hog." Nevertheless, his composition in hudibrastics and Pindarics indicated much more than a superficial knowledge of poetical structure. His second volume of poetry was titled *The Life of Our Blessed Lord and Saviour* (1693), a series of heroic couplets in epic style. The preface to this volume bears the title "Essay on Heroic Poetry" and provides considerable insight into Samuel Wesley's erudition, particularly his acquaintance with Aristotle, Horace (Quintus Horatius Flaccus), Homer, Philo of Alexandria, Flavius Josephus, Abraham Cowley, Virgil, Edmund Spenser, John Milton, John Dryden, and many others.

In 1695 he published *Elegies,* which mourned the deaths of Queen Mary II and Archbishop John Tillotson. In addition to *An Epistle to a Friend Concerning Poetry* (1700), Samuel Wesley published four more volumes of poetry.

A number of Samuel and Susanna (his wife) Wesley's nineteen children were greatly influenced by this wealth of classical and poetical knowledge. Of the ten surviving children, seven girls and three boys, the eldest brother Samuel, also an Anglican priest, was a gifted poet and satirist, as revealed in his volume *Poems on Several Occasions* published in 1736, just three years before his untimely death. Charles Wesley was an admirer of his brother's poetry and on occasion, after Samuel became headmaster of Tiverton School, he would visit him and copy his verse. This is evidenced by the fact that one entry in Charles's manuscript journal for the year 1736[1] during his sojourn in America cites a passage from one of Samuel's poems before it had been published. Either Charles took copies he had made with him to America or he had memorized portions of his brother's verse that he had copied.

All three of the surviving brothers, Samuel, John, and Charles, were excellent students of the classics and mastered Greek, Hebrew, and Latin, and became gifted poets. Their sister, Mehetabel, affectionately known as Hetty, who also became a published poet, could read the Greek New

---

1. Kimbrough and Newport, *CW Journal,* 1:44.

Testament when she was only eight years old. John also mastered German and demonstrated his own poetical gifts by translating many German hymns into eloquent English verse. In addition, John's and Charles's knowledge of Latin was so advanced that they could easily converse in the language.

During his university years at Oxford, Charles combined an ongoing interest in the classics and poetry by writing metrical paraphrases of some of the Latin poets, such as Ovid, Virgil, Juvenal, and Horace, of which a few examples survive. Through such a discipline his gifts in the use of meter, rhyme, assonance, alliteration, and other poetical characteristics were honed. Here is one example from Horace's *Satires* (I.iii.107–110).[2]

> *Fuit ante Helenam mulier*[3] *teterrima belli*
> *Causa: Sed ignotis perierunt mortibus omnes*[4]
> *Quos Venerem incertum rapientes, more ferarum,*
> *Viribus editior caedebat, ut in grege taurus.*

> Full many a war has been for woman waged,
> Ere half the world in Helen's cause engaged;
> But unrecorded in historic verse,
> Obscurely died those savage ravishers:
> Who, like brute beasts, the female bore away,
> Till some superior brute re-seized the prey.
> As a wild bull, his rival bull o'erthrown,
> Claims the whole subject-herd, and reigns alone.[5]

The studies of Henry Bett, *The Hymns of Methodism,* and Frank Baker, *Charles Wesley's Verse,* on the background, content, literary structure, and qualities of Charles Wesley's poetry have demonstrated the importance of his immersion in outstanding Latin, Greek, and English poets. The few surviving English-language paraphrases of Latin classical

2. Henry Moore published five such examples in his *Life of the Rev. John Wesley.* See Frank Baker, *Rep. Verse,* 258–59. Baker's Introduction to this volume, which was later published separately in a revised and expanded edition, *Charles Wesley's Verse,* is the premiere study of the characteristics of Wesley's poetry, particularly vocabulary, structure, meter, rhyme, and rhetoric.

3. Charles is probably quoting from memory, for Horace's original text is "*cunnus*" instead of "*mulier.*"

4. Original text = "*illi*" instead of "*omnes.*"

5. *Unpub. Poetry,* 3:393.

poets by Charles, no doubt from his time at the university, are evidence of an early formative stage of his poetical gifts.

His training in the classics, thorough knowledge of biblical languages and content, in-depth absorption of the language and liturgies of the BCP, broad understanding of theological issues of his time (including a broad reading knowledge of the same), knowledge of significant extrabiblical literature by outstanding writers such as Homer, Cervantes, and Shakespeare, and ability to see humankind and its problems mirrored throughout Scripture—all of these combined to result in one of the most outstanding English-language sacred poets of all time.

It is not the intent of this chapter, nor of this volume as a whole, to provide an extended interpretation of every poem or hymn that is included. Rather, the purpose of this chapter is to examine who Charles Wesley is in his own eighteenth-century context and to explore some of the historical, theological, and literary currents that shaped his poetry and to which he often responded in his lyrics. Thus, the reader will be better equipped to understand and interpret his poetry.

Who, Then, is Charles Wesley?

What is there in Charles Wesley's identity, background, and makeup that aids the reading and interpretation of his lyrical theology?

(1) *Charles Wesley was a biblical interpreter. He was a person of the book, the Holy Scriptures.*[6] It is impossible to understand his poetry without an understanding of the Bible. In fact, having an open Bible alongside his poetry is a necessity. A brief glance at the marginal biblical reference citations prepared by Oliver A. Beckerlegge for *A Collection of Hymns for the Use of the People Called Methodists* (1780)[7] reveals the utter saturation of Charles's lyrics with biblical language, metaphors, figures of speech, events, places, and stories. He wrote long narrative poems about biblical characters such as the Canaanite woman, the Syrophoenician woman, and the Good Samaritan. He produced extensive metrical paraphrases of the Psalms, and in 1762 published a two-volume commentary on the

6. See below the hymns and poems under the heading "The Book of the Church: Holy Scripture" in section 4, "The Community of Faith."

7. Cited throughout as *Collection* (1780). The edition used here is volume 7 in the series *The Works of John Wesley*, edited by Franz Hildebrandt and Oliver A. Beckerlegge (1983).

Bible with the title *Short Hymns on Select Passages of the Holy Scriptures*[8] with over 2,000 hymns and poems based on every book of the Bible. In one sense, it is a poetical counterpart to his brother John's *Explanatory Notes Upon the New Testament*.

Charles's vast knowledge of the Bible was not limited merely to the content he garnered from its reading in English, Hebrew, Greek, and Latin. In some of his poetry, for example, he is known to have appropriated or adapted passages from Matthew Henry's commentary, *Exposition of the Old and New Testaments*.

To understand Charles Wesley's lyrical theology, indeed his sacred poetry as a whole, one must keep in mind that he lived and breathed the Holy Scriptures.

(2) *Charles Wesley was committed to Christ*[9] *and the church.*[10] After his Pentecost-Day conversion on May 21, 1738, which he referred to for the rest of his life as his "day of conversion," he saw that he stood by faith in Christ. While this was a personal realization to which he came in the privacy of his sick room at Mr. John Bray's home, he knew that his salvation was to be lived out in the community of faith, the church. The fullest expression of salvation he knew of was the Church of England, and in no wise would he ever have considered abandoning "the old ship," as he often referred to it.

(3) *Hence, Charles Wesley was an ecclesial theologian.*[11] His theology emerged within and through the church, not outside it. It is fascinating to see him working out a soteriology, which begins in creation and ends in new creation, within the context of ecclesiology. This requires tremendous imagination and it is precisely here that the poet excels. While Charles, like his brother John, is deeply concerned about the salvation of individuals, such salvation is always related to community, the church, the body of Christ.

As an ecclesial theologian Charles was also a liturgical theologian. Just as he lived and breathed the Holy Scriptures, he lived and breathed the liturgies of the church. We find him paraphrasing litanies, canticles,

8. Cited throughout as *Scripture Hymns* (1762).

9. See below the hymns and poems in section 2 under the heading, "The Grace of Jesus Christ."

10. See below the hymns and poems under the heading, "The Nature of the Church," in section 4, "The Community of Faith."

11. Ibid., and see Robinson, "A Single, Steady Aim," 31–57.

and prayers, and using the language of the Nicene Creed and the BCP in his hymns and sacred poems. He read the daily lections and often sang or read the appointed Psalm for the day before retiring.

(4) *Charles Wesley was a sacramental evangelist.*[12] This proclaimer of the good news of Christ did not conceive of the task of evangelization apart from the sacrament of Holy Communion. For him this was impossible. Indeed, according to Charles and his understanding of the church, evangelization is grounded in and flows from the sacrament. It is the body and blood of Christ that draw one into faith and are the expression of divine love for humankind. It is the body and blood of Christ that sustain the Christian and the church for eternity. It is the body and blood of Christ that send one out to live and proclaim God's redemptive love. Charles Wesley believed with all his heart in the evangelical power of the sacrament as stated in the New Testament: when we participate in this sacred meal we "proclaim the Lord's death until he comes" (1 Cor 11:26 NRSV).

One of the Wesley brothers' most significant works is *Hymns on the Lord's Supper*[13] (1745). It is one of the fullest expressions of Wesleyan ecclesial theology and sacramental evangelism. Interestingly this volume is probably the strongest expression of the theological linkage of Charles and John Wesley. John most likely wrote the introduction based on Daniel Brevint's work, *On the Christian Sacrament and Sacrifice* (1672), and Charles wrote the poetical responses to Brevint. In this volume, through Brevint in particular, one finds the strongest link between the Caroline divines and the Eucharistic theology of the Wesleys.

In *HLS* (1745) one sees Charles Wesley, the sacramental evangelist, diligently at work as poet-theologian through dramatic imagination as he combines liturgy and evangelism and turns the congregation into evangelists. The language of these hymns is filled with evangelical imperatives: come, see, and feel "his blood applied."

(5) *Charles Wesley was a person of catholic vision.*[14] As committed as he was to the Church of England (one must remember that this is the church brought into being by the action of King Henry VIII), Charles's

---

12. See below the hymns and poems under the heading, "The Sacraments and Rites of the Church," pages 234–54, in section 4, "The Community of Faith."

13. Cited throughout as *HLS* (1745).

14. See below the hymns and poems under the heading, "United in Christ," pages 217–26, in section 4, "The Community of Faith."

vision of the body of Christ is inclusive. His prayers for the unity of the church are some of the most eloquent and poignant ever written.

A poem by Charles first published in 1755 titled "Catholic Love" was printed at the end of John Wesley's sermon on 2 Kgs 10:15. The poem of seven stanzas expresses a strong evangelical piety coupled with a high ecclesiology, as found in stanzas 2 and 7 respectively:

2. Forth from the midst of *Babel* brought,
       Parties and sects I cast behind;
    Enlarged my heart, and free my thought,
       Where'er the latent truth I find,
    The latent truth with joy to own,
    And bow to Jesus' name alone.
       . . .

7. Joined to the hidden church unknown
       In this sure bond of perfectness,
    Obscurely safe, I dwell alone,
       And glory in the'uniting grace,
    To me, to each believer given,
    To all thy saints in earth and heaven.[15]

Father Francis Frost speaks of the "trans-confessional" nature of Charles Wesley's hymns and poems.[16] They reach far beyond confessions and denominations to the heart of the Holy Scriptures, the gospel, and the life of faith community centered in Christ and the Eucharist.

(6) *Charles Wesley was an advocate for the poor.*[17] As the Wesleys began their work throughout Great Britain, there was no middle class, essentially only the poor and the wealthy. While they certainly reached out to both groups, one of the defining strengths of the Wesleyan movement was its outreach to the poor and marginalized—coal miners, people in workhouses, abused and neglected children, prisoners, etc.

In his journal Charles Wesley avers that the poor are his best friends and he begins a stanza of one of his hitherto unpublished poems with the line, "Help us to make the poor our friends."[18] Charles wrote numerous

---

15. *Poet. Works*, 6:71–72.

16. See his article, "The Christ-Mysticism of Charles Wesley," 11–26.

17. Kimbrough and Young, *Songs for the Poor*; also Kimbrough's "Charles Wesley and the Poor" and "Perfection Revisited."

18. *Unpub. Poetry*, 2:157.

hymns/poems related to life with and among the poor. It is indeed strange, given the commitment of the Wesleyan movement to work among the poor, that most of these poems never appeared in *any* hymnbook of "the people called Methodists." The following stanza is certainly an exception. It is usually the fourth stanza of the hymn "Jesus, the gift divine I know,"[19] a five-stanza hymn that consists of the combination of parts of two different poems from *Scripture Hymns* (1762).

> Thy mind throughout my life be shown,
>   While listening to the sufferer's cry,
> The widow's and the orphan's groan,
>   On mercy's wings I swiftly fly
> The poor and helpless to relieve,
> My life, my all for them to give.

It is a powerful statement of the social conscience of early Methodists. It survives today in the British Methodist hymnal, *Hymns and Psalms* (1983), but it is not included in *The United Methodist Hymnal* (1989).

In one poem in particular Charles lays out a *social manifesto* for the Wesleyan movement, which sees the poor in the world as being there vicariously in the stead of Christ. The mandate of the individual Christian and the church is:

> Work for the weak, and sick, and poor,
> Raiment and food for them procure,
>   And mindful of God's Word,
> Enjoy the blessedness to give,
> Lay out your gettings to relieve
> The members of your Lord.[20]

All of the aspects of Charles Wesley's identity mentioned above are vital to keep in mind as one reads and interprets his poetry. His interpretation of the Christian faith and life integrates biblical, Christological,

---

19. From *Scripture Hymns* (1762), stanzas 1–2, 2:244, Hymn 413, based on John 4:10: "Jesus answered and said unto her, If thou knewest the gift of God, and who it is that saith to thee, Give me to drink; thou wouldest have asked of him, and he would have given thee living water." Stanzas 3–5, 2:380, Hymn 738, are based on James 1:27: "Pure religion and undefiled before God and the Father is this, To visit the fatherless and widows in their affliction, and to keep himself unspotted from the world." (See also selection 11 in Kimbrough, *Songs for the Poor*.)

20. *Unpub. Poetry,* 2:403–4; see also selection 10 in Kimbrough, *Songs for the Poor.*

ecclesial, sacramental, evangelical, catholic, and social outreach foci, all of which impact his lyrical theology.

After a brief examination of the historical and theological contexts in which Charles Wesley is found in the eighteenth century, we turn to three aspects of Charles Wesley's lyrical theology whose understanding is essential for reading and interpreting his hymns: lyrical theology as doxology, lyrical theology as a reflective process, and historically oriented lyrical theology.

Historical and Theological Contexts[21]

An understanding of the historical and theological contexts in which Charles Wesley emerged as a sacred poet and to which he often responded in his poetry is vitally important in order to interpret his texts appropriately. While we cannot establish a *Sitz im Leben* for each poem or hymn included in this volume or written during his lifetime, we can establish an overall picture, and in some instances a very specific one, which sheds interpretive light on his work.

Charles was the son of Susanna and Samuel Wesley, a priest of the Church of England, the church in which he was baptized and grew up. It is by no means insignificant that at an early age he left Epworth to attend Westminster School (at Westminster Abbey) in London where his eldest brother Samuel was an Usher. While there Charles attended worship at the Abbey and, as in his home and the parish of Epworth, became more and more familiar with the BCP and its Coverdale Psalter, which he came to treasure throughout his life. How serious Charles was about the church and liturgical life during these early school years we do not know, but it was the ecclesial context in which he was educated and which sowed theological, liturgical, and linguistic seed that later would bear much fruit in his poetical composition.

Besides the strong ecclesial and poetical influence of his brother Samuel (known as Samuel the Younger), eighteen years his senior and who also became an Anglican priest, it is perhaps by no means a small matter that Samuel modeled for Charles and brother John care for the poor by advocating for the first medical dispensary for the poor at Westminster in London.

21. See below, chapter 5.

We have noted already that it was the Henrician church in which Charles found himself, for King Henry VIII had broken with Rome over marriage issues and established the Church of England. While this church unequivocally lay somewhere between continental Protestantism and traditional Roman Catholicism, by the time of the Wesleys the liturgy had been established in the vernacular of the people. The BCP had had over a century of usage. In addition to the Coverdale Psalter included in the BCP, a tradition of English-language metrical Psalters was well in place through the work of Sternhold and Hopkins, Tate and Brady, and others.

An anti-Rome posture had emerged in many parts of the country with continental Reformation sentiments, which had crossed the Channel from the continent to England. Politically the country had endured monarchial attempts to reestablish Roman Catholicism as the religion of the realm under the short-lived reign of Queen Mary I and the ill-fated invasion of the Pretender to the throne, Bonnie Prince Charlie (Charles Edward Stuart), who had courted the support of the French Roman Catholics.

Two parliamentary measures passed in 1559 set the tone for the immediate future of the Church of England. (1) The Act of Supremacy established Queen Elizabeth I as the head of state, but also as the "Supreme Governor" of the church. Fortunately, however, the Act avoided making her the "head" of the church, so as to prevent the turmoil Henry VIII had caused with his self-declaration as such. (2) The Act of Uniformity standardized the doctrine and liturgy of the church by requiring all parishes to use the BCP and all clergy to subscribe to the Thirty-Nine Articles of Religion. It also acknowledged the Book of Homilies as the standard interpretation of doctrine to be read regularly throughout the Church of England.

These two Acts by no means solved all problematical issues for the Church, for there followed much political turmoil, which greatly affected the attitudes of Christians and the leadership of the Church in England. This was complicated all the more by wave after wave of religious discontent, as the country was overwhelmed with Presbyterians, Baptists, Congregationalists, Quakers, Moravians, and Dissenters of other persuasions.

In 1738, the Wesley brothers, John and Charles, began to lead a reform movement within the Church of England, the adherents of which became known as "Methodists." They were not, however, the only ones within the Church seeking reform. For example, Anglican priest George Whitefield was a primary figure in the evangelical revival, though a protagonist of many aspects of Calvinist theology.

After flirting with unity within the revival, however, the three primary groups split into distinct segments: Moravians, Calvinists, and Methodists. To be sure, some of the Calvinists and Moravians did not stand within the context of the Church of England. The Wesleys, with their strong emphasis on universal salvation, sought to bring these groups together, but ultimately did not prevail.

The eighteenth century was a time of sorting through important theological issues: predestination vs. free will, election vs. universal atonement, stillness vs. good works, Trinitarianism vs. Unitarianism and Deism, full perfection vs. the pilgrimage toward perfection, imputed righteousness vs. Christian perfection, Calvinism vs. Arminianism. While John Wesley addressed these and other theological issues in his prose writings, Charles addressed many of them, as well as numerous moments and events of history, in his poetry.

Lyrical Theology as Doxology

In 1761 John Wesley published the "Directions for Singing" which summarized the doxological posture of the Methodist movement of the past, present, and future.

> Above all sing spiritually. Have an eye to God in every word you sing. Aim at pleasing him more than yourself, or any other creature. In order to do this attend strictly to the sense of what you sing, and see that your heart is not carried away with the sound, but offered to God continually; so shall your singing be such as the Lord will approve here, and reward you when he cometh in the clouds of heaven.[22]

Charles came on the scene as a sacred poet of the evangelical revival within the Church of England in 1738, and grasped from the beginning of the Methodist movement what his brother John would articulate so eloquently twenty-three years later: "see that your heart is not carried away with the sound, but offered to God continually; so shall your singing be

22. *Select Hymns* (1761), vi.

such as the Lord will approve." Therefore, he spent his life articulating for the individual and the worshiping community what it means to live a doxological life, one that continually offers the heart to God in song, praise, and prayer. The adverb "continually" used by John Wesley in the above admonition is vitally important, for doxology is the Christian's lifelong vocation. One lives every hour of every day in praise of God the Creator with thanksgiving in one's heart for life and all creation.

Therefore, the hymnic corpus composed by Charles Wesley for worship is doxological. This does not mean that every hymn text he composed was a hymn of praise and thanksgiving. Rather, in the hymns he wrote for the purposes of worship and devotion he was seeking a continual offering of the human heart and life to God. Hence, the lyrical theology of doxology is multifaceted, multidimensional, and filled with diverse themes.

"O for a thousand tongues to sing" (stanzas 7–12 of a hymn which originally had 18 stanzas) has been the opening hymn in many Methodist hymnbooks. This is not surprising, since its "first" stanza expresses three primary emphases of the Methodist movement: music, praise of God, and God's grace. As important as it is as an expression of Wesleyan doxology, too often it has been sung merely as a hymn of praise divorced from the full context of the eighteen-stanza poem within which it is found. Fortunately in *The United Methodist Hymnal* (1989) all but one stanza of the original hymn appear in the form of poetry without music at selection 58.

Charles Wesley wrote this hymn/poem in 1739 for the anniversary of his conversion, which took place on May 21, 1738. He published it with the title "For the Anniversary Day of One's Conversion." Hence, in reading the first six stanzas, which precede the stanza beginning "O for a thousand tongues to sing," one discovers what it is that makes Charles Wesley want to break continually into song in praise of the Redeemer/Creator God. Those stanzas reflect his experience leading up to his conversion on May 21, 1738. The opening line of the original first stanza is the prologue to Charles Wesley's lyrical theology:

> Glory to God, and praise, and love,
>   be ever, ever given.

Praise of God and the expression of love are two recurring themes and emphases in the hymns of Charles Wesley. They are inseparable. Praise of

God is an expression of love, and an expression of love for God is praise. Hence, from the outset the biblical dimensions of praise and love, be they horizontal or vertical, are expressed by Wesley in a hymn that celebrates conversion. One of the special gifts of Charles Wesley in creating a lyrical theology is his ability to combine a multiplicity of Christian beliefs, values, and morals, sometimes in almost telescopic fashion, in his sacred hymns and poems. For example, within the eighteen stanzas of the original poem, which begins with the line "Glory to God, and praise and love," he integrates the themes of conversion, transformation, faith, the Holy Spirit, emotion, decision, the identity of Jesus, outreach to the marginalized (murderers, harlots, thieves), universal outreach to all, justification, and grace.

Furthermore, the resonance of God's glory in Wesley's lyrical theology is expressed in praise and love, which unite earth and heaven. The voices of ages past join with those of the present in a song that is eternal. It resounds through time and space in praise of the Creator. Hence, whoever sings this song never sings alone! It is a song of a global, *universe-al* community, and often transcends time and space.

Lyrical Theology as Reflection

We will observe below that Charles Wesley often addressed historical moments in a poetical style not intended for worship. The writing of poetical verse for Charles involved much more. It was an avenue of theological reflection and exploration. It was his way of working through theological issues, thought, and concepts, and of shaping theological ideas. Though doxology was often his intent, he did not write poetry solely with a doxological purpose, in other words, to be used specifically by the worshiping community in adoration of God.

We will examine four examples of this kind of poetical writing by Charles Wesley, designated here as a "lyrical theology of reflection," of which one must be aware in reading and interpreting his texts.

HYMNS ON THE LORD'S SUPPER (1745)

In 1745 Charles and John Wesley published *HLS* (1745). It is one of the most significant poetical contributions to Wesleyan theological expression. The opening prose preface to the hymns was no doubt the work of John and is an abridgment of Daniel Brevint's treatise *On the Christian Sacrament and Sacrifice, by way of discourse, meditation, and prayer upon the nature, parts, and blessings of the Holy Communion* (1672). Under the restoration of King Charles II, Brevint (1616–1695) was the Dean of Lincoln College. His treatise expresses a lofty view of the presence of Christ in the sacrament of Holy Communion and stresses the sacrificial nature of the rite. The hymns of the volume are generally understood to be the work of Charles.

There were eight chapters in Brevint's treatise. The first five were on the theme of Holy Communion as a sacrament, and the remaining three were on the theme of the rite "as a sacrifice." Most likely it was John Wesley who condensed Brevint's eight chapters to five sections: (1) "As it is a Memorial of the Suffering and Death of Christ," (2) "As it is a Sign and Means of Grace," (3) "The Sacrament as a Pledge of Heaven," (4) "Concerning the Sacrifice of our Persons," (5) "The Holy Eucharist as it implies Sacrifice." To these a section "After the Sacrament" was added.

Following Brevint, Charles Wesley reflects upon and explores the completeness of Christ's sacrifice as sufficient once and for all. One senses the coherence of Charles Wesley's theological understanding and, contrary to Roman Catholic views, Wesley does not seek to determine "*how* the means transmit the power*" (see Hymns 57–59). Also, the hymns are clearly often anti-Calvinist, rejecting any idea of limited atonement.

In typical Charles Wesley style, he is often taken by a particular word or phrase in Brevint to which he devotes an entire poem. The five sections of poetry are generally understood to be the composition of Charles Wesley and follow Brevint rather closely. In the concluding section of poems, however, Wesley diverges with lyrics that are more doxological in nature. In the first four sections, if one reads Brevint alongside Wesley's poetry, one sees clearly how he is responding to Brevint's theological discussion with considerable consistency. Nevertheless, Wesley moves beyond Brevint, for his lyrical theology is more open-ended. He knows that he can express the mystery of God's presence in the Eucharist, but his verse reveals his full awareness that he cannot "capture" the mystery with finality in words. He cannot lock into words the precise meaning of the mystery, for it transcends human expression. What more fitting genre than poetry can be found to reveal this reality?

1. O the depth of love divine,
        Th'unfathomable grace!
    Who shall say how bread and wine
        God into man conveys?
    How the bread his flesh imparts,
        How the wine transmits his blood,
    Fills his faithful peoples' hearts
        With all the life of God!

2. Let the wisest mortal show
        How we the grace receive:
    Feeble elements below
        A power not theirs to give.
    Who explains the wondrous way?
        How thro' these the virtue came?
    These the virtue did convey,
        Yet still remain the same.

3. How can heavenly spirits rise
        By earthly matter fed,
    Drink herewith divine supplies
        And eat immortal bread?
    Ask the Father's wisdom *how;*
        Him that did the means ordain
    Angels round our altars bow
        To search it out, in vain.

4. Sure and real is the grace,
        The manner be unknown;
    Only meet us in thy ways
        And perfect us in one.
    Let us taste the heavenly powers,
        Lord, we ask for nothing more;
    Thine to bless, 'tis only ours
        To wonder, and adore.[23]

Brevint considers the Lord's Supper as a past, present, and future reality. One sees clearly the theological reflection on this timeframe in three sections of *HLS* (1745):

23. *HLS* (1745) 41, Hymn 57.

I. As it is a Memorial of the Suffering and Death of Christ
    (*past,* Hymns 1–27);

II. As it is a Sign and a Means of Grace (*present,* Hymns 28–92);

III. The Sacrament as a Pledge of Heaven (*future,* Hymns 93–115).

Geoffrey Wainwright has shown that in addition to the Wesleys' theological reflection on Brevint, *HLS* (1745) draws heavily on two ritual sources: the BCP and the Eighth Book of *The Apostolic Constitutions,* which originated in the fourth century and was thought by some in the time of the Wesleys to be apostolic in origin.[24] Some of the ritual elements that find lyrical theological expression in *HLS* (1745) are: *sanctus* (Hymn 161), *sursum corda* (Hymn 21), Institution narrative (Hymn 1), anamnesis-oblation (Hymns 118, 121, 124, 125), *epiclesis* (Hymns 16, 72), elevation of the elements (Hymn 163), *gloria in excelsis* (Hymn 163), *benedictus qui venit* (Hymn 98), Words of Distribution (Hymn 71), Prayer of Humble Access (Hymn 43).

Some of the more closely reasoned hymns are so packed full with biblical imagery and metaphors from line to line that they were most probably not intended for congregational singing. For example, in a rehearsal of some aspects of salvation history Wesley composes the following words for stanza 2 of Hymn 61, "Thou God of boundless power and grace":

> Let but thy ark the walls surround,
> Let but the Rams-horn Trumpets sound,
>   The city boasts its height no more,
> Its bulwarks are at once o'erthrown,
> Its massy walls by air blown down,
>   They fall before Almighty power.
> Jordan at thy command shall heal
> The sore disease incurable,
>   And wash out all the leper's stains;
> Or oil the med'cine shall supply,
> Or cloths, or shadows passing by,
>   If so thy sovereign will ordains.[25]

24. Wainwright, Preface to a facsimile reprint of *HLS* 1745, ix.

25. *HLS* (1745) 45, Hymn 61.

Nevertheless, there are numerous texts in *HLS* (1745) that cry out to be sung, for they are composed with eloquence, combining depth of perception with human experience.

1.   Author of life divine,
        Who hast a table spread,
    Furnished with mystic wine
        And everlasting Bread,
    Preserve the life thyself hast given,
    And feed, and train us up for heaven.

2.   Our needy souls sustain
        With fresh supplies of love,
    Till all thy life we gain,
        And all thy fullness prove,
    And strength'ned by thy perfect grace,
    Behold without a veil thy face.[26]

Without question the Wesleys intended many of their poems to be sung as hymns by the worshiping community and hence many may be considered in the context of a doxological theology. One should not assume, however, that such a theology cannot also be reflective and intellectually disciplined. *HLS* (1745) illustrates this indeed—in substance, structure, and theological ideas, especially when one reads these hymns alongside Brevint, the *Apostolic Constitutions,* and the BCP.

HYMNS ON THE TRINITY (1767)

The second example of Charles Wesley's lyrical reworking of a theological treatise is *Trinity Hymns* (1767), which is based on William Jones's *The Catholic Doctrine of the Trinity, proved by above an hundred short and clear arguments, expressed in terms of the Holy Scriptures* (1756). Wesley's work contains 188 sacred poems divided into two parts. In Part 1 (Hymns 1–136) Wesley works his way carefully through Jones's treatise: "Hymns on the Divinity of Christ" (Hymns 1–57), "The Divinity of the Holy Ghost" (Hymns 58–86), "The *Plurality* and *Trinity* of Persons" (Hymns 87–109), "The Trinity in Unity" (Hymns 110–136). Just as Jones bases most of his discussion on the strength of argument from Holy Scripture, in Hymns 1–136 Wesley prefaces almost every lyric with a passage from

26. Ibid., 30, Hymn 40.

the Scriptures. Once again, his closely reasoned verse reflects his wrestling with the meaning and understanding of the Trinity, but at times the lyric is more for reflection than singing. He packs so much into the first stanza of Hymn 42, which is based on 1 Cor 11:3, "The head of Christ is God" (RSV), that it is difficult to imagine these lines in congregational song.

> The Partner of our flesh and blood,
> As man, inferior is to God:
> The lower part of Christ, the heel
> Was bruised, and did our sorrows feel;
> But though he would his life resign,
> His part superior is divine,
> And doth, beyond the reach of pain,
> God over all for ever reign.[27]

What happens with Jones's treatise is precisely what happens with Brevint's treatise in *HLS* (1745): Wesley transforms the prose apologetic into what Wilma J. Quantrille calls "lyrical theological discourse."[28] The result is often the language of praise and thanksgiving. Though Wesley follows Jones very closely in the concluding Part 2, "Hymns and Prayers to the Trinity" (Hymns newly numbered 1–52), he transcends Jones's treatise and moves to the realm of experience. The link between knowledge and practice is experienced in worship, private devotion, and daily living. So important is the aspect of articulating the mystery of the Trinity in song that for the first twenty-four hymns in Part 2 Wesley prescribes the twenty-four tunes of John Lampe in *Festival Hymns* (1746) to be sung with the hymns so designated.

Here is an eloquent example of how Wesley moves from the glory of God to the human experience of goodness and love:

> Make thy goodness pass before me,
> Glorious God thyself proclaim,
> To my first estate restore me,
> Re-imprest with thy new name,
> In the likeness of my Maker
> Re-begotten from above,
> Of thy holiness partaker,
> Filled with all the life of love.[29]

27. *Trinity Hymns* (1767) 28, stanza 1, Hymn 62.

28. Quantrille, Introduction to a facsimile reprint of *Trinity Hymns* (1767) ix.

29. *Trinity Hymns* (1767) 120, stanza 2, Hymn 35.

Knowledge of God without the experience of the "life of love" is for Wesley unthinkable.

On a number of occasions Charles Wesley turned the prose and poetry of distinguished writers into poetry: Daniel Brevint, Matthew Henry, John Dryden, Edward Young, Ovid, Juvenal, and Virgil, and he drew as well on Shakespeare and Milton. Wesley processed his thought through verse. Did he intend all of such sacred poetry for hymn singing? No. In the case of *Trinity Hymns* (1767), as singable as many of the texts may be, Wesley was probably more interested in faithfulness to Jones's treatise than in creating every stanza of every poetical text for singing. He presents his poetry in the same categories used by Jones: "The Divinity of Christ," "The Divinity of the Holy Spirit," "The Plurality and Trinity of Persons," and "The Trinity in Unity."

As in the case with *HLS* (1745), Wesley writes his own concluding section to *Trinity Hymns* (1767) entitled "Hymns and Prayers to the Trinity" in a highly doxological manner. Here he is not following Jones but rather creating his own theological commentary in the language of praise and adoration.

A major difference in Charles Wesley's style from either Jones or Brevint is that he is neither polemical nor apologetic in his approach to theological expression. He is evangelical and doxological. His approach has never been viewed as scholarly or academic. This is, in the strict sense of the two words, one reason why proponents of theology as a highly academic discipline often look down on poetical expressions of theology as less worthy of serious theological study. Such a view, however, does not take into consideration the values of theopoetic art in the understanding of faith and faith expression.

In *Trinity Hymns* (1767) Wesley seeks to give life to what the church taught about the Trinity. In his poetry the Trinity is a dynamic, living, life-giving reality. Those who think his hymns to be detached, sporadic expressions of theological ideas will find in *Trinity Hymns* (1767) continuity and coherence of thought, process, and theology.

SHORT HYMNS ON SELECT PASSAGES OF THE HOLY SCRIPTURES (1762)

The third example of Charles Wesley's lyrical theology that illustrates a serious discipline of theological reflection and exploration is his two-volume work *Scripture Hymns* (1762),[30] published in 1762. Volume 1 included 1,160 poems on the Old Testament, and volume 2 contained 318 poems on the Old Testament and 871 poems on the New Testament, for a total of 2,349. *Scripture Hymns* (1762) appeared only in one additional, but abbreviated posthumous edition (Charles Wesley died in 1788): volume 1 in 1794 and volume 2 in 1796.

Scripture Hymns (1762) is one of the largest lyrical commentaries on the Holy Scriptures in the English language. In most instances John edited his brother's poetry before publication. However, Charles published the 1762 work, as he had *HSP* (1749), independently of John. Thus, Charles expressed himself without the theological, linguistic, or literary editing of his brother, and in *Scripture Hymns* (1762) shaped his thoughts on gradual sanctification, perfection, and mysticism, which John might have altered had he edited the work.[31] The 1762 volumes contain valuable biblical, theological, social, ecclesial, and poetical insight for the study of Holy Scripture, English and church history, literature, and theology.

Scripture Hymns (1762) is a collage of biblical allusions. Wesley begins with Genesis and concludes with the book of Revelation, writing over 2,000 poems that encompass every book of the Bible. He generally proceeds chronologically through the Scriptures except in poems on the Gospel of Luke, where he fills out the seven last words of Jesus from the cross with passages from the Gospels of Matthew and John.[32] Unlike many of his lengthy poetical expositions of biblical passages[33] in other publications, the poems in *Scripture Hymns* (1762) are usually brief, consisting of one or two stanzas. Poems of five or six stanzas do occur, but they are not the norm. Therefore, the focus is generally on a central idea, word, or phrase of a passage. Wesley preceded each poem with a scriptural quotation and reference. To save space he often abbreviated lengthy verses and

30. See the brief discussion of *Scripture Hymns* (1762) by Jackson, *Life of the Rev. Charles Wesley*, 2:199–210. See also this author's more detailed discussion of the work in the next chapter.

31. John made extensive marginal notes in his own copy of *Scripture Hymns* (1762), which is currently located in the Wesley house in City Road, London. They indicate very clearly many editorial changes and adjustments he would have made, had Charles allowed him to edit the two volumes. See this author's collation and interpretation of John's notes in Kimbrough, "John Wesley: Editor—Poet—Priest," 131–52.

32. See *Scripture Hymns* (1762) 2:232–34.

33. See the poems in *HSP* (1742) based on Romans 6 (182–83), Isaiah 4 (184–86), Isaiah 12 (186–87).

added "etc." at the point of interruption. At times he wrote more than one poem on the same biblical passage. In such instances he quoted the biblical verses only before the first poem in the series.

The title contains the word "hymns" and suggests that all of the 2,349[34] poetical entries in the two volumes are hymns. That is far from the case. More properly they should be called "hymns and sacred poems," as the Wesleys had done in earlier works. Although some of the poems did make their way into hymnbooks,[35] one may not consider the 1762 work as a two-volume hymnbook.

It should be noted that "O thou who camest from above"[36] is of particular historical and theological importance, since John Wesley is reported by Samuel Bradburn in his *Sketch of Mr. Wesley's Character* (1791) to have referred to the first two lines as expressive of his own testimony of faith.[37]

> Jesus, confirm my heart's desire
> To work, and speak, and think for thee,
> Still let me guard the holy fire,
> And still stir up thy gift in me,
> Ready for all thy perfect will
> My acts of faith and love repeat,
> 'Till death thy endless mercies seal,
> And make my sacrifice compleat.

"Come, let us use the grace divine"[38] is also very important, for it became known as the "Covenant Hymn" included in John Wesley's Covenant Service, which was celebrated at the turn of each new year.

---

34. The total number of poems in both volumes according to the printed number of poems is 2,348, but in volume 2 on page 293 there are two poems with the number 556, hence, the total number is 2,349.

35. "Captain of Israel's host and guide," 1:42, Hymn 133; "O thou who camest from above," 1:57, Hymn 183; "A charge to keep I have," 1:58, Hymn 188; "Lord, in the strength of grace," 1:194, Hymn 621; "Thou shepherd of Israel, and mine," 1:294, Hymn 931; "'Tis finished! the Messiah dies," 2:234, Hymn 387; "Come, let us use the grace divine," 2:36, Hymn 1242; "Come then, and dwell in me," 2:298, Hymn 569; "The causeless, unexhausted love," 1:53, Hymn 169.

36. *Scripture Hymns* (1762) 1:57, Hymn 183.

37. Young, *Companion to The United Methodist Hymnal*, 533.

38. *Scripture Hymns* (1762) 2:36, Hymn 1242.

THEOLOGICAL WRITINGS OF JOHN WESLEY

There is yet a fourth arena of prose literature to which Charles responded in verse, namely, theological writings of his brother John. Though Charles refused to let John edit his poems in *Scripture Hymns* (1762), there are also instances of his lyrical theological reflection that resulted specifically from working in concert with John and in responding to his brother's theological writings. One example of this is seven hymns of Charles, which are attached to the conclusion of John's 1758 publication, *Reasons Against a Separation from the Church of England*. In this treatise John described twelve reasons against separation and presented them in a rather conciliatory tone. "Whether it be *lawful* or no, (which itself may be disputed, being not so clear a Point as some imagine,) it is by no Means *expedient,* for us to separate from the Establish'd Church."[39]

To his hymns, which concluded John's publication, Charles prefixed a much stronger statement:

> I think myself bound in duty, to add my testimony to my brother's. His twelve reasons against our ever separating from the Church of England are mine also. I subscribe to them with all my heart. Only with regard to the first, I am quite clear that it is neither expedient nor lawful for *me* to separate: and I never had the least inclination or temptation to do so. My affection for the Church is as strong as ever; and I clearly see my calling; which is, to live and die in her communion. This, therefore, I am determined to do, the Lord being my helper.
>
> I have subjoined the hymns for the lay-preachers; still further to secure this end, to cut off all jealously and suspicion from our friends, or hope from our enemies, of our having any design of ever separating from the Church. I have no secret reserve, or distant thought of it. I never had. Would to God all the Methodist preachers were, in this respect, like-minded with CHARLES WESLEY.[40]

In these seven hymns Charles addresses the fallen state of the established Church as regards doctrine, and he views discipline, morality, devotion, and self-denial as important characteristics of Methodist preachers. In these hymns one finds a high ecclesiology and a fervent evangelical spirit. Note, for example, Hymn 5:5, and 4:5:

39. John Wesley, *Reasons Against Separation from the Church of England,* 3.

40. Ibid., 12.

We pray these dry bones may live:
　　We see the answer of our prayer!
Thou dost a thousand tokens give,
　　That *England's* Church is still thy care,
Ten thousand witnesses appear,
Ten thousand proofs, that God is here!

Here let us spend our utmost zeal,
　　Here let us all our powers exert,
To testify thy gracious will,
　　Inform the world how kind thou art,
And nothing know, desire, approve,
But Jesus—and thy bleeding love.[41]

Though four specific instances have been noted in which Charles's reflective lyrical theology is a response to three theological treatises and to the Bible as a whole, there are many other poetical texts of Charles that may or may not have been written specifically to be sung by the faith community. In numerous poetical texts, without responding specifically to theological works in print, he reflected on theological concepts such as sanctification, perfection, love, grace, sin, redemption, salvation, etc. Often he succeeded in writing enduring lyrics that provide an ongoing means for the faith community to rehearse the content, ethics, and action of its faith in song. Thus, Wesley contributes to the creation of a theological memory of depth within the church that sustains it in times of difficulty and suffering, as well as in times of joy and wellbeing. Learning to read and sing his poetry with sensitivity to the importance of theological memory for Christians and the church as a whole is vitally important.

Historically Oriented Lyrical Theology

If we are to read and interpret his poetry and lyrical theology with integrity, it is important to recognize that poetry is the means whereby Charles Wesley responded theologically to important historical events, moments, and persons of his time.

41. *Poet. Works*, 6:103–4.

Hymns for Times of Trouble and Persecution (1744)

One of the early examples of Charles Wesley writing hymns in response to contemporary events is the booklet titled *Hymns for Times of Trouble* (1744). The period of time immediately before and after the Jacobite Revolution of 1745 resulted in grave difficulties for the Methodists. The mob violence directed against them resulted often in destruction of property and physical injury. Their loyalty to the British Crown was questioned, and some labeled them Papists and Jacobites. Charles responded to this chaos with a call to stand firm in their faith:

> The waves of the sea have lift up their voice,
> Sore troubled that we in Jesus rejoice;
> The floods they are roaring, but Jesus is here,
> While we are adoring, he always is near.
>
> Men, devils engage, the billows arise,
> And horribly rage, and threaten the skies:
> Their fury shall never our stedfastness shock,
> The weakest believer is built on a rock.[42]

By and large the language of the hymns in this booklet is general in nature, although four prayers in the first section indicate the Wesley brothers' allegiance to King George II. Three prayers are titled "A Prayer for His Majesty King George" and another "For the King and the Royal Family."

A few additional examples underscore Charles Wesley's lyrical and theological response to contemporary events.

Hymns for the Public Thanksgiving-Day, October 9, 1746[43]

A day of public thanksgiving was declared by the government in response to defeat of rebels at the Battle of Culloden (April 16, 1746), in which supporters of the Stuart takeover of the throne were defeated. For this event

---

42. Stanzas two and three of the hymn, "Ye servants of God, your Master proclaim," which are usually excluded in modern versions of the hymn. See *HTTP* (1744) 43, Hymn 1.

43. Cited throughout as *Thanksgiving Hymns* (1746).

Wesley published seven hymns in *Thanksgiving Hymns* (1746). Stanza one of Hymn 2 reads:

> Thanks be to God, the God of Power,
> Who sheltered us in Danger's Hour,
> The God of Truth, who heard the Prayer,
> Let all his Faithfulness declare,
> Who sent us Succours from above,
> Let all adore the God of Love.[44]

Hymns Occasioned by the Earthquake, March 8, 1750[45]

On February 8, 1750, Charles recorded in his journal, "There was an earthquake in London." At this time he was in Bristol, and his brother John, who was in London, recorded this account of the earthquake:

> It was about a quarter after twelve that the earthquake began at the skirts of the town. It began in the south-east, went through Southwark, under the river, and then from one end of London to the other. It was observed at Westminster and Grosvenor-square a quarter before one (perhaps, if we allow for the difference of the clocks, about a quarter of an hour after it began in Southwark). There were three distinct shakes, or wavings to and fro, attended with a hoarse, rumbling noise, like thunder.[46]

On March 8, 1750, Charles Wesley was in London and John in Bristol. Charles recorded in his *Journal* on that day: "There was an earthquake in London." John was in Bristol at the time and on the same day Charles wrote to John:

> This morning, at a quarter after five, we had another shock of an earthquake, far more violent than that of February 8th. I was repeating my text, when it shook the Foundery so violently, that we all expected it to fall upon our heads. A great cry followed from the women and the children. I immediately cried out, "Therefore will we not fear, though the earth be moved, and the hills be carried into the midst of the sea: for the Lord of hosts is with us; the

---

44. *Pentecost Hymns* (1746) 4.

45. Cited throughout as *Earthquake Hymns* (1750).

46. W. Reginald Ward and Richard P. Heitzenrater, *Journal and Diaries III* (1743–54), vol. 20:320. In the series *The Works of John Wesley*.

God of Jacob is our refuge." He filled my heart with faith, and my mouth with words, shaking their souls, as well as their bodies.[47]

And on Wednesday, April 4, he recorded:

Fear filled our chapel, occasioned by a prophecy of the earthquake's return this night. I preached my written sermon on the subject,[48] with great effect, and gave out several suitable hymns. It was a glorious night for the disciples of Jesus.[49]

In less than one month Charles Wesley had begun, if not completed, the nineteen hymns for his pamphlet *Earthquake Hymns* (1750). Part 1 included six hymns, and Part 2 consisted of thirteen hymns.

The primary emphases of these hymns were: the power and sovereignty of God, God's mercy, and God's righteous dealing with humankind; divine forbearance and long-suffering, uncertainty of life, and earthly possessions. What endures is the joy, which comes from Christ. The hymns are primarily devotional in nature and plead for serenity amid all the turmoil rampant in England. Hymn 5, "From whence these dire Portents around" begins with the identical first line of one of his brother Samuel's texts in *Poems on Several Occasions* (1736), pages 136–37. The poem is entitled "On the Passion of Our Saviour" and focuses upon the earthquake at the crucifixion. Charles takes his brother's first line and makes a connection with the experience of the 1750 earthquake.

1.   From whence these dire Portents around,
       That Earth and Heav'n amaze?
    Wherefore do Earthquakes cleave the Ground?
    Why hides the Sun his Rays?[50]

The years of 1755–56 and following were a difficult period for England. In June 1755 the Seven Years' War had begun. Because of a plague among livestock, cattle were dying at a rapid rate. The French and British colonies in North America were moving toward confrontation. There were conflicts between Protestants and Catholics. France was becoming more and more hostile toward England, as opposition to

47. Ibid., 323.

48. Charles Wesley, *The Cause and Cure of Earthquakes*; Newport, *The Sermons of Charles Wesley*, 227–37.

49. Kimbrough and Newport, *CW Journal*, 2:591.

50. *Earthquake Hymns* (1750), 8, first four lines of stanza 1, Hymn 5.

Protestantism grew and France threatened to invade England. Lisbon was severely damaged by an earthquake on November 1, 1755. Yet, amid all this turmoil the British were lethargic about arming themselves.

February 6, 1756, was declared a National Fast Day, and Methodists, to be sure, sounded the alarm. George Whitefield published his "Address to Persons of all Denominations, occasioned by the Alarm of an intended invasion," which included strong opposition to the Roman Catholic Church. John Wesley wrote and printed "Serious Thoughts occasioned by the late Earthquake at Lisbon." He contends that the best preparation for all calamities is true religion. Wesley calls all to the repentance of personal and national sins and summons the clergy to be leaders in shaping the nation.

Hymns for the Year 1756

Caught up in the spirit of these events, Charles Wesley composed and published seventeen hymns under the title *Hymns for the Year 1756*. The hymns are a call to the observance of the National Fast Day and emphasize national guilt, the need for repentance, God's impending judgment, and God as the only refuge. Three hymns in this small collection were published in the *Collection* (1780):

- "Righteous God, whose vengeful vials" (Hymn 15), four of six stanzas, vv. 1–2, 5–6, Hymn 59 in the *Collection* (1780)

- "Stand th'omnipotent decree" (Hymn 16), Hymn 60 in *Collection* (1780)

- "How happy are the little flock" (Hymn 17), Hymn 61 in *Collection* (1780)

Note a stanza of "Righteous God, whose vengeful vials," which John Wesley omitted from the *Collection* (1780):

> Earth, unhinged as from her basis,
>> Owns her great Restorer nigh;
> Plunged in complicate distresses,
>> Poor distracted sinners cry:

Men their instant doom deploring,
 Faint beneath their fearful load:
Ocean working, rising, roaring
 Claps his hands to meet his God.[51]

The last two lines seem to echo a passage in John Wesley's *Serious Thoughts Occasioned by the Late Earthquake at Lisbon*:

Who can account for the late motion in the waters? Not only that of the sea, and rivers communicating therewith, but even that in canals, fishponds, cisterns, and all other large or small bodies of water? It was particularly observed, that while the water itself was so violently agitated, neither did the earth shake at all, nor any of the vessels which contained the water. Was such a thing ever known or heard of before![52]

This resonates also in Hymn 14, stanza 5:

Outstretching his hand
 O'er mountains and seas,
He shakes the dry land,
 And watry abyss!
A marvelous motion
 Thro' nature is spread,
And *peacable* ocean
 Starts out of his bed![53]

Hymns on the Expected Invasion[54]

During the summer of 1759 a frenzy of public fear broke out over the threat of a French invasion of England. News of the French successes in the Seven Years' War had spread, and it was genuinely believed that the French had built boats specifically for an invasion. In the face of the public panic Charles wrote *Hymns for the Invasion* (1750) and *Hymns to Be Used on the Thanksgiving-Day, Nov. 29, 1759, and After It.*[55]

On November 20, the French fleet was engaged by Admiral Edward Hawke and defeated between Belleisle and Cape Quiberon. Thereafter

51. *Hymns for the Year 1756*, 21, stanza 4 of Hymn 15.
52. Dublin, 1756, 14.
53. *Hymns for the Year 1756*, stanza 5 of Hymn 14.
54. Cited throughout as *Hymns for the Invasion* (1759).
55. Cited throughout as *Thanksgiving Hymns* (1746/1759).

public thanksgivings were offered to God for deliverance, and once again Charles Wesley offered his poetical response this time in *Thanksgiving Hymns* (1759). This publication of sixteen very patriotic hymns bore no date of publication or place of publication. Note the tone that Wesley gives to *The Song of Moses* (Hymn 12):

> 3.   The Lord, He is a man of war,
>   In every age the same:
> Let Britain saved, with shouts declare
>   The great Jehovah's name:
> Jehovah on our foes did frown
>   Amidst their furious boast,
> And cast their chosen captains down,
>   And drowned half their host.
>
> 4.   Into the depths they sunk as lead,
>   Who Thee and Thine opposed,
> They sunk at once, and o'er their head
>   The mighty waters closed!
> Thine own right hand with power supreme,
>   With glorious, dreadful power,
> In pieces dashed their ships and them,
>   And bade the gulf devour.[56]

Funeral Hymns

One final aspect of Charles Wesley's historically oriented lyrical theology will be mentioned, namely, his poems about individuals. Some of the poems are hymnic in nature, such as those dedicated to individuals in *Funeral Hymns*. In 1746 Charles had printed his first series of *Funeral Hymns,* which contained sixteen hymns, only three of which were dedicated to specific individuals. In 1759 he published a much larger second series with the same title, including forty-three hymns, sixteen of which were dedicated to specific persons. It was often Wesley's practice to celebrate the lives of others in poems occasioned by their deaths. Of special interest are the poems dedicated to Rev. John Meriton, John Hutchinson, Grace Bowen, Thomas Walsh, and the Rev. James Hervey. Many of these

56. *Thanksgiving Hymns* (1759) 28, Hymn 12.

poems are quite lengthy and have numerous parts, which receive hymn numbers, though one cannot imagine they were to have been sung as hymns.

There are other non-hymnic poems written by Charles about individuals, such as *An Epistle to the Reverend Mr John Wesley* (1755) and the lengthy *An Epistle to the Reverend Mr George Whitefield* (1771), written on the occasion of Whitefield's death. One finds these epic-like poems filled with theological sensitivity and insight.

Conclusion

It is important to realize that Charles was creating an art form for which the eighteenth-century Church of England had no use in its liturgy. It was not a hymn-singing church, though there was perhaps a sequence hymn and/or a gradual hymn at the Eucharist. John Wesley, of course, introduced the innovation of hymn singing at the time of the administration of the bread and wine during the Eucharist, which prepared the way for some of his brother's hymns to be used.

Where, then, did the people called Methodists sing the Wesley hymns and those of other writers? It was largely in their Society meetings, bands, classes, and informal gatherings. The Societies augmented what took place in the parish church with the following: praising God in song, sound preaching of the Word, the study of Scripture, the inner witness of the Spirit, fervent prayer, and service to the poor. The Society members were encouraged, however, to go to the parish church to receive Holy Communion.

Here we find an example of the tension mentioned earlier in this chapter that Charles Wesley sustained throughout his life and ministry between conformity and nonconformity. He relates in his journal[57] an instance of the colliers of Kingswood being turned away from the table of Holy Communion by the clergy in Bristol. While he was fully committed to and conformed to the practice of the administration of the sacrament within the parish church by an ordained priest of the Church of England, on this occasion he broke with conformity and served the elements to the colliers in Kingswood beyond the bounds of the parish church.

57. Kimbrough and Newport, *CW Journal*, 1:297.

I: Lyrical Theology

As the Methodist movement grew, other theological issues emerged which John (in prose) and Charles (primarily in poetry) addressed: (1) lay preaching, (2) ordination, (3) administration of the sacrament outside the parish church and by the non-ordained, (4) separation of the Methodists from the Church of England. Hence, much of what Charles Wesley writes in his poetry is oriented to what the Methodist movement and the Church of England were experiencing at a given time in the eighteenth century. While some of his lyrics are unquestionably so strongly time-bound that they do not speak readily to the experiences and needs of the twenty-first century, others are timeless and speak to the needs of human beings in any age. They continue to summon nonbelievers to faith and believers to deeper faith and more faithful living. Charles Wesley does so through poetry and song, which create a vibrant, lyrical theological memory individually and corporately for Christians and the church as a whole.

4

Literary and Ecclesial Sources Used in Charles Wesley's Poetry[1]

Wesley's hymnody is often read as a sacred literary corpus in isolation, but to do so is a great injustice to his work. Literary critics have also made a great mistake by considering hymn literature as unworthy of careful study. Charles Wesley is a man of his times whose hymns emerge from his education and literary influences of the period. Donald Davie has rightly observed in his book *A Gathered Church: The Literature of the English Dissenting Interest, 1700–1930*:

> One looks for a long time before finding any attempt to place Charles Wesley, or Isaac Watts either, in relation to the more secular poetry of their times—in relation to Pope, or Thomson, or Gray or Goldsmith. One consequence is that the eighteenth century is thought to have produced little *lyric* poetry, whereas the eighteenth-century lyric is to be found in the hymn books just as surely as seventeenth-century lyric is in George Herbert's *Temple*. The dependence of line after line of Wesley on the precedent of Matthew Prior has been duly noted, but no one has explored the significance, stylistically and historically, of this surprising connection with the suave and frequently improper author of "Henry and Emma."[2]

1. Portions of this chapter have appeared in the "Hymnody of Charles Wesley" by this author in the *T. & T. Clark Companion to Methodism*, edited by Charles Yrigoyen, Jr., 36–60, and are used here by permission.

2. Davie, *Gathered Church*, 48.

Charles Wesley's Literary Sources

One of the earliest significant attempts to explore the literary influences on Charles Wesley is the work of Henry Bett, *The Hymns of Methodism*. Of particular interest is his concluding chapter, "The Hymns and the Poets." Bett traces the influences of Virgil's *Aeneid*, Edward Young's *Night Thoughts*, Homer's *Illiad*, John Milton's *Paradise Lost*, and recollections in Wesley's poetry of William Shakespeare, John Dryden, Matthew Prior, and others.

An extremely important volume, *Hymns Unbidden*, by Martha Winburn England and John Sparrow, was published by the New York Public Library in 1966. England's contributions to the volume include a series of erudite chapters comparing the work of Wesley to that of his contemporary William Blake, as well as to that of John Milton. Her literary analysis is exemplary for all students of the Wesleys. She is able to see beyond details to the larger strokes of continuity and discontinuity, particularly in her study of Wesley's *Hymns for the Nation, in 1782*.

> What *Hymns for the Nation* has in common with Blake is belligerence, exuberance, excess.[3]

> . . . Wesley and Blake are comparable in arrogance, vulgarity, and excess. These traits of enthusiasm poetry entered into all their poetic successes and can be seen with greatest clarity in their poetic failures.[4] . . . Their poetry is prophetic and evangelical, the messages are intensely personal and aimed at reformation of the social order. They meant to bring about an inner change, in the heart, the imagination, and hoped that social changes would come about as a result.[5]

Fortunately in more recent times others have explored in depth the rich literary sources from which Wesley draws and which shape his diction, style, meters, phraseology, imagery, and grammar. In *Collection* (1780), volume 7 (1983) of the series *The Works of John Wesley*, James Dale addressed "The Literary Setting of Wesley's Hymns"[6] with a strong emphasis on the Wesleys' reliance on works of James Thomson, John

3. England and Sparrow, *Hymns Unbidden*, 66.

4. Ibid., 93.

5. Ibid., 71.

6. *Collection* (1780) 38–44.

Milton, Alexander Pope, John Dryden, and others. These influences are not merely ones of diction and poetical structure, for as Dale avers, "even a passing acquaintance with the verse of Dryden and Pope, of [Samuel] Johnson and [Thomas] Gray, makes clear that reason and emotion can coexist, that strong feeling gains in intensity when it is given controlled and concise utterance."[7] Most certainly the coexistence of reason and emotion plays a vital role in the thought and theology of Charles Wesley and is reflected in his hymns.

One of the most helpful recent discussions titled "The Hymns of Charles Wesley and the Poetic Tradition" by J. R. Watson appeared as chapter twenty-one in the collection of essays *Charles Wesley, Life, Literature and Legacy*, edited by Kenneth G. C. Newport and Ted A. Campbell. Watson makes a convincing case for the strong influence of Greek and Latin poets on Charles Wesley. His discussion of the importance of Ovid's *Metamorphoses* is particularly valuable for understanding some of the hymns in Wesley's *HLS* (1745), an influence often overlooked by students and teachers of that important volume.

Watson has eloquently summarized Wesley's assimilation and articulation of a vast array of literary influences.

> The idea of the text as a tissue of quotations has an obvious application to Charles Wesley's hymns. His choice of culture-centres comes from his education, his reading, his memory, his understanding and appreciation, his critical sense, his personal needs. He takes them in to his hymns, and then sends them out, filled with their accumulated meaning, for the readers and singers to take in to themselves: the words come down to us from Charles Wesley's many sources, but enriched by him. They are from different places—the Bible, the Prayer Book, other poets, such as Herbert, Matthew Prior, Elizabeth Singer Rowe, Samuel Wesley— but the very fact that Charles Wesley has used them gives them a new lustre. His hymns shine with words he has transformed.[8]

James Dale illustrates[9] beautifully what Watson asserts by exploring words, phrases, and concepts that Wesley borrows and/or appropriates

7. Ibid., 43.

8. Newport and Campbell, *Charles Wesley, Life, Literature and Legacy*, 363.

9. James Dale, "Charles Wesley and the Line of Piety: Antecedents of the Hymns in English Devotional Verse." See also his article, "Holy Larceny? Elizabeth Rowe's Poetry in Charles Wesley's Hymns."

from Elizabeth Singer Rowe in his well-known hymn "Christ, whose glory fills the skies." The line, "Visit then this soul of mine," Dale sees as a virtual quotation of Rowe's line "O! visit then thy servant, Lord" from a poem of Rowe that John Wesley included in *Moral and Sacred Poems* (1744). Dale notes further the quotation by Charles Wesley in his *Hymns occasioned by an Earthquake* (1750) of the phrase "amaranthine bowers" from Rowe's poem "On Heaven": " . . . those blest shades, and amaranthine bowers."[10]

It is clear from the hitherto unpublished poetry of Charles Wesley that he was capable of writing secular verse that would have stood on its own among the poets of his time. For example, he composed Alexandrine verse, and wrote in heroic epic style "The American War,"[11] a poem of 615 octosyllabic lines of rhyming couplets with occasional rhyming triplets. Furthermore, he addressed a variety of subjects, such as music, contemporary events, patriotism, and political ideas, and composed charming poems for the entertainment of his children. Yet Wesley did not publish such verse.[12] "He chose instead," as Kenneth D. Shields appropriately states, "to employ his considerable talents to serve his Lord as a priest and evangel of His Word. In his pursuit of Christian Perfection, he rejected . . . the pursuit of a literary reputation."[13] He chose to be a sacred poet, a purpose to which God had called him. While all of his sacred verse by no means reaches heights of literary eloquence, much of his lyricism does, and it deserves to stand among the best poets of his time and their works.

It is not by chance that John and Charles Wesley selected the title *Hymns and Sacred Poems* for their first joint publication in 1739, and for two succeeding volumes in 1740 and 1742, and that Charles used the same title for a two-volume work he published as the sole author in 1749. In the *HSP* 1739 volume John included sacred poems by a number of authors that were not written specifically as hymns for use in worship. Throughout his career as a poet of religious verse Charles would also write much non-hymnic poetry, such as *An Epistle to the Reverend Mr John Wesley* (1755),

10. *Miscellaneous Works in Prose and Verse of Mrs. Elizabeth Rowe*, No. 65, line 25. This work was published posthumously and was, according to Dale, most certainly read by Charles Wesley.

11. *Unpub. Poetry*, 1:41–57.

12. All of Wesley's known secular verse has been published in volumes 1 and 3 of *Unpub. Poetry*.

13. Kenneth D. Shields, "Charles Wesley as Poet," 67.

An Epistle to the Reverend Mr George Whitefield (1771), and *An Elegy on the Late Reverend George Whitefield, M.A.* (1771). He wrote numerous sacred poems on the occasion of the deaths of individuals.

As noted elsewhere in this volume, Charles did not necessarily intend all of the poems he wrote in hymnic style to be sung. An example from the second edition (1756) of *Earthquake Hymns* (1750) illustrates this point. A hymn titled "An Hymn upon the pouring out of the Seventh Vial, Rev. xvi, xvii, &c. Occasioned by the Destruction of Lisbon" is added at the conclusion of Part I. It follows the heading "To which are added An Hymn for the English in America, and another for the Year 1756." It is very clear from Part 2 of the poem on Lisbon that Charles would not have intended it to be sung in the Methodist Societies, as illustrated by stanza 3:

> Then let the thundering trumpet sound;
>   The latest lightning glare;
> The mountains melt; the solid ground
>   Dissolve as liquid air;
> The hugh celestial bodies roll,
>   Amid that general fire,
> And shrivel as a parchment scroll,
>   And all in smoke expire![14]

Charles Wesley's Ecclesial Sources

Having established that Charles Wesley's poetry and style of writing were greatly influenced by the Latin and Greek classics and a number of British poets, we turn now to the sources which shaped the content and theology of his hymns: the Thirty-Nine Articles of Religion, the BCP, the Holy Scriptures, and the early Fathers of the Church.

The Thirty-Nine Articles of Religion of the Church of England

Unquestionably Charles Wesley was a man educated and nurtured within the life, liturgy, and beliefs of the Church of England. Hence it is not surprising that this rich ecclesiastical heritage surfaces quite often in his sacred poetry. J. R. Watson has explored the importance of understanding

---

14. *Earthquake Hymns*, 11–12.

the Thirty-Nine Articles of Religion of the Church of England as the fulcrum of the theological ideas one encounters in Wesley hymns.[15] It is not so much that Wesley made use of direct quotations from the Thirty-Nine Articles, as it is his ability to convey in his verse their theological perspectives and posture. For example, as the theological matrix of Wesley's thought in a stanza of "Hark! How all the Welkin rings," Watson quotes the following passage from Article II, "Of the Word or Son of God, which was made very Man":[16]

> The Son, which is the Word of the Father, begotten from everlasting of the Father, the very and eternal God, and of one substance with the Father, took Man's nature in the womb of the blessed Virgin, of her substance: so that two whole and perfect Natures, that is to say the Godhead and Manhood, were joined together in one Person, never to be divided, whereof is one Christ, very God, and very Man.

Wesley affirms this in these words:

> Christ, by highest heaven adored,
> Christ, the everlasting Lord,
> Late in time behold him come,
> Offspring of a virgin's womb.
> Veiled in flesh the Godhead see!
> Hail the incarnate Deity![17]

The BCP (1662)

A number of scholars have explored the influence of the language, metaphors, images, and ideas of the BCP on Charles Wesley's hymns. He attended Westminster School, adjacent to Westminster Abbey, where he experienced the daily offices and Eucharistic liturgy of the BCP. While there are many examples of the presence of the BCP imprimatur on Wesley's hymns, perhaps this is nowhere clearer than in the volume *HLS* (1745), published jointly by John and Charles Wesley.

15. Watson, "Charles Wesley and the Thirty-Nine Articles," 27–38.
16. Ibid., 32.
17. Stanza three of "Hymn for Christmas-Day," *HSP* (1739) 206–7.

Some of the Eucharistic hymns are metrical versions of passages from the BCP liturgy such as "Lord, and God of heavenly powers," which is preceded with the words of the BCP liturgical *Preface* to the *Sanctus*: "Therefore with angels and archangels":

> Lord, and God of heavenly powers,
> Theirs—yet oh! benignly ours;
> Glorious King, let earth proclaim,
> Worms attempt to chant thy name.
>
> Thee to laud in songs divine,
> Angels and Arch-angels join;
> We with them our voices raise,
> Echoing thy eternal praise.
>
> Holy, holy, holy Lord,
> Live by heaven and earth adored!
> Full of thee they ever cry
> Glory be to God most high![18]

Another example is the hymn "Glory be to God on high," a metrical paraphrase of the *Gloria in excelsis Deo,* which Wesley prefaces in his text with the words "Glory be to God on high, and on earth peace, etc." The first three stanzas of the seven-stanza hymn suffice to illustrate the influence of the language of the liturgy.

> Glory be to God on high,
> God whose glory fills the sky;
> Peace on earth to man forgiven,
> Man the well-beloved of heaven!
>
> Sovereign Father, heavenly King,
> Thee we now presume to sing,
> Glad thine attributes confess,
> Glorious all and numberless.
>
> Hail by all thy works adored,
> Hail the everlasting Lord!
> Thee with thankful hearts we prove,
> Lord of power, and God of love.[19]

18. Ibid., 134–35.
19. Ibid., 136.

The hymn "Meet and right it is to sing," another metrical paraphrase of the *Preface* and *Sanctus*, reveals Wesley's reliance on the words, imagery, and language of the Eucharistic rite.

Hymn 7, "Jesu, show us thy salvation" in *Resurrection Hymns* (1746) is based on *The Great Litany*, which in Wesley's time would have been read regularly at the Eucharist. The following portion of the liturgical text precedes Wesley's metrical paraphrase.

> By the Mystery of thy holy Incarnation; by thy holy nativity and circumcision; by thy baptism, fasting, and temptation; by thine agony, and bloody sweat; by thy cross and passion; by thy precious death and burial; by thy glorious resurrection and ascension; and by the coming of the Holy Ghost, good Lord, deliver us.

Stanza one illustrates what Wesley accomplishes throughout the nine-stanza poem, namely, the eloquent lyrical rendering of the language and imagery of the liturgical text.

> Jesu, show us thy salvation,
>   (In thy strength we strive with thee)
> By thy Mystic Incarnation,
>   By thy pure nativity,
> Save us Thou, our New-Creator,
>   Into all our Souls impart,
> Thy divine unsinning nature,
>   Form thyself within our heart.[20]

One must hasten to add, however, that it is not merely Wesley's repetition of BCP's language, imagery, and theology that is of importance. It is his further development of all three. He enriches the affirmations of the Great Litany by introducing the Pauline idea of new creation, thus emphasizing not only deliverance from sin but the formation of the divine nature within the human heart. This is for Wesley the evangelical focus of deliverance. J. R. Watson rightly asserts:

> The significant and creative element of Charles Wesley's hymnody is his ability to take a familiar phrase or idea from the Bible or the Prayer Book and transform it, to use it in a way which "de-familiarises" it or gives it new and unexpected meaning. It is not,

20. *Resurrection Hymns* (1746) 10.

therefore, the actual repetition or seizure of a phrase which is important, but the felicitous development of it.[21]

Wesley's hymns are filled with phrases and echoes of the BCP, such as the Order for Morning Prayer, diverse collects, the Order for the Service of Holy Communion, and the BCP Psalter. What is truly extraordinary is his ability to appropriate this material to Christian meaning and living, and this he most often does by the turn of an artful poetical phrase or line.

Robin Leaver summarizes superbly Wesley's use of the BCP:

> Charles Wesley's many allusions to the BCP are not mere quotation but rather sophisticated recreations of Prayer Book imagery, theologically understood and poetically expressed. It is witness to a man who was not only aware of the verbal content of the Anglican book of worship but who had also imbibed its basic thought-forms and images to form an essential part of his creative genius.[22]

The Holy Scriptures

The sacred book of the church, the Holy Scriptures, is the primary source of most of Charles Wesley's sacred verse. He literally consumed its content and spirit through his reading of it in Hebrew, Greek, Latin, and English. He lived and breathed its words, imagery, metaphors, similes, phraseology, stories, and parables. He saw within himself the potential for the full spectrum of emotions that he found there. The English of the Authorized Version (AV) was normative biblical language for him and often made its way into his poetical lines, yet his knowledge of Hebrew and Greek often provided him correctives for the AV's English translation. "He sometimes corrected errors of translation in the Authorized Version and even anticipated the emendations of the revisers."[23] Frank Baker has claimed: "His [Charles Wesley's] verse is an enormous sponge filled to saturation with Bible words, Bible similes, Bible metaphors, Bible stories, Bible ideas."[24]

21. Watson, "Charles Wesley's Hymns and the *Book of Common Prayer*," 206. See also Nichols, "Charles Wesley's Eucharistic Hymns."

22. Leaver, "Charles Wesley and Anglicanism," 167. See also Bett, *Hymns of Methodism*, 129–35, and Watson, "Charles Wesley's Hymns and the *Book of Common Prayer*," 205–8.

23. Rattenbury, *Evangelical Doctrines of Charles Wesley's Hymns*, 48.

24. *Rep. Verse*, xxv.

J. Ernest Rattenbury makes yet a stronger claim: "A skilful man, if the Bible were lost, might extract much of it from Wesley's hymns. They contain the Bible in solution. . . . His language was the language of Israel. His complete mastery of the Holy Scriptures was really amazing."[25]

Two volumes illustrate superbly how line after line of Charles Wesley's poetry reflects his saturation with the language and content of the Scriptures. In *Collection* (1780), volume 7 in the series, *The Works of John Wesley*, one of the editors, Oliver A. Beckerlegge, provided a very helpful tool for the study of Charles Wesley's hymns, namely the marginal scriptural references which indicate Wesley's use of biblical language, imagery, figures of speech, metaphors, etc., as well as scriptural quotations and allusions. Similarly, in *The Wesley Hymns: As a Guide to Scriptural Teaching*[26] John Lawson has selected fifty-three Wesley hymns and suggested biblical references for almost every line of poetry. Lawson's marginal scriptural references are more prolific than Beckerlegge's and some of them fall short of certainty. Nevertheless, they remind the reader of how skilled Wesley was in weaving together multiple threads of the Scriptures throughout his poetry.

Wesley is unquestionably a master at creating scriptural hymns. Very early in his published poetry he often prefaces a poem with a specific biblical passage on which it is based. At other times, while he does not cite a passage, it is clear that the background is biblical. This occurs in numerous publications from the Wesley brothers' first joint publication, *HSP* (1739), onward.[27]

In addition to his use of typology and allegory,[28] Wesley had a special gift in paraphrasing entire passages. His paraphrases often integrate textual content and language with personal experience. He is able to internalize the scriptural moment. For example, in *HSP* (1749), in a poem titled "Desiring to Love" Wesley eloquently paraphrases and appropriates Peter's response to Jesus' question in John 21:15, "Simon, son of Jonas,

---

25. Rattenbury, *Evangelical Doctrines of Charles Wesley's Hymns*, 48.

26. See also the study of Waterhouse, *The Bible in Charles Wesley's Hymns*.

27. See also: *HSP* (1740), *HGEL* (1741), *HSP* (1742), *HTTP* (1744), *HLS* (1745), *Nativity Hymns* (1745), *Resurrection Hymns* (1746), *Ascension Hymns* (1746), *Pentecost Hymns* (1746), *HSP* (1749), *Trinity Hymns* (1767).

28. See Kimbrough, "Charles Wesley as a Biblical Interpreter."

lovest thou me more than these? He saith unto him, Yea, Lord; thou
knowest that I love thee." Wesley responds:

> O that with humbled Peter I
> Could weep, believe, and thrice reply
>   My faithfulness to prove,
> Thou know'st (for all to thee is known),
> Thou know'st, O Lord, and thou alone,
>   Thou know'st that thee I love![29]

During his latter years Wesley devoted considerable time to the
composition of metrical paraphrases of the Psalms. Much of this material remained unpublished at his death and some of the paraphrases were
published posthumously in *The Arminian Magazine.*

In 1762 Charles Wesley published a two-volume lyrical commentary
on the Bible, *Short Hymns on Select Passages of the Holy Scriptures,*[30] beginning with the Book of Genesis and continuing through the Revelation
to John. In this and succeeding works his Scripture hymns are more
closely reasoned. At times these hymns can be somewhat pedantic, but at
others, particularly in *Scripture Hymns* (1762), Wesley rises to the heights
of lyrical eloquence of his earlier verse.

Scripture Hymns (1762) is a lyrical commentary[31] on the entire
Bible. Below is a tabulation of Charles's productivity in *Scripture Hymns*
(1762):

Vol. No.	No. of Poems	Lines of Poetry	Stanzas
1 (Old Testament)	1,160	10,903	1,241
2 (Old Testament)	318	3,320	446
2 (New Testament)	871	8,912	1,306
Totals	2,349	23,135	2,993

29. *HSP* (1749) 1:59, stanza 5.

30. Cited throughout as *Scripture Hymns* (1762).

31. See Kimbrough, "Charles Wesley's Lyrical Commentary on the Holy Scriptures."

As impressive as these figures are, this is less than half of the biblical poetry Charles composed from 1762 onwards. Much of it was left unpublished at his death, for example, hundreds of poems in *MS Scripture Hymns 1783* were not put into print. Though some unpublished poems appeared posthumously in *The Arminian Magazine,* still over 1200 hymns and poems were unpublished until the three volumes of *Unpub. Poetry*[32] appeared in 1988, 1990, and 1992.

What do we learn about Charles Wesley's biblical interpretation in *Scripture Hymns* (1762)? While he has the utmost confidence in the authority of Holy Scripture and in the knowledge of it as sufficient to the salvation of humankind, he is not a literalist in the strict sense. While he trusts completely that the promises of the Bible will indeed be fulfilled according to "the Word" (e.g., the return of Christ), he says:

> Thy word in the bare *literal* sense,
>   Though heard ten thousand times, and read,
> Can never of itself dispense
>   The saving power which wakes the dead;
> The meaning *spiritual* and true
>   The learned expositor may give,
> But cannot give the virtue too,
>   Or bid his own dead spirit live.[33]

First and foremost, as this poem makes clear, Wesley is concerned with what the Scriptures mean. There are various levels of understanding: literal, spiritual, and experiential. This three-dimensional aspect of his interpretation surfaces time and again in his hymns and poems.

In the preface to *Scripture Hymns* (1762) Charles expresses his debt in biblical interpretation to three scholars: Matthew Henry (1662–1714), Dr. Robert Gell (1595–1665), and Iohannes Albertus Bengelius (1687–1752). Matthew Henry's commentary, *Exposition of the Old and New Testaments* (1708–1710), was well known and widely read. Gell, a London biblical scholar, produced an "Amended Translation" of the Pentateuch with which Charles had apparently become acquainted, since he associates his debt to Gell with the Pentateuch. Charles had become familiar with the work of Bengelius, a Lutheran scholar, while assisting

---

32. Of particular interest to this discussion is volume 2, which bears the subtitle *Hymns and Poems on Holy Scripture.*

33. *Scripture Hymns* (1762) 2:337, Hymn 663.

his brother John with *Explanatory Notes Upon the New Testament,* due to John's strong reliance on Bengelius's work. Charles also makes clear in the preface that he has written these two volumes of *Scripture Hymns* (1762) in order to rectify certain wrong ideas about holiness and perfection. He was no protagonist of instantaneous perfection, as numerous satirical poems throughout both volumes make clear.

Scripture Hymns (1762) illustrates Wesley's ongoing interest in translation. Though he usually quotes texts from the AV immediately prior to every poem, the abbreviations [Heb.] and [Gk.] are inserted often, indicating what he considers to be the appropriate translation of the Hebrew or Greek word or phrase. In the section on the Psalms, though he does not indicate it in the printed text, he often quotes from the BCP Psalter instead of the AV.

As important as *Scripture Hymns* (1762) is for insight into the Scriptures and into Charles Wesley's biblical interpretation, it would be misleading to ignore other aspects of biblical interpretation in his hymnody. He is often at his best in biblical narrative poems, though few of these survive in contemporary hymnody. For example, in his lyrical interpretation of Jesus' encounter with the woman of Canaan in Matthew 15, he intertwines and personalizes reality, symbol, and allegory.

1.   Lord, regard my earnest cry,
      A postsherd of the earth,
    A poor guilty worm am I,
      A Canaanite by birth:
  Save me from this tyranny,
From all the power of Satan save,
   Mercy, mercy upon me,
     Thou Son of David have.

2.   Still Thou answerest not a word
      To my repeated prayer;
    Hear thine own disciples, Lord,
      Who in my sorrows share;
  O let them prevail with thee
To grant the blessing which I crave:
   Mercy, mercy upon me.
     Thou Son of David have.

3.   Send, O send me now away,
      By granting my request,
   Still I follow thee, and pray,
      And will not let thee rest;
   Ever crying after thee,
Till thou my helplessness relieve,
   Mercy, mercy upon me
      Thou Son of David have.

4.   To the sheep of Israel's fold,
      Thou in thy flesh wast sent,
   But the gentiles now behold
      In thee their covenant.
   See me then, with pity see,
A sinner, whom thou cam'st to save;
   Mercy, mercy upon me
      Thou Son of David have.

5.   Still to thee, my God, I come,
      And mercy I implore,
   Thee (but how shall I presume)
      Thee trembling I adore,
   Dare not stand before thy face,
But lowly at thy feet I fall,
   Help me, Jesu, show thy grace:
      Thy grace is free for all.

6.   Still I cannot part with thee,
      I will not let thee go,
   Mercy, mercy unto me,
      O Son of David show,
   Vilest of the sinful race,
On thee importunate I call,
   Help me, Jesu, show thy grace:
      Thy grace is free for all.

7.   Nothing am I in thy sight,
      Nothing have I to plead;
   Unto dogs it is not right
      To cast the children's bread:

Yet the dogs the crumbs may eat,
That from their Master's table fall,
Let the fragments be my meat:
Thy grace is free for all.

8.   Give me, Lord, the victory,
My heart's desire fulfil,
Let it now be done to me
According to thy will;
Give me living bread to eat,
And say, in answer to my call,
"Canaanite, thy faith is great,
"My grace is free for all."

9.   If thy grace for all is free,
Thy call *now* let *me* hear,
Show this token upon me,
And bring salvation near;
Now the gracious word repeat,
The word of healing to my soul,
"Canaanite, thy faith is great,
"Thy faith has made thee whole."[34]

It is fascinating how Wesley's poetic imagination deals with the hidden meaning of this biblical story, which has troubled interpreters for many generations. While some might accuse him of psychologizing the story by moving the reader to the inmost thoughts of the Canaanite woman, he sees beyond the things in the story which have troubled interpreters: calling the woman *kunária*, in Greek a diminutive for dog, Jesus' silence or lack of response to her, acknowledging faith in a Gentile, and the exclusivity of his response, "I was sent *only* to the lost sheep of Israel" (Matt 15:24 NRSV). Through poetic and theological imagination Wesley tells the story in the first person from the perspective of the woman. He wants the reader to feel and sense her plight.

If the Matthew 15 story has been seen by many as evidence of the tension between Jews and Gentiles in the New Testament period, Wesley is able to see beyond this to the woman herself: her humility and desire for mercy, the triumph of faith, and the universality of God's grace

34. *HSP* (1742) 96–98.

and covenant. Ever the evangelical poet-priest, he focuses on the person, God's universal grace, and the importance of faith. Thus Wesley is able to transcend the difficulties of the text through the art of poetry and keen theological insight and to evoke the reader's sensibilities to these emphases just mentioned.

The Early Fathers of the Church

Nicholas Lossky has made a convincing case for the strong influence of the Early Fathers of the Church and patristic theology through John Wesley's reading of Lancelot Andrewes, particularly his *Preces Privatae*. While one might labor to find numerous quotations of the Early Fathers in Charles Wesley's poetry, his theology exudes the spirit of much of their theology. Lossky maintains:

> Here in poetical form, we find an expression of the Church's experience of God. Much of the theology is of the school of Andrewes. It is a trinitarian theology, with a Christology inseparable from pneumatalogy. As for the divine dispensation, Charles Wesley insists many times on the fact that Christ "died for all" and that grace is offered to all. The poetical form, often magnificent, is also something that links Charles Wesley with Orthodox practice: the non-Greek Orthodox should never forget that in the original, most of our Syro-Byzantine hymnography is in rhythmic poetry (most of the time untranslatable).[35]

We do not have the same kind of bibliographical evidence of the Early Fathers in the writings of Charles that one finds in his brother John's writings, though most certainly Charles had read John's *A Plain Account of Genuine Christianity*, where the following are mentioned: Clemens Romanus, Ignatius of Antioch, Polycarp (bishop of Smyrna), Justin Martyr, Irenaeus, Origin (Origines Adamantius), Clemens Alexandrinus, Cyprian (Thascius Caecilius Cyprianus, bishop of Carthage), Macarius, and Ephrem Cyrus. Furthermore, in the brothers' first joint publication, *HSP* (1739), their appreciation of one of the Fathers just cited was expressed by the inclusion of a poem titled "On Clemens Alexandrinus's Description of a Perfect Christian."[36] While John may have agreed with

35. Lossky, "Lancelot Andrewes," 154.
36. *HSP* (1739) 37–38.

the spirit of the poem, Charles probably identified more strongly with the imagery of a long desert struggle toward holiness, as expressed in stanza one:

> Here from afar the finished height
>   Of holiness is seen:
> But O what heavy tracts of toil,
>   What deserts lie between?

Peter Bouteneff finds resonances of Gregory of Nyssa in Charles's poetry. The "themes of salvation as restoration, and as change and movement from glory to glory,"[37] are evident in these words:

> Finish then thy new creation,
>   Pure and sinless let us be;
> Let us see thy great salvation
>   Perfectly restored in thee;
>
> Changed from glory into glory,
>   Till in heaven we take our place,
> Till we cast our crowns before thee,
>   Lost in wonder, love and praise.[38]

One matter of theological concern that surfaces time and again in Charles Wesley's poetry in concert with many of the Early Fathers of the Church is *theosis*. A. M. Allchin addressed this eloquently in a chapter on Charles Wesley in his important study *Participation in God: A Forgotten Strand in Anglican Tradition*. Wesley understood that, as Bishop Kallistos Ware says, "God's Incarnation opens the way to man's deification."[39] Wesley emphasized this a number of times in his *Nativity Hymns* (1745). Stanza 2 of Hymn 14 reads:

> 2. The Creator of all
>   To repair our sad Fall,
>   From his Heav'n stoops down,
>   Lays hold of our Nature, and joins to his own.[40]

Stanzas 5 and 8 of Hymn 8 give even stronger voice to this emphasis:

37. Bouteneff, "All Creation in United Thanksgiving," 194.
38. *Redemption Hymns* (1747) 12.
39. Ware, *Orthodox Way*, 74.
40. *Nativity Hymns* (1745) 18.

> 5.   Made flesh for our sake,
> That we might partake
> The Nature Divine,
> And again in his image, his holiness shine.
> . . .
> 8.   And while we are here
> Our King shall appear,
> His Spirit impart,
> And form his full image of love in our heart.[41]

Wesley's understanding of *theosis* is intimately bound to Holy Communion. "It is a means of grace by which the Incarnation is imparted to the life of the Christian and by which and through which God makes divine. Here . . . Charles Wesley stands close to Ephrem Cyrus for whom Holy Communion was the cradle of *theosis*."[42] This is clear from many passages in Wesley's *HLS* (1745):

> What streams of sweetness from the bowl
> Surprize and deluge all my soul,
>   Sweetness which is, and makes Divine,
> Surely from God's right-hand they flow,
> From thence derived to earth below,
>   To cheer us with immortal wine.[43]

Perhaps more familiar are the lines from two additional Eucharistic hymns:

> Christ in us; in him we see
> Fulness of the Deity,
> Beam of the Eternal Beam;
> Life Divine we taste in him.[44]

> Who thy mysterious supper share,
>   Here at thy table fed,
> Many, and yet but One we are,
>   One undivided Bread.

---

41. Ibid.

42. Kimbrough, "Theosis in the Writings of Charles Wesley," 207.

43. *HLS* (1745) 133, stanza 2 of Hymn 160.

44. Ibid., 138, stanza 7 of Hymn 164.

> One with the Living Bread Divine,
>   Which now by faith we eat,
> Our hearts, and minds, and spirits join,
>   And all in Jesus meet.[45]

Conclusion

One cannot read Charles Wesley's poetry in isolation, for it is shaped by a repertory of intellectual and experiential sources. He possessed an amazing ability to absorb that which he read, reasoned, processed, and experienced, and to articulate these phenomena in eloquent poetical diction. He readily cross-fertilized the seeds of sacred and secular thought because he had a holistic view of creation that did not draw such a sharp distinction. It is precisely the fusion of language and thought from ecclesial and non-ecclesial realms that makes the interpretation of his work at times more difficult and yet exciting and challenging, for one tends to read him as a priest or poet, but he was a poet/priest. It is important to read the literature he so eagerly devoured, be it Shakespeare or the Bible, if one wishes to sound the depths of his expression and understanding. Nevertheless, one will often be left with an open-ended mystery because he himself was willing to let mystery be mystery.

---

45. Ibid., 138, stanzas 2 and 3 of Hymn 165.

5

The Wesleyan Poetical Sources Used in This Volume

Since the importance of reading Wesley's poetry in the context of the time in which he lived has been emphasized, it is essential to set the Wesleyan poetical sources from which the poetical selections for this volume have been drawn in their own context. As one reads the poems, one should refer back to the contextual explanations for the sources listed below in order to grasp more fully how, when, and why the poems were published. In some instances this will be more obvious than others. It is hoped that these contextual elaborations will assist the reader in the understanding and interpretation of Charles Wesley's hymns and poems.

Context

One often tends to read poetry in isolation, divorced from its original context. Without question much poetry transcends the milieu in which it was created, and it is possible for it to speak effectively in other contexts and times. This may certainly be said of much of Charles Wesley's poetry, especially since some of the spiritualized language and theological ideas articulated in his verse are still used and addressed by the church and Christians today. Nevertheless, there are risks in reading his poetry devoid of its context.

What is meant by context? (1) Context refers to Wesley's *Sitz im Leben*, the life situation in which a lyric is born or that precipitates its composition. For example, a variety of conflicts, theological controversies, and events evoked many poems from the pen of Wesley. His second volume of *Hymns on God's Everlasting Love* (*HGEL* [1742]) was written as direct opposition to the doctrine of unconditional election supported by Calvinism. *Earthquake Hymns* (1750) was composed and published as a direct response to the London earthquake of February 8, 1750. *Hymns for Times of Trouble* (1744) and *HTTP* (1744) were a response to the turbulent times preceding the Jacobite Revolution of 1745 and a possible French invasion. At other times Wesley wrote verse in response to specific theological treatises, e.g., *HLS* (1745) (responding to Daniel Brevint's *The Christian Sacrament and Sacrifice* [1673]) and *Trinity Hymns* (1767) (responding to William Jones's *Catholic Doctrine of the Trinity proved by above an Hundred Short and Clear Arguments* [1756]).

(2) Context may also refer to the social location of Charles Wesley's literary production as part of the evangelical revival of the Church of England in the eighteenth century. What does his poetry reveal about the social, political, economic, and religious milieu of eighteenth-century England? Since hymn singing was not characteristic of the liturgy of the Church of England of that period, one must ask—What was its place in the emerging Methodist movement? And—What does Wesley's poetry reveal about his response to eighteenth-century English society, its problems, and its opportunities?

(3) A third dimension of context has to do with the literature itself. Charles Wesley often wrote lengthy poems that sometimes have been abbreviated or edited for the purpose of hymn singing. Such abbreviation or editing of his poems, however, has led frequently to misrepresentations of the narrative scope of his poems and a truncation of their message. Three examples suffice to illustrate this point. (a) The poem "Wrestling Jacob" originally had fourteen stanzas but often only four survive in many hymnbooks today. This is most unfortunate since the poem is somewhat autobiographical and the first six stanzas reflect the period before Wesley's conversion in 1738, and they explain why he bursts into a doxology of praise in stanza seven. In the poetical narrative, which is a reflection on Jacob's wrestling with the angel in Genesis 32, the poet is depicted in stanzas 1–8 as wrestling to know who God is. He says he will not let the angel, with whom he is wrestling, go until he knows the angel's name, a metaphor for knowing the name of God. Stanzas 3, 4, 5, and 7 end with the line "Till I thy name, thy nature know." Stanza 8 concludes with the imperative "And tell me if thy name is Love." Stanza 9 is the key to the poet's quest with the realization "'Tis Love! 'tis Love! thou diedst for me"

(line 1) and "Thy nature, and thy name is Love" (line 6). The acknowledgment or confession of faith—"Thy nature, and thy name is Love"—is the closing line for stanzas 9–14. When the poem is reduced to four stanzas for the purpose of singing, the *denouement* of Wesley's poetical narrative is radically crippled and the climax of stanzas 8-14 is completely lost.

(b) The hymn "O for a thousand tongues to sing" is an excerpt usually of six stanzas (7–12) from an eighteen-stanza poem of Charles Wesley written in 1739 on the anniversary of his conversion (May 21, 1738). The first six stanzas, however, reveal his pre-conversion struggles and underscore why he builds to the doxology of stanza 7, which begins with the familiar words, "O for a thousand tongues to sing." While it is by no means necessary to sing stanzas 1–6 in order for stanzas 7–12 to have meaning and an effective impact on worshippers, as a commentary on the faith quest of an individual the opening stanzas are extremely important.

(3) The hymn "Ye servants of God, your Master proclaim" was first published in *HTTP* (1744). The original stanzas 2 and 4, which use language that speaks of opponents to the faithful, are usually not included in contemporary hymnals.

> 2. The waves of the sea have lift up their voice,
> Sore troubled that we in Jesus rejoice;
> The floods they are roaring, but Jesus is here,
> While we are adoring, he always is near.

> 4. Men, devils engage, the billows arise,
> And horribly rage, and threaten the skies:
> Their fury shall never our steadfastness shock,
> The weakest believer is built on a Rock.

Without these stanzas one has a very upbeat hymn of praise but has no idea that this hymn was composed to encourage believers to stand up and be counted for their faith in the face of all adversities.

In reading the poetry included in this volume it is important, as far as possible, to understand the context that has given it birth. It will not be possible, however, to delineate the specific contextual background of all Wesley texts used here. A careful study of the period in which the Methodist movement emerged, however, will be extremely helpful. There are ample resources available for such study, and it is not the purpose here to review such history. Highly recommended for such a review is Richard

P. Heitzenrater's *Wesley and the People Called Methodists.* Also very helpful for historical overview is Rex D. Matthews' *Timetables of History for Students of Methodism.*

Annotated Bibliography of Wesleyan Sources Used in this Volume

Below is an annotated bibliography of the sources from which the poems used here were taken. It is hoped that it will assist the reader's understanding of the background of the literature in general and in some instances very specifically.

Hymns and Sacred Poems of 1739, *HSP* (1739), published by John and Charles Wesley in 1739, was their first joint publishing venture. While John was no doubt the collector and editor of the volume, which included poetry from a number of authors, one finds here Charles Wesley's first published verse. Since the brothers elected to attach both of their names to the volume and leave undesignated their own authorship of particular poems, there remain some questions regarding who composed which poems. It is generally accepted, however, that most of the Wesleyan verse comes from Charles's pen. From his earlier *Collection[s] of Psalms and Hymns,* John brought twenty-seven poems into the 1739 volume. The authors of an additional sixty texts included by John are identifiable. Charles Wesley is probably the author of most of the remaining poetry in the collection.

An examination of the poetry most likely by Charles Wesley in the volume reveals that the Wesley brothers set the tone in *HSP* (1739) for succeeding publications throughout their lifetime. They emphasize the importance of prayer life through the inclusion of numerous prayers related to private and public devotion. There are graces for meals, prayers for recovery from sickness and when one is at work, paraphrases of the *Gloria,* the *Sanctus,* and the *Magnificat* from the liturgy of the church, a prayer to be offered after receiving the sacrament, and prayers for moral strength in the face of adversities. Celebration of the high feast days of the Christian year is punctuated with hymns for Christmas, Epiphany, Easter, Ascension, and Pentecost. There is a strong emphasis on the centrality of the Persons of the Holy Trinity and of sin and redemption through God's act in Jesus Christ. In addition, many of the hymns or poems are based on specific passages of the Bible, thus stressing the importance of the Holy Scriptures in the life of the believer.

Hymns and Sacred Poems of 1740, *HSP* (1740), was the second volume of sacred verse published jointly by the Wesley brothers. As the primary editor, John included two hymns from his *CPH* (1738) and five Wesley hymns from *HSP* (1739). Though there were texts by other English authors (George Herbert, George Sandys, John Norris, Samuel Wesley, Sr.) and seven new translations of German hymns (no doubt by John), the majority of the hymns and poems were first publications of lyrics most certainly by Charles Wesley. Nevertheless, again the brothers' decision not to affix their names to the texts leaves open the question in some instances of whether John or Charles is the author.

There is a definite continuation of the emphases of *HSP* (1739) mentioned above, but these are unquestionably expanded to address issues related to the emergence of the Methodist movement and the development of the societies. One sees how Charles is writing and John is editing out of the context of the emerging movement. One hymn is included with the title "On the Admission of Any Person into the Society." There are poems to be read or sung before the reading of the Scriptures and before and after preaching, both central activities of the societies. No doubt the "Love Feast" was being introduced, as there is a series of hymns with that title. One finds here keynote emphases of Wesleyan theology such as universal redemption, sanctification, and the means of grace. The texts reveal Charles's ability to write out of the context of everyday life: "A Hymn to Be Sung at Sea," "In a Storm," "Written in Sickness," "In Temptation," "On a Journey," "After a Journey," "To Be Sung While at Work," etc. Throughout the volume there are numerous paraphrases and expositions of biblical texts, and it concludes with an extended series of poems on "The Communion of Saints" and two poems based on Isaiah 64 and Heb 4:9.

The third and last joint publication of John and Charles Wesley under the title *Hymns and Sacred Poems* was published in 1742, *HSP* (1742). Its format was quite similar to the other two. However, this volume contained a definite foreshadowing of later volumes of Charles Wesley. There are numerous poems that reveal his practice of basing a lyric on a specific passage of the Holy Scriptures. This unquestionably anticipates his two-volume lyrical Bible commentary published twenty years later, *Scripture Hymns* (1762). There is, however, one major difference. The poems in the

1762 volumes tend to be quite brief, one to six stanzas. In *HSP* (1742) many of the biblically based poems are long narrative lyrics, e.g., "The Woman of Canaan" (Matt 15:22), "The Pool of Bethesda" (John 5:2), "The Good Samaritan" (Luke 10:30), "Wrestling Jacob" (Genesis 32), and a series of poems based on passages from chapters 2, 3, and 22 of the Book of Revelation. Other foreshadowings of Charles Wesley's later works are "Before the Sacrament" (*HLS* [1745]), "Groaning for Redemption" (*Redemption Hymns* [1747]), "Hymn to the Trinity" (*Trinity Hymns* [1767]), "A Funeral Hymn" (*Funeral Hymns* published in 1746 [first series], 1759 [second series]), "Hymn for the Day of Pentecost" (*Pentecost Hymns* [1746]), "Hymns for Children" (*Hymns for Children* [1763]). Many of the poems are pastoral in nature in that they express concerns for the everyday life of the Christian: humility, temptation, sin, love, recovery from sickness, doubt, hope, holiness, and thanksgiving.

John Wesley published a series of collections of hymns and poems under the title *A Collection of Psalms and Hymns* (*CPH*). The two editions of 1741 and 1743 included some hymns by his brother Charles, though there remains a question as to whether John or Charles is the author of the fifteen unidentified hymns in *CPH* (1741). In the 1741 edition John included ninety-four selections from previous publications (forty-four from *CPH* [1737] and fifty from *CPH* [1738]). *CPH* (1743) was a second edition of *CPH* (1741) with major revisions. Charles's name was added to the title page of *CPH* (1743), probably because John removed sixty poetical selections to make room for thirty-seven new psalms in the second section of the volume, which were most likely all by Charles since the majority are found in his extant manuscripts. John's commitment to make the Psalter accessible through metrical versions for hymn singing is very evident in these collections.

HGEL (1742) was an unequivocal response to Calvinism with a strong emphasis on universal redemption, namely, that God offered saving grace freely to all people. John Wesley's sermon titled *Free Grace* was one of the first attempts to articulate the Wesleyan view. In 1741 Charles had published another collection under the same title, *Hymns on God's Everlasting Love*, which evoked an attack by Anne Dutton, an advocate of unconditional election, in her *A Letter to the Rev. Mr. John Wesley* (1741). Charles responded with the second collection (1742) filled with satirical verse and lines such as:

> *You are elect*, and once forgiven
> Can never fall from grace.[1]
>
> . . .
>
> Cut off you shall not be,
> You never shall remove,
> Secure from all eternity
> In his *electing love*.[2]

Though both collections were initially published anonymously, the evidence points to Charles Wesley as the author of both.

Since satire does not lend itself to good hymn singing, most of this material does not survive in hymnals today. One of the exceptions "Sinners, turn, why will you die?" is included in this volume. John Wesley, however, clearly thought these poems were an effective expression of Wesleyan views of God's offer of salvation to all people, for when he founded *The Arminian Magazine* in 1778, an important tool for defending against Calvinism, he included six of them in the first issue.

Two collections, *Hymns for Times of Trouble* (1744) and *Hymns for Times of Trouble and Persecution* (1744), were published in 1744 as a response to a heated political controversy and the threat of a French invasion. The son of King James II, a Roman Catholic, had been forced into exile in France, where support had been rallied for an invasion of England that would return him to the throne. In the year 1744 the threat of such an invasion became imminent. Desiring to express support for the Hanoverian line and King George II, Charles Wesley published the first small collection of six poems, *Hymns for Times of Trouble* (1744). Though published anonymously, the manuscript evidence supports Charles's authorship. While this first group of poems does not mention details of the conflict, the language is, one might say, in coded metaphors, such as "the accusing serpent" and "blood-thirsty Rome."

The first collection appeared in March of 1744. Though the French fleet shortly afterwards was pushed back by stormy seas, nevertheless the threat remained. Desiring to show full support for King George II, Charles put together a larger second collection of thirty-three poems, *HTTP* (1744), in three sections: "Hymns for Times of Trouble," "Hymns for Times of Persecution," and "Hymns to Be Sung in a Tumult." The names

1. *HGEL* (1742) 8.
2. Ibid., 9.

of John and Charles Wesley were affixed to this collection, underscoring their undivided support of the current king. On the whole the language is general in nature, though four prayers in the first section by title reveal the Wesley brothers' allegiance to King George II. Three prayers bear the title "A Prayer for His Majesty King George" and a fourth "For the King and the Royal Family."

The early collections of *Hymns and Sacred Poems* (*HSP* [1739], [1740], [1742]), as indicated, already reflected some of the ongoing concerns of the Wesleys for public and private worship and devotion. Many of these grew out of the worship life of the Church of England with which they were intimately familiar: paraphrases of Psalms, the *Gloria*, the *Sanctus*, The Lord's Prayer, and hymns for the Christian year and the sacrament. While there was very little liturgical place for hymn singing in the worship life of the eighteenth-century Church of England, the Wesleys had learned the didactic, doxological, and evangelical value of wedding the message of faith with music. It provided the theological memory for the Methodist movement. John Wesley's introduction of hymn singing at the time of the reception of the elements during Holy Communion was a liturgical innovation of the Methodist movement and was not a direct interruption of the liturgy. Perhaps this is the reason the practice was tolerated by some Anglicans. This innovation was perhaps a motivation for the preparation of one of the most important contributions of the Wesleys, and particularly Charles as the poet: *Hymns on the Lord's Supper* published in March 1745 (*HLS* [1745]). What role this volume actually played in early "Methodist worship" is a question, for Holy Communion was not included as a practice apart from the parish church. The Wesleys encouraged the "Methodist" followers to attend the local parish of the Church of England to receive Holy Communion. Most certainly at the time of its publication in 1745 there was no practice of Methodist administration of the sacrament of Holy Communion beyond the prescriptions of the liturgical canons of the Church of England.

HLS (1745) is quite unique in that it is one of the largest collections of poetry in the English language ever devoted to the theology and practice of Holy Communion. It underscores the centrality of this liturgical practice in the life and evangelical witness of the Methodist movement.

John Wesley was no doubt responsible for the preparation of the preface to the volume, which is an extract of Daniel Brevint's *The Christian*

Sacrament and Sacrifice (1673), a compendium of theological perspectives on communion, particularly the centrality of sacrifice. Charles is generally considered to be the author of most of the hymns, seven of which are taken over from *HSP* (1739), and three of those are adaptations from other authors. The 166 hymns included in the volume are organized into six sections outlined in the preface, following Brevint. The last section of *HLS* (1745), however, is more freely composed by Charles in a doxological style. The volume is one of the first examples by Charles Wesley of theological reflection based on the close reading and evaluation of a theological treatise by another author.

In December 1745 Charles Wesley began a series of publications of hymns for the Christian year. As already noted, these publications had been anticipated by a number of hymns for Christian year festivals in *HSP* (1739). The first in the series was titled *Hymns for the Nativity of our Lord* (*Nativity Hymns* [1745]). It contained eighteen Nativity hymns in fourteen different meters and reveals Charles's creativity in poetical structure and diction. There is a strong emphasis on *kenosis*, God's self-emptying disclosure in the Incarnation, and *theosis*, human participation in God's nature through the divine revelation in Jesus Christ, and the mystery of the Incarnation. The hymns contain some of his most memorable images of the divine-human paradox of the Incarnation:

> Our God contracted to a span,
> Incomprehensibly made man.[3]

> Wrapt in swaths th' immortal stranger
>   Man with men
>   We have seen,
> Lying in a manger.[4]

This little booklet of hymns was one of Charles's most popular collections, going through some twenty-five printings during his lifetime, which indicates his own editorial efforts and skill.

In 1746 came a flurry of additional hymn collections for the Christian year from Charles's pen, which reveals his continuing affection for the festival days in the church's calendar connected with major events in the life of Christ. In March 1746, just before Easter, he published *Hymns for our*

---

3. *HNL* (1745), 7.

4. *HNL* (1745), 4.

Lord's Resurrection (*Resurrection Hymns* [1746]). This small collection contained fourteen hymns and, like *Nativity Hymns* (1745), remained in print throughout his life, though with fewer printings and revisions. This booklet of hymns concludes with a hymn for Ascension-Day. One finds in the collection once again the influence of the liturgy of the Church of England (BCP), in Hymn 7, which is based on the litany that begins "By the mystery of thy Incarnation; by thy holy nativity. . . ." The most familiar hymn in *Resurrection Hymns* (1746) is "Rejoice, the Lord is King!" Charles emphasized that through the resurrection God has released saving and redemptive love for all humankind. He weaves in and out of this reality one's moral and ethical obligation as a resurrected believer and emphasizes that in the Eucharist the mystery of the Incarnation and resurrection are made known.

> Honour the means ordained by thee,
>> The great unbloody sacrifice,
> The deep tremendous mystery;
>> Thyself in our inlighten'd eyes
> Now in the broken bread make known,
> And shew us thou art all our own.

Two additional Christian year hymn collections were published in May 1746: *Hymns for Ascension-Day* (*Ascension Hymns* [1746]) and *Hymns of Petition and Thanksgiving for the Promise of Father* or *Hymns for Whitsunday* (*Pentecost Hymns* [1746]). The texts of *Ascension Hymns* (1746) are in large measure outbursts of praise to God for the gift of Christ, the redemptive act of his death upon the cross and his resurrection, and his ascent into heaven, which foreshadows the union of all his followers with the Triune God beyond death. Hymn 2 of the collection issues the following invitation:

> Join all on earth, rejoice, and sing,
> Glory ascribe to glory's King.

Pentecost Hymns (1746) was the largest of the collections of hymns for special Christian year festivals and the last to be published jointly under the names of both brothers. Following his practice of many years, at the beginning of fifteen of the thirty-two hymns for Pentecost Charles states the specific passages of Scripture on which the hymns are based (in this instance, they are from the Gospel of John). He emphasizes throughout the small volume the importance of the indwelling of God's Spirit in the individual and in the community, the church. This is amplified by stressing that the Spirit is the bringer of truth, love, peace, and grace, all of which are essential to a healthy or whole individual and community of faith. The hymns are some of Charles's most fervent and effective prayers for the individual and corporate yearning for the gift of God's Spirit.

In 1747, nine years after his conversion, Charles published, though anonymously, *Hymns for those that seek and those that have Redemption in the Blood of Jesus Christ* (*Redemption Hymns* [1747]). He did not marry until two years later (1749); hence, at this time he devoted all of his energies to his own spiritual journey with Christ and the church and that of the followers, and potential followers, in the evangelical movement. In *Redemption Hymns* (1747) he shaped a narrative for the Christian pilgrimage and revealed the kinds of pastoral concerns he faced daily. Wesley asserted in these hymns that thanksgiving and prayer were to sustain the believer in all circumstances: business, conflict, death, traveling, relation to God and others, rest, and daily living. At the center, of course, is the emphasis that all life issues from the redemptive blood of Christ, the fullest expression of God's love for all. While these hymns or poems are decidedly evangelical, once more the centrality of the liturgy of the Church of England surfaces, as in Charles's poignant paraphrase of the *Te Deum* (Hymn 13) and in the twenty-four stanza poem, "Come, sinners, to the Gospel-Feast," titled "The Great Supper" (Hymn 50) and based on Luke 14:16–24.

The Wesley brothers, according to their journals, began gatherings on December 31 (Watch-Night) and January 1 (New Year's Day) to address the intent of the Christian community at the beginning of the New Year. John Wesley records such a gathering on January 1, 1748 (London) and Charles on January 1, 1750 (Bristol). One assumes that preaching, prayer, praise, and thanksgiving were integral elements of such assemblies. Following his practice of writing inspirational texts for singing on special occasions which challenged the individual and community to a sincere faith journey, Charles wrote *Hymns for New Year's Day, 1750,* which were most certainly intended for use at such gatherings. He takes his cue from the Gospel of Luke (chapter 4) and celebration of the Gospel year of Jubilee. Though there are only seven hymns in this collection (one of which was first published in *HSP* [1749]), two of them have enjoyed sustained presence in diverse hymnals: "Away with our fears" and "Blow ye the trumpet, blow" with its memorable refrain, "The year of jubilee is come; / return, ye ransomed sinners, home."

In 1749, as a demonstration to Sarah Gwynne's parents that he was capable of financially providing for their daughter, whom he intended to marry, Charles published a two-volume work bearing the name of the earlier joint publications with his brother John, *Hymns and Sacred Poems* (*HSP* [1749]). These two volumes, however, were exclusively the work of Charles and are the first major publication in which his brother John did not participate as either editor or author. The contents were comprised of hymns and poems he had written over the previous decade. Once again, one finds him writing as a biblical interpreter or expositor and as a pastor. Volume 1 opens with a series of expositions, and partial paraphrases, of six chapters or portions thereof from the Book of Isaiah and the New Testament Beatitudes. These are followed by a lengthy section of poems for "One Convinced of Unbelief." This is quite interesting since part two of the volume begins with a series of forty-two "Hymns for Believers." One encounters in both volumes Charles addressing the kinds of concerns and challenges with which he was confronted in daily ministry and his personal spiritual journey: sickness and recovery, temptation and penitence, life and death, desiring love, falling from grace, faith, prayer, intercession, redemption. As the Methodist movement had grown considerably by 1749, Charles also addressed the subject of preachers and preaching. In some of his poems he posed the questions—How does one approach the task of preaching? How does one respond after one has preached? While there are a number of homogenous sections in both volumes, e.g., the very interesting series of "Hymns for Widows" in volume 2, there is a *potpourri* of hymns or poems on diverse subjects that do not fit into cohesive thematic sections: "On a Journey," "Hymn for the Kingswood Colliers," "The Physician's Hymn," "An Hymn for a Mother," "The True Use of Musick," etc. This is, of course, not surprising since the volumes were hurriedly put together to underscore Charles's financial capability to the parents of his bride-to-be, Sarah Gwynne.

The following couplet from volume 1 is a superb summary of the central focus of both volumes:

> To thy church the pattern give,
> Show how true believers live.[5]

Though many of Charles Wesley's hymns and poems were written in the form of prayer, in 1758 he dedicated a publication of forty hymns solely to intercessory prayer, *Hymns of Intercession for all mankind* (*Intercession Hymns* [1758]). This type of prayer characterized many of the gatherings of "the people called Methodists." The Wesley brothers often appointed the noon hour on Fridays as the time for them to gather for intercessory prayer. This volume reflects the breadth of concerns that Charles found appropriate for such prayer. It opens with three hymns that embrace very broad subjects: "For All Mankind," "For Peace," and "For the Church Catholic." Then he moves to more specific themes, e.g., "For the Church of England," "For Ministers of the Gospel." Given the period of turmoil in which England found itself with the Seven Years' War (1756–1763), Charles offered prayers for King George, the Prince of Wales, the King of Prussia, the British Nation and its magistrates, nobility, Parliament, the Fleet, and the army. There are prayers for travel, childbirth, orphans, prisoners, widows, enemies, people of other religions, and the coming of God's kingdom. The all-encompassing nature of these intercessory prayers—from the marginalized of society to the aristocracy of the nation—underscores the breadth of the Wesleys' outreach in ministry.

In 1746 Charles Wesley published his first set of sixteen poems titled *Funeral Hymns.*[6] One of those hymns, "Ah lovely appearance of death" (Hymn 5), expressed not a grim preoccupation with death, of which many have accused Charles, but rather the deep yearning of the true believer to hope for and trust in full union with God at death. In this little volume he published a few "death" poems about individuals, that is, poems he wrote on the occasion of someone's death, usually holding the individual up to the community of faith as an example of how to live for Christ and the church. In 1759 Wesley published a second series of *Funeral Hymns* that included forty-three poems. In this second volume there were many more death poems written about specific individuals whom he had known in and through the Methodist movement. In addition, there was a very

---

5. *HSP* (1749), 1:248, hymn titled "For a Family."

6. In *HSP* (1742) Charles had published a set of funeral hymns in selections 124 to 131.

moving eight-part poem written on the death of his first child, John, in January 1754.

Short Hymns on Select Passages of the Holy Scriptures, a two-volume work published by Charles Wesley in 1762 (*Scripture Hymns* [1762]), might be considered his lyrical counterpart to his brother John's *Explanatory Notes Upon the New Testament* (1755). Charles employed a style established early in his publishing career of quoting a passage of Scripture (usually from the Authorized Version) followed by a poem based on the passage. As was the case with *HSP* (1749), Charles did not seek the editorial assistance of his brother John, but rather he published the two volumes on his own.

The 2,249 hymns in *Scripture Hymns* (1762) are indeed true to the title, for they are brief, usually one to four stanzas (occasionally six) in length. Many are reflective and devotional in nature, some are expository, and others are brief paraphrases. In some instances Wesley shaped an entire poem around a word or words from a scriptural passage, which sometimes had little to do with the biblical passage quoted.

While Wesley stated in the preface to the two volumes that his reflections and interpretations had been inspired by biblical specialists such as Johann Bengel (Iohannes Albertus Bengelius), Robert Gell, and Matthew Henry, he exercised as well his own interpretive skills. Occasionally he made his own translations from the Greek and Hebrew Scriptures. When quoting passages from the Book of Psalms, he often followed the BCP Psalter, namely, the Coverdale translation of 1535.

Wesley also affirmed in the preface that it was his intent to rectify some misdirected views on Christian perfection. He adamantly opposed the concepts of instantaneous perfection and instantaneous holiness and advocated a gradual pilgrimage toward perfection and holiness throughout one's life.

Hymns on the Trinity (*Trinity Hymns* [1767]) is another example of Charles Wesley's lyrical response to a theological treatise. As he had done with Brevint's volume on the sacrifice of Christ in *HLS* (1745), in *Trinity Hymns* (1767), Wesley worked through a process of theological reflection following closely *Catholic Doctrine of the Trinity, proved by an Hundred Short and Clear Arguments* (1756) by Anglican priest William Jones, whose study was a strong apologetic for the divine nature of the three Persons of the Holy Trinity. *Trinity Hymns* (1767) contained 188 hymns, though unquestionably many were not intended for singing. In the first 136, one finds Wesley's close lyrical theological assessment of and response to Jones's volume. In the concluding fifty-two hymns, as in the final section of *HLS* (1745), Wesley composed in a freer, more doxological style, resulting in a number of memorable hymns of praise to the Trinity.

In 1767 Wesley published yet another volume of poetry, *Hymns for the Use of Families* (*Family Hymns* [1767]). It was quite different from *Trinity Hymns* (1767) in that it did not have a closely reasoned theological structure. One encounters a variety of themes that appear in many of his earlier volumes of poetry but here the central focus is the family: childbirth, baptism of a child, birthdays, parenthood, sickness, education, death, grief, belief, morning, evening, Sunday. There is even a poem titled "For a Child Cutting His Teeth." No doubt he was writing out of the context of his own family experience and his pastoral ministry. Unquestionably many of the poems were written in response to specific situations involving his wife and children. He even included the hymn he wrote for his marriage to Sarah Gwynne. There are numerous poems dealing with the sickness and death of children. This is not surprising since smallpox, diphtheria, measles, and other illnesses were primary causes of infant and child death in the eighteenth century, and five of the eight children born to Sarah and Charles died within the first year of life. Wesley attempted to cope with these grim realities from the standpoint of one's faith in God.

MS Scriptural Hymns (1783) is a large volume left unpublished by Charles Wesley at his death. It has two main sections: Old Testament (128 pages with 126 poems based on Old Testament passages) and New Testament (139 pages with 128 poems based on New Testament passages). George Osborn published most of this material in his thirteen-volume collection of *The Poetical Works of John and Charles Wesley*. Though the style corresponds to *Scripture Hymns* (1762), the poetical material does not overlap between these two sources. However, they do have one thing in common. One finds in *MS Scriptural Hymns* (1783) many poems that are also addressed to those who claim to have achieved Christian perfection in this life, which Charles viewed as being consummated only at death in full union with God.

Into the twentieth century there remained over a thousand hymns and poems of Charles Wesley that had not been published. Some of them had been included in whole or in part by George Osborn in his thirteen-volume collection of Wesley hymns and poems. In 1988, 1990, 1992, respectively, three volumes titled *The Unpublished Poetry of Charles Wesley* were edited by S T Kimbrough, Jr., and Oliver A. Beckerlegge and published in the Kingswood Books series of Abingdon Press. Volume 1 contains five sections: (1) "The American War and Other Poems on Patriotism," (2) "Epistles" (to individuals), (3) "Courtship and Marriage," (4) "Family Hymns and Poems," (5) "John Wesley's Marriage." Volume 2 carries the subtitle "Hymns and Poems on Holy Scripture." It includes six sections: (1) "The Gospel of Matthew" (MS Matthew), (2) "The Gospel of Mark" (MS Mark), (3) "The Gospel of Luke" (MS Luke), (4) "The Gospel of John" (MS John), (5) "The Book of Acts" (MS Acts), (5) "Other Scriptural Passages." Volume 3 has the subtitle "Hymns and Poems for Church and World" and has eleven sections: (1) "Hymns for Preachers," (2) "Hymns and Poems for Ordination," (3) "Hymns and Poems for Festivals," (4) "Devotional Hymns and Poems," (5) "Intercessory Hymns and Poems," (6) "Hymns for Malefactors," (7) "Epitaphs and Other Poems on Death," (8) "Epigrams," (9) "Miscellaneous Hymns and Poems," (10) "Fragments," (11) "Hymns and Poems of Doubtful Authorship." Volume 3 also includes the indexes for all three volumes: Index of First Lines, Index of Personal Names, and Index of Scriptural Passages (for volumes 1 and 3 only).

As one reads Charles Wesley's poetry in this volume, it will be wise to refer to these brief contextual annotations of the sources from which the diverse poems have been taken.

II

Poetical Selections

Part 1:

The Glory of the Triune God

Praise and Thanksgiving (1–6)

1. Hymn to the Trinity[1]

1.   God of unexhausted grace,
      Of everlasting love,
    Overpowered before thy face
      I fall, and dare not move.
    What hast thou for sinners done,
      For so poor a worm as me?
    Thou hast given thine[2] only Son,
      To bring us back to thee.

2.   Suffering, sin-atoning God,
      Thy hallowed name I bless;
    Jesus, lavish of thy blood
      To buy the sinner's peace!
    Gushing from thy sacred veins
      Let it now my soul o'erflow,
    Purge out all my sinful stains,
      And wash me white as snow.

---

1. *HSP* (1742) 121; original title.
2. First edition has "thy" but was changed to "thine" in second edition (1745).

3.   Holy Ghost, set to thy seal,
       The life of Jesus breathe;
    The deep things of God reveal,
       Apply *my* Saviour's death:
    With the Father and the Son
       Soon as one in thee I am,
    All my nature shall make known
       The glories of the Lamb.

4.   Father, Son, and Holy Ghost,
       Thy Godhead we adore,
    Join with the triumphant host
       Who praise thee evermore;
    Live, by heaven and earth adored,
       Three in One, and One in Three,
    Holy, holy, holy Lord,
       All glory be to thee!

2. To the Trinity[3]

1.   Father, in whom we live,
       In whom we are and move,
    The glory, power, and praise receive
       Of thy creating love.
       Let all the angel-throng
       Give thanks to God on high,
    While earth repeats the joyful song
       And echoes to the sky.

2.   Incarnate Deity,
       Let all the ransomed race
    Render in thanks their lives to thee,
       For thy redeeming grace;

3. *Redemption Hymns* (1747) 44–45, No. 34; original title.

        The grace to sinners showed
        Ye heavenly choirs proclaim,
    And cry Salvation to our God,
        Salvation to the Lamb.

3.   Spirit of holiness,
        Let all thy saints adore
    Thy sacred energy, and bless
        Thine heart-renewing power.
        Not angel-tongues can tell
        Thy love's ecstatic height,
    The glorious joy unspeakable,
        The beatific sight.

4.   Eternal, Triune God,
        Let all the hosts above,
    Let all the sons of men record
        And dwell upon thy love.
        When heaven and earth are fled
        Before thy glorious face,
    Sing all the saints thy love hath made
        Thine everlasting praise.

3. *Three Persons Divine inexpressibly One*[4]

1.   While the Army above
        Overwhelmed by his love
        The Trinity sings,
    With their faces inwrapt in their shadowing wings;
        Holy Father, we cry,
        Holy Son we reply!
        Holy Spirit of grace!
    And extol the Three-One in a rapture of praise!

2.   Many gods we disclaim
        For the Three are the same

---

4. *Trinity Hymns* (1767) 90, Hymn 3.

In a *manner* unknown
Three Persons Divine inexpressibly One;
Who all homage demands
From the work of his hands
Re-created to know
And resemble his God manifested below.

3.   Their omnipotent Lord
By angels adored
When their being began,
And in Eden extolled by the primitive man;
As it was, and as now
To the Triad we bow,
Men and angels shall fall,
And eternally praise the Creator of all.

4. Lord of hosts, we bow before thee[5]

1.   Lord of hosts, we bow before Thee
God made known, Three in One,
One in Three, adore thee;
Far above our comprehending,
God of grace, take the praise
Never, never ending.

2.   Thee, the bright harmonious choir
Three and One, on thy Throne
Joyfully admire;
With triumphant acclamation
Night and day thee we pay
Threefold adoration.

3.   Glorious God, like them we bless thee,
God most high magnify,
Lord of all confess thee;

5. *Trinity Hymns* (1767) 89–90, Hymn 2.

'Till we mount through Jesus' merit,
    There to gaze, there to praise
    Father, Son and Spirit.

5. For the Anniversary Day of One's Conversion[6]

1.   Glory to God, and praise, and love
        Be ever, ever given;
    By saints below, and saints above,
        The church in earth and heaven.

2.   On this glad day the glorious Sun
        Of Righteousness arose,
    On my benighted soul he shone,
        And filled it with repose.

3.   Sudden expired the legal strife,
        'Twas then I ceased to grieve;
    My second, real, living life
        I then began to live.

4.   Then with my *heart* I first believed,
        Believed, with faith divine,
    Power with the Holy Ghost received
        To call the Saviour *mine.*

5.   I felt my Lord's atoning blood
        Close to *my* soul applied;
    Me, me he loved, the Son of God—
        For *me,* for *me* he died!

6.   I found, and owned his promise true,
        Ascertained of *my* part,
    My pardon passed in heaven I knew
        When written on my heart.

6. *HSP* (1740) 120–23; original title.

7.   O for a thousand tongues to sing
        My dear Redeemer's praise!
    The glories of my God and King,
        The triumphs of his grace.

8.   My gracious Master, and my God,
        Assist me to proclaim,
    To spread thro' all the earth abroad
        The honours of thy name.

9   Jesus the name that charms our fears,
        That bids our sorrows cease;
    'Tis music in the sinner's ears,
        'Tis life, and health, and peace!

10.   He breaks the power of cancelled sin,
        He sets the prisoner free;
    His blood can make the foulest clean;
        His blood availed for me.

11.   He speaks; and listening to his voice,
        New life the dead receive,
    The mournful, broken hearts rejoice,
        The humble poor *believe*.

12.   Hear him ye deaf, his praise ye dumb
        Your loosened tongues employ,
    Ye blind, behold your Saviour come,
        And leap, ye lame, for joy.

13.   Look unto him, ye nations, own
        Your God, ye fallen race!
    Look, and be saved thro' faith alone;
        Be justified, by grace!

14. See all your sins on Jesus laid;
       The Lamb of God was slain,
   His soul was once an offering made
       For *every soul* of man.

15. Harlots, and publicans, and thieves
       In holy triumph join!
   Saved is the sinner that believes
       From crimes as great as mine.

16. Murderers, and all ye hellish crew,
       Ye sons of lust and pride,
   Believe the Saviour died for you;
       For me the Saviour died.

17. Awake from guilty nature's sleep,
       And Christ shall give you light,
   Cast all your sins into the deep,
       And wash the *Ethiop* white.

18. With me, your chief, you then shall *know*,
       Shall feel your sins forgiven;
   Anticipate your heaven below,
       And own, that love is heaven.

6. Praise the Lord who reigns above[7]

1. Praise the Lord who reigns above
       And keeps his court below;
   Praise the holy God of love
       And all his greatness show;
   Praise him for his noble deeds,
       Praise him for his matchless power;
   Him from whom all good proceeds
       Let earth and heaven adore.

7. *CPH* (1743) 122.

2.   Publish, spread to all around
           The great Jehovah's name,
       Let the trumpet's martial sound
           The Lord of hosts proclaim:
       Praise him, in the sacred dance,
           Harmony's full concert raise,
       Let the virgin-choir advance,
           And move but to his praise.

3.   Celebrate th'eternal God
           With harp and psaltery,
       Timbrels soft and cymbals loud
           In his high praise agree:
       Praise with every tuneful string,
           All the reach of heavenly art,
       All the powers of music bring,
           The music of the heart.

4.   Him, in whom they move and live,
           Let every creature sing,
       Glory to their Maker give,
           And homage to their King:
       Hallowed be thy name beneath,
           As in heaven on earth adored;
       Praise the Lord in every breath;
           Let all things praise the Lord!

God's Nature (7–11)

GOD AS MYSTERY (7–9)

7. 'Tis all a mystery[8]

           What angel can explain
           The love of God to man,
           The secret cause assign
           Of charity divine?

8. *Scripture Hymns* (1762) 1:93.

Nothing in us could move,
Deserve, or claim his love:
'Tis all a mystery,
And must for ever be!

8. Incomprehensible—Unsearchable[9]

1. Shall foolish, weak, short-sighted man
      Beyond archangels go,
   The great almighty God explain,
      Or to perfection know?
   His attributes divinely soar
      Above the creatures' sight,
   And prostrate *Seraphim* adore
      The glorious Infinite.

2. *Jehovah's* everlasting days
      They cannot numbered be,
   Incomprehensible the space
      Of thine immensity;
   Thy wisdom's depths by reason's line
      In vain we strive to sound,
   Or stretch our labouring thought t'assign
      Omnipotence a bound.

3. The brightness of thy glories leaves
      Description far below;
   Nor man, nor angels' heart conceives
      How deep thy mercies flow:
   Thy love is *most* unsearchable,
      And dazzles all above;
   They gaze, but cannot count or tell
      The treasures of thy love!

9. *Scripture Hymns* (1762) 1:231–32, based on Job 10:7: "Canst thou by searching find out God? Canst thou find out the Almighty unto perfection?"

9. *Incomprehensible thou art*[10]

When he did our flesh assume
  That everlasting Man,
Mary held him in her womb
  Whom heaven could not contain!
Who the mystery can believe!
  Incomprehensible thou art;
Yet we still by faith conceive,
  And bear thee in our heart.

GOD AS DIVINE ENERGY AND DIVINE ESSENCE (10–11)

10. *The energy divine*[11]

1.   Can these dry bones perceive
        The quickening power of grace,
  Or Christian infidels retrieve
        The life of righteousness?
  All-good, almighty Lord,
        Thou know'st thine own design,
  The virtue of thine own great word,
        The energy divine.

2.   Now for thy mercy's sake
        Let thy great word proceed,
  Dispensed by whom thou wilt, to wake
        The spiritually dead;
  Send forth to prophesy
        Thy chosen messenger,
  And thou the gospel-word apply,
        And force the world to hear.

10. *Scripture Hymns* (1762) 2:32, based on Jer 31:22: "A woman shall compass a man."

11. *Scripture Hymns* (1762) 2:51, based on Ezek 37:3–4: "And he said unto me, Son of man, can these" bones live?

11. *Essence incomprehensible*[12]

Essence incomprehensible
Jehovah, who can know,
Who was, and is, and comes to dwell
With all his saints below!
Then the whole world shall be restored
And bow to Jesu's name,
Filled with the knowledge of the Lord,
The infinite I AM.

Providence (12)

12. *Providential care*[13]

1. Where is the Hebrews' God,
Who kept them night and day,
Where is the heavenly fire and cloud,
Which showed thy church their way?
No symbol visible
We of thy presence find,
Yet all who would obey thy will,
Shall know their Father's mind.

2. Father, thou still dost lead
The children of thy grace,
The spiritual, believing feed
Throughout this wilderness:
Our chart thy written word,
Thy Spirit is our guide,
And Christ, the glory of the Lord,
Doth in our hearts reside.

---

12. *Scripture Hymns* (1762) 2:33, based on Jer 31:34: "They shall all know me."

13. *Scripture Hymns* (1762) 1:63–64, based on Num 9:16: "So it was always: the cloud covered the tabernacle by day, and the appearance of fire by night."

3.   Thy providential care,
   Lord, we with joy confess,
 Assured thou wilt our paths prepare
   And order all our ways;
   Thy presence shall direct
   Our journeys here beneath,
 And convoy home thine own elect
   Through a triumphant death.

Creation (13)

13. Psalm 104[14]

1.   Author of every work divine,
   Who dost through both creations shine,
    The God of nature and of grace!
   Thy glorious steps in all we see,
   And wisdom attribute to thee,
    And power, and majesty, and praise.

2.   Thou didst thy mighty wings outspread,
   And, brooding o'er the chaos, shed
    Thy life into th'impregned abyss,
   The vital principle infuse,
   And out of nothing's womb produce
    The earth and heaven, and all that is.

3.   That All-informing Breath thou art,
   Who dost continued life impart,
    And bidd'st the world persist to be:
   Garnished by thee yon azure sky,
   And all those beauteous orbs on high
    Depend in golden chains from thee.

14. *Pentecost Hymns* (1746) 31–32, Hymn 28.

4. Thou dost create the earth anew,
   (Its Maker and Preserver too)
      By thine almighty arm sustain;
   Nature perceives thy secret force,
   And still holds on her even course,
      And owns thy providential reign.

5. Thou art the Universal Soul,
   The Plastic Power that fills the whole,
      And governs earth, air, sea, and sky:
   The creatures all thy breath receive;
   And who, by thy inspiring live,
      Without thy inspiration die.

6. Spirit immense, Eternal Mind,
   Thou on the souls of lost mankind
      Dost with benignest influence move,
   Pleased to restore the ruined race,
   And new create a world of grace
      In all the image of thy love.

Part 2:

The Grace of Jesus Christ

In Praise of Christ (14–18)

14. Thou hidden source of calm repose[1]

1.   Thou hidden source of calm repose,
       Thou all sufficient love divine,
    My help and refuge from my foes,
       Secure I am, if thou art mine;
    And lo! From sin, and grief, and shame
    I hide me, Jesus, in thy name.

2.   Thy mighty name salvation is,
       And keeps my happy soul above;
    Comfort it brings, and power, and peace,
       And joy, and everlasting love;
    To me with thy dear name are given
    Pardon, and holiness, and heaven.

3.   Jesus, my all in all thou art,
       My rest in toil, my ease in pain,
    The med'cine of my broken heart,
       In war my peace, in loss my gain,

---

1. *HSP* (1749) 1:245–46, Hymn 144 (Hymn 31 in the series of poems titled Hymns for Believers); original title. On pages 214 and 216 of volume 1 of *HSP* (1749) the same number (126) appears for two successive hymns; hence, the numbering from that point is off by one. Therefore, 143, though printed, should be 144.

My smile beneath the tyrant's frown,
In shame my glory and my crown,

4.   In want my plentiful supply,
In weakness my almighty power,
In bonds my perfect liberty,
My light in Satan's darkest hour,
In grief my joy unspeakable,
My life in death, my heaven in hell.

15. Through Jesus I can do all things[2]

My God, from whom the precept came,
Doth power divine therewith impart,
When Jesus I desire, and name,
The Word is in my mouth and heart;
I feel it intimately near,
Soon as my heart believes him true,
And conscious of his presence here,
Through Jesus I can all things do.

16. Jesus, Son of God, the Rock[3]

Jesus, Son of God, thou art
Omnipotence divine,
Tell it to my faithful heart
That what thou art is mine;
Rock of everlasting love,
If on thee my hopes I build,
I thy perfect work shall prove
With all thy fullness filled.

---

2. *Scripture Hymns* (1762) 1:104, based on Deut 30:14: "The word is very nigh unto thee, in thy mouth and in thy heart."

3. *Scripture Hymns* (1762) 1:105, based on Deut 32:4: "He is the Rock; his work is perfect."

17. To Be Sung in a Tumult[4]

1.   Ye servants of God, your Master proclaim,
      And publish abroad his wonderful name;
      The name all-victorious of Jesus extol,
      His kingdom is glorious and rules over all.

2.   The waves of the sea have lift up their voice,
      Sore troubled that we in Jesus rejoice;
      The floods they are roaring, but Jesus is here,
      While we are adoring, he always is near.

3.   Men, devils engage, the billows arise,
      And horribly rage, and threaten the skies:
      Their fury shall never our steadfastness shock,
      The weakest believer is built on a Rock.

4.   God ruleth on high, almighty to save,
      And still he is nigh, his presence we have;
      The great congregation his triumph shall sing,
      Ascribing salvation to Jesus, our King.

5.   Salvation to God, who sits on the throne!
      Let all cry aloud and honor the Son;
      Our Jesus's praises the angels proclaim,
      Fall down on their faces and worship the Lamb.

6.   Then let us adore and give him his right,
      All glory and power, all wisdom and might;
      All honour and blessing, with angels above,
      And thanks never ceasing, and infinite love.

---

4. *HTTP* (1744) 43, No. 1; original title of section "Hymns to be Sung in a Tumult."

18. After Preaching (in a Church)[5]

1.   Jesu, accept the grateful song,
            My wisdom and my might,
        'Tis thou hast loosed the stammering tongue,
            And taught my hands to fight.

2.   Thou, Jesus, thou my mouth hast been,
            The weapons of thy war,
        Mighty through thee, I pull down sin,
            And all thy truth declare.

3.   Not without thee, my Lord, I am
            Come up unto this place,
        Thy Spirit bade me preach thy name,
            And trumpet forth thy praise.

4.   Thy Spirit gave me utterance now,
            My soul with strength endued,
        Hardened to adamant my brow,
            And armed my heart with God.

5.   Thy powerful hand in all I see,
            Thy wondrous workings own,
        Glory, and strength, and praise to thee
            Ascribe, and thee alone.

6.   Gladly I own the promise true
            To all whom thou dost send,
        "Behold, I always am with you,
            "Your Saviour to the end!"

7.   Amen, amen, my God and Lord,
            If thou art with me still,
        I still shall speak the gospel-word,
            My ministry fulfill.

5. *HSP* (1749) 1:305–8, Hymn 195; original title.

8.   Thee I shall constantly proclaim,
        Though earth and hell oppose,
    Bold to confess thy glorious name
        Before a world of foes.

9.   Jesus the name high over all,
        In hell or earth or sky,
    Angels and men before it fall,
        And devils fear and fly.

10.   Jesus the name to sinners dear,
        The name to sinners given,
    It scatters all their guilty fear,
        It turns their hell to heaven.

11.   Balm into wounded spirits it pours,
        And heals the sin-sick mind;
    It hearing to the deaf restores,
        And eyesight to the blind.

12.   Jesus the prisoner's fetters breaks,
        And bruises Satan's head,
    Power into strengthless souls it speaks,
        And life into the dead.

13.   O that the world might taste and see
        The riches of his grace!
    The arms of love that compass me
        Would all mankind embrace.

14.   O that my Jesu's heavenly charms
        Might every bosom move!
    Fly sinners, fly into those arms
        Of everlasting love.

15.   The Lover of your souls is near,
        Him I to you commend,
    Joyful the Bridegroom's voice to hear,
        Who calls a worm his friend.

16. He hath the Bride, and he alone,
    Almighty to redeem,
I only make his mercies known,
    I send you all to him.

17. Sinners, behold the Lamb of God,
    On him your spirits stay;
He bears the universal load,
    He takes your sins away.

18. His only righteousness I show,
    His saving grace proclaim;
'Tis all my business here below
    To cry, Behold the Lamb!

19. For this a suffering life I live,
    And reckon all things loss;
For him my strength, my all I give,
    And glory in his cross.

20. I spend myself, that you may know
    The Lord our righteousness,
That Christ in you may live, and grow,
    I joyfully decrease.

21. Gladly I hasten to decay,
    My life I freely spend,
And languish for the welcome day,
    When all my toil shall end.

22. Happy, if with my latest breath
    I might but gasp his name,
Preach him to all, and cry in death,
    Behold, behold the Lamb!

Christ's Gracious Life (19–25)

PROMISED COMING (19)

19. *Come, thou long-expected Jesus*[6]

1. Come, thou long-expected Jesus,
  Born to set thy people free;
From our fears and sins relieve[7] us,
  Let us find our rest in thee.
Israel's strength and consolation,
  Hope of all the earth thou art;
Dear desire of every nation,
  Joy of every longing heart.

2. Born thy people to deliver,
  Born a child and yet a King,
Born to reign in us forever,
  Now thy gracious kingdom bring.
By thine own eternal spirit
  Rule in all our hearts alone;
By thine all-sufficient merit,
  Raise us to thy glorious throne.

BIRTH AND INCARNATION / *KENOSIS* (20–25)

20. *Hymn for Christmas-Day*[8]

1. Hark how all the Welkin rings,
  "Glory to the King of kings;
  "Peace on earth, and mercy mild,
  "God and sinners reconciled!"

---

6. *Nativity Hymns* (1745) 14, Hymn 10.

7. "Relieve" changed to "release" in the edition of 1777 and thereafter.

8. *HSP* (1739) 206–8; original title. George Whitefield (*Hymns*, 1753) altered the opening couplet to "Hark! the herald angels sing, / Glory to the new-born King," and made other changes which have survived.

2.   Joyful, all ye nations rise,
   Join the triumph of the skies;
   Universal Nature say,
   "Christ the Lord is born today!"

3.   Christ, by highest heaven adored;
   Christ, the everlasting Lord;
   Late in time behold him come,
   Offspring of a virgin's womb.

4.   Veiled in flesh, the Godhead see;
   Hail th'incarnate Deity!
   Pleased as man with men t'appear,
   Jesus, our Emmanuel here!

5.   Hail the heavenly Prince of Peace!
   Hail the Sun of Righteousness!
   Light and life to all he brings,
   Risen with healing in his wings.

6.   Mild he lays his glory by,
   Born—that man no more may die,
   Born—to raise the sons of earth,
   Born—to give them second birth.

7.   Come, Desire of Nations, come,
   Fix in us thy humble home,
   Rise, the woman's conquering seed,
   Bruise in us the Serpent's head.

8.   Now display thy saving power,
   Ruined nature now restore,
   Now in mystic union join
   Thine to ours, and ours to thine.

9.   Adam's likeness, Lord, efface,
   Stamp thy image in its place,

> Second Adam from above,
> Reinstate us in thy love.

10.   Let us thee, though lost, regain,
> Thee, the life, the inner Man:
> O! to all thyself impart,
> Formed in each believing heart.

21. *Rejoice in Jesu's birth*[9]

1.   Rejoice in Jesu's birth!
> To us a Son is given,
> To us a child is born on earth,
> Who made both earth and heaven!
> His shoulder props the sky,
> This universe sustains!
> The God supreme, the Lord most high,
> The king *Messiah* reigns!

2.   His name, his nature, soars
> Beyond the creatures' ken:
> Yet whom th'angelic host adores,
> He pleads the cause of men!
> Our Counselor we praise,
> Our Advocate above,
> Who daily in his Church displays
> His miracles of love.

22. *Away with our fears*[10]

1.   Away with our fears!
> The Godhead appears
> In Christ reconciled,
> The Father of mercies in Jesus the child.

9. *Scripture Hymns* (1762) 1:312, based on Isa 9:6: "Unto us a child is born, unto us a son is given, and the government shall be upon his shoulder: and his name shall be called Wonderful, Counselor."

10. *Nativity Hymns* (1745) 11–12, Hymn 8.

2.   He comes from above,
In manifest love,
The desire of our eyes,
The meek Lamb of God, in a manger he lies.

3.   At Emmanuel's birth
What a triumph on earth!
Yet could it afford
No better a place for its heavenly Lord.

4.   The Ancient of Days
To redeem a lost race,
From his glory comes down,
Self-humbled to carry us up to a crown.

5.   Made flesh for our sake,
That we might partake
The nature divine,
And again in his image, his holiness shine;

6.   An heavenly birth
Experience on earth,
And rise to his throne,
And live with our Jesus eternally One.

7.   Then let us believe,
And gladly receive
The tidings they bring,
Who publish to sinners their Savior and King.

8.   And while we are here,
Our King shall appear,
His Spirit impart,
And form his full image of love in our heart.

23. *Let earth and heaven combine*[11]

1.   Let earth and heaven combine,
        Angels and men agree,
     To praise in songs divine
        Th'incarnate Deity,
     Our God contracted to a span,
     Incomprehensibly made man.

2.   He laid his glory by,
        He wrapped him in our clay,
     Unmarked by human eye,
        The latent Godhead lay,
     Infant of days he here became;
     And bore the loved[12] Immanuel's name.

3.   See in that infant's face
        The depths of Deity,
     And labour while ye gaze,
        To sound the mystery;
     In vain ye angels gaze no more,
     But fall and silently adore.

4.   Unsearchable the love,
        That hath the Saviour brought,
     The grace is far above,
        Or man[13] or angel's thought:
     Suffice for us that God we know,
     Our God is manifest below.

5.   He deigns in flesh t'appear,
        Widest extremes to join,
     To bring our vileness near,
        And make us all divine;

11. *Nativity Hymns* (1745) 7–8, Hymn 5.
12. "Loved" changed to "mild" in second edition of 1745 and thereafter.
13. "Men" altered to "man" in the edition of 1778 and thereafter.

And we the life of God shall know
For God is manifest below.

6.   Made perfect first in love,
      And sanctified by grace,
We shall from earth remove,
      And see his glorious face;
His love shall then be fully showed,
And man shall all be lost in God.

24. Christmas Day[14]

Stupendous mystery!
      God in our flesh is *seen*
(While angels ask, how can it be?)
      And dwells with sinful men!
Our nature he assumes,
      That we may his retrieve;
He comes, to our dead world he comes,
      That all through him may live.

25. All-wise, all-good, Almighty Lord[15]

1.   All-wise, all-good, Almighty Lord,
Jesus, by highest heaven adored,
      E'er time its course began,
How did thy glorious mercy stoop
To take the fallen nature up,
      When thou thyself wert man?

2.   Th'eternal God from heaven came down,
The King of Glory dropped his crown,
      And veiled his mystery,
Emptied of all but love he came;
Jesus, I call thee by the name
      Thy pity bore for me.

14. *Unpub. Poetry*, 3:106; original title.
15. *Nativity Hymns* (1745) 19–20, Hymn 15.

3.   O holy child, still let thy birth
      Bring peace to us poor worms of earth,
          And praise to God on high!
      Come, thou who didst my flesh assume,
      Now to the abject sinner come,
          And in a manger lie.

4.   Didst thou not in thy person join
      The natures human and divine,
          That God and man might be
      Henceforth inseparably One?
      Haste then, and make thy nature known
          Incarnated in me.

5.   In my weak sinful flesh appear,
      O God, be manifested here,
          Peace, righteousness, and joy,
      Thy kingdom, Lord, set up within
      My faithful heart, and all my sin,
          The devil's works destroy.

6.   I long thy coming to confess
      The mystic power of Godliness,
          The life divine to prove,
      The fullness of thy life to know,
      Redeemed from all my sins below,
          And perfected in love.

7.   O Christ, my hope, make known in me
      The great, the glorious mystery,
          The hidden life impart:
      Come, thou Desire of Nations, come,
      Formed in a spotless virgin's womb,
          A pure believing heart.

8.   Come quickly, dearest Lord, that I
      May own, though Antichrist deny,

Thy Incarnation's power,
May cry, a witness to my Lord,
"Come in my flesh is Christ, the Word,
"And I can sin no more!"

LIFE AND TEACHING (26–28)

26. O that all mankind might hear him[16]

O that all mankind might hear him,
Teacher, Friend of all mankind,
Every ransomed soul revere him,
In his blood remembrance find!
Sinners, know your present Saviour,
Listen to his love's advice,
Find in him the Father's favour,
Find the way to paradise.

27. Saviour, instruct us to declare[17]

1.   Saviour, instruct us to declare
Thy word as every one can bear,
Milk, or strong meat to give,
As every soul hath gain'd from thee
A large or small capacity
Thy doctrines to receive.

2.   Who the first elements would know,
To these we cannot stoop too low,
Or speak in words too plain,
While step by step we bring them on,
Till all thy saints through faith alone,
Come to a perfect man.

16. *Scripture Hymns* (1762) 1:173, based on Matt 17:5: "While he yet spake, behold, a bright cloud overshadowed them: and behold a voice out of the cloud, which said, This is my beloved Son, in whom I am well pleased; hear ye him."

17. MS Mark, 43. See *Poet. Works*, 10:477, based on Mark 4:33: "Spake he the word unto them, as they were able," etc.

28. Spirit of Truth, descend[18]

1. Spirit of Truth, descend,
  And with thy Church abide,
Our Guardian to the end,
  Our sure unerring Guide,
Us into the whole counsel lead
Of God revealed below,
And teach us all the truth we need
To life eternal know.

2. Whate'er thou hear'st above
  To us with power impart,
And shed abroad the love
  Of Jesus in our heart:
One with the Father and the Son
Thy record is the same,
O make to us the Godhead known,
Through faith in Jesu's name.

3. To all our souls apply
  The doctrine of our Lord,
Our conscience certify,
  And witness with the Word,
Thy realizing light display,
And show us things to come,
The after-state, the final day,
And man's eternal doom.

4. The Judge of quick and dead,
  The God of truth and love,
Who doth for sinners plead,
  Our Advocate above;
Exalted by his Father there
Thou dost exalt below,
And all his grace on earth declare,
And all his glory show.

18. *Pentecost Hymns* (1746) 25–27, Hymn 23; original title "John 16:13, 14, 15."

5.   Sent in his name thou art,
       His work to carry on,
     His Godhead to assert,
       And make his mercy known:
Thou searchest the deep things of God,
       Thou know'st the Saviour's mind,
And tak'st of his atoning blood
       To sprinkle all mankind.

6.   Now then of his receive,
       And show to us the grace,
     And all his fullness give
       To all the ransomed race,
Whate'er he did for sinners buy
       With his expiring groan,
By faith, in us reveal, apply,
       And make it all our own.

7.   Descending from above
       Into our souls convey
His comfort, joy and love,
       Which none can take away,
His merit and his righteousness
       Which makes an end of sin,
Apply to every heart his peace,
       And bring his kingdom in!

8.   The plenitude of God
       That doth in Jesus dwell,
On us through him bestowed
       To us secure and seal:
Now let us taste our Master's bliss
       The glorious heavenly powers,
For all the Father hath is his,
       And all he hath is ours.

PASSION AND DEATH (29–35)

29. *Christ, our Passover, is slain*[19]

> Christ, our passover, is slain,
> To set his people free,
> Free from sin's Egyptian's chain,
> And Pharaoh's tyranny:
> Lord, that we may now depart,
> And truly serve our pard'ning God,
> Sprinkle every house and heart
> With thine atoning blood.

30. *To Me Thy Death is Life*[20]

> Oft have I unconcerned passed by,
> Nor stopped on Calvary,
> So small a thing, that thou should'st die,
> O nothing, Lord, to me!
> But now I see, the bleeding cross
> Is all in all to man,
> To me thy death is life, thy loss
> Is mine eternal gain.

31. *God of unexampled grace*[21]

> 1.　God of unexampled grace,
> Redeemer of mankind,
> Matter of eternal praise,
> We in thy Passion find:
> Still our choicest strains we bring,
> Still our joyful theme pursue,
> Thee the Friend of sinners sing
> Whose love is ever new.

19. *Scripture Hymns* (1762) 1:41, Hymn 129, based on Exod 12:7: "They shall take of the blood, and strike it on the two side-posts, and on the upper door posts of the houses."

20. *Scripture Hymns* (1762) 2:39, based on Lam 1:12: "Is it nothing to you, all ye that pass by?"

21. *HLS* (1745) 16–17, Hymn 21.

2. Endless scenes of wonder rise
       With that mysterious tree,
    Crucified before our eyes
       Where we our Maker see:
    Jesus, Lord, what hast thou done!
       Publish we the death divine,
    Stop, and gaze, and fall, and own
       Was never love like thine!

3. Never love nor sorrow was
       Like that my Jesus showed;
    See him stretched on yonder cross
       And crushed beneath our load!
    Now discern the deity,
       Now his heavenly birth declare!
    Faith cries out 'Tis he, 'tis he,
       My God that suffers there!

4. Jesus drinks the bitter cup;
       The wine-press treads alone,
    Tears the graves and mountains up
       By his expiring groan:
    Lo! The powers of heaven he shakes;
       Nature in convulsions lies,
    Earth's profoundest centre quakes,
       The great Jehovah dies!

5. Dies the glorious cause of all,
       The true Eternal *Pan*,
    Falls to raise us from our fall,
       To ransom sinful man:
    Well may *Sol* withdraw his light,
       With the sufferer sympathize,
    Leave the world in sudden night,
       While his Creator dies.

6. Well may heaven be clothed with black
       And solemn sackcloth wear,
    Jesu's agony partake
       The hour of darkness share:
    Mourn th'astonished hosts above,
       Silence saddens all the skies,
    Kindler of seraphic love
       The God of angels dies.

7. O my God, he dies for me,
       I feel the mortal smart!
    See him hanging on the tree—
       A sight that breaks my heart!
    O that all to thee might turn!
       Sinners, ye may love him too,
    Look on him ye pierced, and mourn
       For one who bled for you.

8. Weep o'er your desire and hope
       With tears of humblest love;
    Sing, for Jesus is gone up,
       And reigns enthroned above!
    Lives our Head, to die no more:
       Power is all to Jesus given,
    Worshiped as he was before
       Th'immortal King of heaven.

9. Lord, we bless thee for thy grace,
       And truth which never fail,
    Hast'ning to behold thy face
       Without a dimming Veil:
    We shall see our heavenly King,
       All thy glorious love proclaim,
    Help the Angel-choirs to sing
       Our dear triumphant Lamb.

32. Let me on thy passion gaze[22]

1. Lord, to thee I feebly look,
    Thou my cause hast undertook,
    Author of my faith thou art,
    Stamping pardon on my heart.

2. But that every moment I,
    May on thy dear cross rely,
    Still the mystery reveal
    Of thy love unspeakable.

3. What thou gav'st me once to know,
    O continue to bestow,
    Give me, every moment give
    By thy precious death to live.

4. This my sole employment be,
    Station'd here on Calvary,
    Let me on thy passion gaze,
    See thee dying in my place.

5. While I thus my pattern view,
    I shall bleed and suffer too,
    With the Man of sorrow joined
    One become in heart and mind.

6. More and more like Jesus grow,
    'Till the Finisher I know,
    Gain the final victor's wreath,
    Perfect love in perfect death.

22. *Scripture Hymns* (1762) 2:370, based on Heb 12:2: "Looking unto Jesus, the author and finisher of our faith."

33. Hearts of stone, relent, relent[23]

1.   Hearts of stone, relent, relent,
      Break by Jesu's cross subdued,
    See his body mangled, rent,
      Covered with a gore of blood!
    Sinful soul, what hast thou done?
    Murdered God's eternal Son!

2.   Yes, our sins have done the deed,
      Drove the nails that fix him here,
    Crowned with thorns his sacred head,
      Pierced him with the soldier's spear,
    Made his soul a sacrifice;
    For a sinful world he dies.

3.   Shall we let him die in vain?
      Still to death pursue our God?
    Open tear his wounds again,
      Trample on his precious blood?
    No; with all our sins we part,
    Saviour, take my broken heart!

34. 'Tis finished! the Messiah dies[24]

1.   'Tis finished! the Messiah dies,
      Cut off for sins, but not his own!
    Accomplished is the sacrifice,
      The great redeeming work is done.

2.   'Tis finished! all the debt is paid,
      Justice Divine is satisfied,
    The grand and full atonement's made,
      God for a guilty world hath died.

23. *HLS* (1745) 18–19, Hymn 23.

24. Charles Wesley wrote the stanzas of this hymn at different times and never wrote or published all of them in the same place. See MS Thirty, 193–95. Stanzas 1–4, 6, 8–10 appear in Osborn's *Poet. Works,* 12:99–100; stanzas 1, 5, 7, 10 appear with slight variations in *Scripture Hymns* (1762) 2:234, and in MS John, 412–13. The sequence of ten stanzas as published here appears in *Unpub. Poetry,* 2:277–79.

3. The veil is rent, the way is shown,
   The living way to heaven is seen;
   The middle wall is broken down,
   And all mankind may enter in.

4. The types and figures are fulfilled,
   Exacted is the legal pain,
   The precious promises are sealed,
   The spotless Lamb of God is slain.

5. Finished the first transgression is,
   And purged the guilt of actual sin,
   And everlasting righteousness
   Is now to all the world brought in.

6. The reign of sin and death is o'er,
   And all may live from sin set free;
   Satan hath lost his mortal power;
   'Tis swallowed up in victory.

7. 'Tis finished! All my guilt and pain,
   I want no sacrifice beside;
   For me, for me the Lamb is slain;
   'Tis finished! I am justified!

8. Saved from the legal curse I am,
   My Savior hangs on yonder tree;
   See there the dear expiring Lamb,
   'Tis finished! He expires for me.

9. Accepted in the well-beloved
   And clothed in righteousness divine,
   I see the bar to heaven removed,
   And all thy merits, Lord, are mine.

10. Death, hell, and sin are now subdued,
    All grace is now to sinners given,
    And lo! I plead th'atoning blood,
    And in thy right, demand thy heaven.

35. Another [Desiring to Love] 25

1. O Love divine, what hast thou done!
    Th'immortal God hath died for me!
   The Father's co-eternal Son
    Bore all my sins upon the tree;
   Th' immortal God for me hath died!
   My Lord, my Love, is crucified!

2. Behold him, all ye that pass by,
    The bleeding Prince of life and peace,
   Come see, ye worms, your Maker die,
    And say, was ever grief like his!
   Come feel with me his blood applied:
   My Lord, my Love, is crucified!

3. Is crucified for me and you,
    To bring us rebels near to God;
   Believe, believe the record true:
    Ye all are bought with Jesu's blood.
   Pardon for all flows from his side;
   My Lord, my Love, is crucified!

4. Then let us sit beneath his cross,
    And gladly catch the healing stream,
   All things for him account but loss,
    And give up all our hearts to him;
   Of nothing think or speak beside:
   My Lord, my Love is crucified!

RESURRECTION AND ASCENSION (36–40)

36. Hymn for Easter-Day²⁶

1. "Christ the Lord is risen today,"
   Sons of men and angels say,

---

25. *HSP* (1742) 26–27; original title.
26. *HSP* (1739) 209–11; original title.

Raise your joys and triumphs high,
Sing, ye heavens, and earth reply.

2. Love's redeeming work is done,
    Fought the fight, the battle won;
    Lo! Our sun's eclipse is o'er,
    Lo! He sets in blood no more.

3. Vain the stone, the watch, the seal;
    Christ has burst the gates of hell!
    Death in vain forbids his rise:
    Christ has opened paradise!

4. Lives again our glorious King,
    Where, O death, is now thy sting?
    Dying once he all doth save,
    Where thy victory, O grave?

5. Soar we now where Christ has led?
    Following our exalted Head;
    Made like him, like him we rise,
    Ours the cross—the grave—the skies!

6. What though once we perished all,
    Partners in our parent's fall?
    Second life we all receive,
    In our heavenly Adam live.

7. Risen with him, we upward move,
    Still we seek the things above,
    Still pursue, and kiss the Son
    Seated on his Father's throne.

8. Scarce on earth a thought bestow,
    Dead to all we leave below,
    Heaven our aim, and loved abode,
    Hid our life with Christ in God!

9.   Hid, till Christ our life appear,
Glorious in his members here:
Joined to him, we then shall shine
All Immortal, all Divine!

10.   Hail the Lord of earth and heaven!
Praise to thee by both be given:
Thee we greet triumphant now;
Hail the Resurrection, Thou!

11.   King of glory, soul of bliss,
Everlasting life is this:
Thee to know, thy power to prove,
Thus to sing, and thus to love!

37. Jesu, show us thy salvation[27]

By the Mystery of thy Incarnation; by thy holy nativity and circumcision; by thy baptism, fasting, and temptation; by thine agony, and bloody sweat; by thy cross and passion; by thy precious death and burial; by thy glorious resurrection and ascension; and by the coming of the Holy Ghost, Good Lord, deliver us. Litany.

1.   Jesu, show us thy salvation,
    (In thy strength we strive with thee)
By thy Mystic Incarnation,
    By thy pure nativity,
Save us thou, our New-Creator,
    Into all our souls impart,
Thy divine unsinning nature,
    Form thyself within our heart.

27. *Resurrection Hymns* (1746) 10–12, Hymn 7. The quotation from the BCP, which appears here, precedes the poem in *Resurrection Hymns*.

2.   By thy first blood-shedding heal us;
       Cut us off from every sin,
    By thy circumcision seal us,
       Write thy law of love within;
    By thy Spirit circumcise us,
       Kindle in our hearts a flame;
    By thy baptism baptize us
       Into all thy glorious name.

3.   By thy fasting and temptation
       Mortify our vain desires,
    Take away what sense, or passion,
       Appetite, or flesh requires:
    Arm us with thy self-denial,
       Every tempted soul defend,
    Save us in the fiery trial,
       Make us faithful to the end.

4.   By thy sorer sufferings save us,
       Save us when conformed to thee,
    By thy miseries relieve us,
       By thy painful agony;
    When beneath thy frown we languish,
       When we feel thine anger's weight
    Save us by thine unknown anguish,
       Save us by thy bloody sweat.

5.   By that highest point of passion,
       By thy sufferings on the tree,
    Save us from the indignation
       Due to all mankind and me.
    Hanging, bleeding, panting, dying,
       Gasping out thy latest breath,
    By thy precious death's applying
       Save us from eternal death.

6.   From the world of care release us,
         By thy decent burial save,
     Crucified with thee, O Jesus,
         Hide us in thy quiet grave:
     By thy power divinely glorious,
         By thy resurrection's power
     Raise us up, o'er sin victorious,
         Raise us up to fall no more.

7.   By the pomp of thine ascending,
         Live we here to heaven restored,
     Live in pleasures never ending,
         Share the portion of our Lord:
     Let us have our conversation
         With the blessed spirits above,
     Saved with all thy great salvation,
         Perfectly renewed in love.

8.   Glorious Head, triumphant Saviour,
         High enthroned above all height,
     We have now through thee found favour,
         Righteous in thy Father's sight:
     Hears he not thy prayer unceasing?
         Can he turn away thy face:
     Send us down the purchased blessing,
         Fullness of the gospel-grace.

9.   By the coming of thy Spirit
         As a mighty rushing wind,
     Save us into all thy merit,
         Into all thy sinless[28] mind;
     Let the perfect gift be given,
         Let thy will in us be seen,
     Done on earth as 'tis in heaven:
         Lord, thy Spirit cries Amen!

28. "Sinless" is altered to "spotless" in the edition of 1764 and thereafter.

38. Rejoice, the Lord is King![29]

1.   Rejoice, the Lord is King!
        Your Lord and King adore,
      Mortals, give thanks, and sing,
        And triumph evermore;
Lift up your heart, lift up your voice,
Rejoice, again, I say, rejoice.

2.   Jesus the Saviour reigns,
        The God of truth and love,
      When he had purged our stains,
        He took his seat above.
Lift up your heart, lift up your voice,
Rejoice, again, I say, rejoice.

3.   His kingdom cannot fail,
        He rules o'er earth and heaven;
      The keys of death and hell
        Are to our Jesus given:
Lift up your heart, lift up your voice,
Rejoice, again, I say, rejoice.

4.   He sits at God's right hand,
        Till all his foes submit,
      And bow to his command,
        And fall beneath his feet.
Lift up your heart, lift up your voice,
Rejoice, again, I say, rejoice.

5.   He all his foes shall quell,
        Shall all our sins destroy,
      And every bosom swell
        With pure seraphic joy;
Lift up your heart, lift up your voice,
Rejoice, again, I say, rejoice.

29. *Resurrection Hymns* (1746) 12–13, Hymn 8.

6.   Rejoice in glorious hope,
           Jesus the Judge shall come;
       And take his servants up
       To their eternal home:
       We soon shall hear th'archangel's voice,
       The trump of God shall sound, Rejoice.

39. *Christ, our Living Head, draw near*[30]

1.   Christ, our Living Head, draw near,
       At our call, quicken all
       Thy true members here.

2.   Filled with faith's eternal Spirit,
       Grant that we, dead with thee,
       May thy life inherit.

3.   All thy resurrection's power,
       All thy love, from above,
       On thy servants shower.

4.   Perfect Love! We long t'attain it,
       Following fast, if at last
       We, ev'n we may gain it.

5.   Partners of thy death and passion,
       O that we all might see
       All thy great salvation.

6.   Saved beyond the dread of falling,
       Let us rise to the prize
       Of our glorious calling.

---

30. *Resurrection Hymns* (1746) 19, Hymn 15,

7. Children of the resurrection,
   Lead us on to the crown
   Of our full perfection.

8. There, where thou art gone before us,
   Christ, our hope, take us up,
   To thy heaven restore us.

40. Hymn for Ascension-Day[31]

1. Hail the day that sees him rise,
   Ravished from our wishful eyes!
   Christ, awhile to mortals given,
   Re-ascends his native heaven!

2. There the pompous triumph waits:
   "Lift your heads, eternal gates!
   Wide unfold the radiant scene,
   Take the King of glory in!"

3. Circled round with angel powers,
   Their triumphant Lord, and ours,
   Conqueror over death and sin,
   Take the King of Glory in!

4. Him though highest heaven receives,
   Still he loves the earth he leaves;
   Though returning to his throne,
   Still he calls mankind his own.

5. See! He lifts his hands above!
   See! He shows the prints of love!
   Hark! His gracious lips bestow
   Blessings on his church below!

31. *HSP* (1739) 211–13; original title.

6.   Still for us his death he pleads;
     Prevalent, he intercedes;
     Near himself prepares our place,
     Harbinger of human race.

7.   Master, (will we ever say)
     Taken from our Head today;
     See thy faithful servants, see!
     Ever gazing up to thee.

8.   Grant, though parted from our sight,
     High above yon azure height,
     Grant our hearts may thither rise,
     Following thee beyond the skies.

9.   Ever upward let us move,
     Wafted on the wings of love,
     Looking when our Lord shall come,
     Longing, gasping after home.

10. There we shall with thee remain,
     Partners of thy endless reign,
     There thy face unclouded see,
     Find our heaven of heavens in thee!

Part 3:

The Power of the Holy Spirit

In Praise of the Holy Spirit (41–44)

41. *Father of everlasting grace*[1]

1. Father of everlasting grace,
    Thy goodness and thy truth we praise,
        Thy goodness and thy truth we prove:
    Thou hast in honour of thy Son
    The gift unspeakable sent down
        The Spir't of life, and power, and love.

2. Thou hast the prophecy fulfilled,
    The grand orig'nal compact sealed,
        For which thy Word and oath were joined:
    The promise to our Fallen Head
    To every child of Adam made,
        Is now poured out on all mankind.

3. The purchased Comforter is given,
    For Jesus is returned to heaven,
        To claim, and then the grace impart:
    Our Day of Pentecost is come,
    And God vouchsafes to fix his home
        In every poor expecting heart.

1. *Pentecost Hymns* (1746) 3–4, Hymn 1.

4.   Father, on thee whoever call,
Confess thy promise is for all,
    While every one that asks receives,
Receives the gift, and Giver too,
And witnesses that thou art true,
    And in thy Spirit walks, and lives.

5.   Not to a single age confined,
For every soul of man designed,
    O God, we now that Spirit claim:
To us the Holy Ghost impart,
Breathe him into our panting heart,
    Thou hear'st us ask in Jesu's name.

6.   Send us the Spirit of thy Son,
To make the depths of Godhead known,
    To make us share the life divine;
Send him the sprinkled blood t'apply,
Send him, our souls to sanctify,
    And show, and seal us ever thine.

7.   So shall we pray, and never cease,
So shall we thankfully confess
    Thy wisdom, truth, and power, and love,
With joy unspeakable adore,
And bless, and praise thee evermore,
    And serve thee like thy hosts above:

8.   Till added to the heavenly choir,
We raise our songs of triumph higher,
    And praise thee in a bolder strain,
Outsoar the firstborn seraph's flight,
And sing with all our friends in light
    Thine everlasting love to man.

42. *Praying for a blessing*[2]

1.   Spirit of faith, come down,
       Reveal the things of God,
And make to us the Godhead known,
       And witness with the blood.
       'Tis thine the blood t' apply
       And give us eyes to see,
Who did for every sinner die
       Hath surely died for *me*.

2.   No man can truly say
       That Jesus is the Lord,
Unless thou take the veil away
       And breathe the living Word.
       Then, only then, we feel
       Our interest in his blood,
And cry with joy unspeakable,
       Thou art my Lord, my God.

3.   I know my Saviour lives,
       He lives who died for me,
My inmost soul his voice receives
       Who hangs on yonder tree:
       Set forth before my eyes
       Ev'n now I see him bleed,
And hear his mortal groans and cries
       While suffering in my stead.

4.   O that the world might know
       My dear atoning Lamb!
Spirit of faith, descend and show
       The virtue of his name;
       The grace which all may find,
       The saving power impart,
And testify to all mankind,
       And speak in every heart.

2. *Pentecost Hymns* (1746) 30–31, Hymn 27.

5.   Inspire the living faith
        (Which whosoe'er receives
The witness in himself he hath,
    And consciously believes),
    The faith that conquers all,
    And doth the mountain move,
And saves whoe'er on Jesus call,
    And perfects them in love.

43. John 16:24[3]

Ask, and ye shall receive, that your joy may be full.

1.   Rise, my soul, with ardor rise,
Breathe thy witness to the skies;
Freely pour out all thy mind,
Seek, and thou art sure to find;
Ready art thou to receive?
Readier is thy God to give.

2.   Heavenly Father, Lord of all,
Hear, and show thou hear'st my call;
Let my cries thy throne assail
Entering now within the veil:
Give the benefits I claim—
Lord, I ask in Jesu's Name!

3.   Friend of sinners, King of saints,
Answer my minutest wants,
All my largest thoughts require,
Grant me all my heart's desire,
Give me, till my cup run o'er,
All, and infinitely more.

3. *HSP* (1739) 219–21; original title.

4. Meek and lowly be my mind,
   Pure my heart, my will resigned!
   Keep me dead to all below,
   Only Christ resolved to know,
   Firm and disengaged and free,
   Seeking all my bliss in thee.

5. Suffer me no more to grieve
   Wanting what thou long'st to give,
   Show me all thy goodness, Lord,
   Beaming from th'Incarnate Word,
   Christ, in whom thy glories shine,
   Efflux of the Light Divine.

6. Since the Son hath made me free
   Let me taste my liberty;
   Thee behold with open face
   Triumph in thy saving grace,
   Thy great will delight to prove,
   Glory in thy perfect love.

7. Since the Son hath bought my peace,
   Mine thou art, as I am his:
   Mine the Comforter I see,
   Christ is full of grace for me:
   Mine (the purchase of his blood)
   All the Plenitude of God.

8. Abba, Father! hear thy child,
   Late in Jesus reconciled!
   Hear, and all the graces shower,
   All the joy, and peace, and power,
   All my Saviour asks above,
   All the life and heaven of love.

9.   Lord, I will not let thee go,
Till the blessing thou bestow:
Hear my Advocate Divine;
Lo! to his my suit I join:
Joined to his it cannot fail—
Bless me, for I *will* prevail.

10.   Stoop from thy eternal throne,
See, thy promise calls thee down!
High and lofty as thou art,
Dwell within my worthless heart!
Here, a fainting soul revive;
Here for ever walk and live.

11.   Heavenly Adam, Life Divine,
Change my nature into thine;
Move and spread from out my soul,
Actuate and fill the whole;
Be it I no longer now
Living in the flesh, but thou.

12.   Holy Ghost, no more delay,
Come, and in thy temple stay;
Now thy inward witness bear
Strong and permanent, and clear;
Spring of Life, thyself impart
Rise eternal in my heart!

44. Come, O thou breath divine[4]

1.   Come, O thou breath divine,
From every quarter blow,
And whom thou didst together join,
On them thine influence show;

4. *Scripture Hymns* (1762) 2:52, Hymn 1276, based on Ezek 37:9–10: "Come from the four winds, O breath, and breathe upon these slain, that they may live," etc.

Thy wonder-working power
Be here again displayed,
And now to sudden life restore
The long-forgotten dead.

2.   Inspired at God's command
By thee, the Spirit of grace,
Let the whole house of Israel stand
And their Restorer praise.
Host of the living God
Throughout the earth declare
The heavenly gift on all bestowed,
Th'indwelling Comforter.

The Fruit of the Spirit (45)

45. For the Fruits of the Spirit[5]

1.   Jesus, God of peace and love,
Send thy blessing from above,
Take, and seal us for thine own,
Touch our hearts, and make them one.

2.   By the sense of sin forgiven
Purge out all the former leaven,
Malice, guile, and proud offence,
Take the stone of stumbling hence.

3.   Root up every bitter root,
Multiply the Spirit's fruit,
Love, and joy, and quiet peace,
Meek long-suffering gentleness;

4.   Strict and general temperance
Boundless pure benevolence,
Cordial firm fidelity;
ALL THE MIND, which was in thee.

5. *Pentecost Hymns* (1746) 28–29, Hymn 25; original title.

II: Poetical Selections

Prevenient Grace (46–48)

INVITATION (46–47)

46. The Great Supper[6]
Luke 14:16–24

1. Come, sinners, to the Gospel-Feast;
   Let every soul be Jesu's guest.
   Ye need not one be left behind,
   For God hath bidden all mankind.

2. Sent by my Lord, on you I call,
   The invitation is to all:
   Come, all the world; come, sinner, thou,
   All things in Christ are ready now.

3. Jesus to you his fullness brings,
   A feast of marrow, and fat things;
   All, all in Christ is freely given,
   Pardon, and holiness, and heaven.

4. Do not begin to make excuse,
   Ah! do not you his grace refuse;
   Your worldly cares and pleasures leave,
   And take what Jesus hath to give.

5. Your grounds forsake, your oxen quit,
   Your every earthly thought forget,
   Seek not the comforts of this life,
   Nor sell your Saviour for a wife.

6. "Have me excused," why will ye say?
   Why will ye for damnation pray?
   Have you excused—from joy and peace!
   Have you excused—from happiness!

6. *Redemption Hymns* (1747) 63–66, Hymn 50, based on Luke 14:16–24; original title.

162

7.   Excused from coming to a feast!
        Excused from being Jesu's guest!
        From knowing *now* your sins forgiven,
        From tasting *here* the joys of heaven!

8.   Excused, alas! Why would you be
        From health, and life, and liberty,
        From ent'ring into glorious rest,
        From leaning on your Saviour's breast.

9.   Yet must I, Lord, to thee complain,
        The world have made thy offers vain,
        Too busy, or too happy they,
        They will not, Lord, thy call obey.

10.   Go then, my angry Master said,
        Since these on all my mercies tread,
        Invite the rich and great no more,
        But preach my gospel to the poor.

11.   Confer not thou with flesh and blood,
        Go quickly forth, invite the crowd,
        Search every lane and every street,
        And bring in all the souls you meet.

12.   Come then, ye souls, by sin oppressed,
        Ye restless wanderers after rest,
        Ye poor, and maimed, and halt, and blind,
        In Christ an hearty welcome find.

13.   Sinners my gracious Lord receives,
        Harlots, and publicans, and thieves,
        Drunkards, and all the hellish crew,
        I have a message now to you.

14.   Come, and partake the Gospel-Feast,
        Be saved from sin, in Jesus rest,
        O taste the goodness of our God,
        And eat his flesh, and drink his blood.

15. 'Tis done; my All-redeeming Lord,
     I have gone forth, and preached thy Word,
     The sinners to thy feast are come,
     And yet, O Saviour, there is room.

16. Go then, my Lord, again enjoined,
     And other wand'ring sinners find,
     Go to the hedges and highways,
     And offer all my pard'ning grace.

17. The worst unto my supper press,
     Monsters of daring wickedness,
     Tell them my grace for all is free,
     They cannot be too bad for me.

18. Tell them their sins are all forgiven,
     Tell every creature under heaven,
     I died to save them from all sin,
     And force the vagrants to come in.

19. Ye vagrant souls, on you I call,
     (O that my voice could reach you all)
     Ye all are freely justified,
     Ye all may live, for God hath died.

20. My message as from God receive;
     Ye all may come to Christ and live.
     O let his love your hearts constrain,
     Nor suffer him to die in vain.

21. His love is mighty to compel,
     His conqu'ring love consent to feel,
     Yield to his love's resistless power,
     And fight against your God no more.

22. See him set forth before your eyes,
     Behold the bleeding sacrifice,
     His offered love make haste t' embrace,
     And freely now be saved by grace.

23.   Ye who believe his record true,
Shall sup with him, and he with you;
Come to the Feast; be saved from sin,
For Jesus waits to take you in.

24.   This is the time, no more delay,
This is the acceptable day;
Come in, this moment, at his call,
And live for him who died for all.

47. *"Why will ye die, O house of Israel?"*[7]
Ezekiel 18:31

1.   Sinners, turn: why will you die?
God, your Maker, asks you why?
God, who did your being give,
Made you with himself to live;
He the fatal cause demands,
Asks the work of his own hands.
Why, you thankless creatures, why
Will you cross his love, and die?

2.   Sinners, turn: why will you die?
God, your Savior, asks you why?
God, who did your souls retrieve,
Died himself that you might live:
Will you let him die in vain?
Crucify your Lord again?
Why, you ransomed sinners, why
Will you slight his grace, and die?

---

7. *Hymns on God's Everlasting Love* (1742) 43–46, Hymn 15 (since the prior hymn is not numbered, this would be originally Hymn 14); original title. The poem is based on Ezek 18:31: "Cast away from you all your transgressions, whereby ye have transgressed; and make you a new heart and a new spirit; for why will ye die, O house of Israel?"

3.   Sinners, turn: why will you die?
God, the Spirit, asks you why?
God, who all your lives hath strove,
Wooed you to embrace his love:
Will you not his grace receive?
Will you still refuse to live?
Why, you long-sought sinners, why
Will you grieve your God, and die?

4.   Dead, already dead within,
Spiritually dead in sin,
Dead to God, while here you breathe,
Pant ye after second death?
Will ye still in sin remain,
Greedy of eternal pain?
O ye dying sinners, why,
Why will you for ever die?

5.   Let the beasts their breath resign,
Strangers to the life divine,
Who their God can never know,
Let their spirit downward go:
Ye for higher ends were born,
Ye, may all to God return,
Live with him above the sky;
Why will you for ever die?

6.   You, on whom he favours showers,
You, possessed of nobler powers,
You, of reason's powers possessed,
You, with will and mem'ry blest,
You, with finer sense endued,
Creatures capable of God;
Noblest of his creatures, why,
Why will you for ever die?

7.   You, whom he ordained to be
Transcripts of the Trinity,
You, whom he in life doth hold,
You, for whom himself was sold,
You, on whom he still doth wait,
Whom he would again create;
Made by him, and purchased, why,
Why will you for ever die?

8.   You, who own his record true,
You, his chosen people, you,
You, who call the Saviour Lord,
You, who read his written word,
You, who see the gospel-light,
Claim a crown in Jesu's right;
Why will you, ye Christians, why
Will the house of Israel die?

9.   You, his own peculiar race,
Sharers of his special grace,
All his grace to you is given,
You, the favourites of heaven;
And will you unfaithful prove,
Trample on his richest love,
Jesus asks the reason, why,
Why will you resolve to die?

10.   What could your Redeemer do,
More than he hath done for you?
To procure your peace with God,
Could he more than shed his blood?
After all his waste of love,
All his drawings from above,
Why will you your Lord deny?
Why will you resolve to die?

11.   Will you die, because his grace
Cannot reach to all the race?

Life because you cannot have,
You because he will not save?
Dare you say he doth not call,
Doth not offer life to all,
Doth not ask his creatures, why,
Why will you resolve to die?

12. Saith he what he never meant,
Calls on all men to repent,
Calls, while his decree withstands,
Mocks the work of his own hands!
Will you die because you must?
Dare you make your God unjust?
He would have you live; O why
Why will you resolve to die?

13. Turn, he cries, ye sinners, turn;
By his life your God hath sworn
He would have you turn and live,
He would all the world receive;
He hath brought to all the race
Full salvation by his grace;
He hath no one soul passed by;
Why will you resolve to die?

14. Hath he pleasure in your pain?
Did he you to death ordain,
Vow you never should return,
Damn, or ever you were born?
If your death were his delight,
Would he you to life invite,
Would he ask, obtest, and cry,
Why will you resolve to die?

15. Sinners, turn, while God is near,
Dare not think him insincere:
Now, ev'n now your Saviour stands,
All day long he spreads his hands,

> Cries, "Ye will not happy be,
> No, ye will not come to me,
> Me, who life to none deny;
> Why will you resolve to die?

16.   Can ye doubt, if God is love,
> If to all his bowels move?
> Will ye not his word receive?
> Will ye not his oath believe?
> See, the suffering God appears!
> Jesus weeps! Believe his tears!
> Mingled with his blood they cry,
> Why will you resolve to die?

REPENTANCE (48)

48. After a Relapse into Sin[8]

1.   Depth of mercy! Can there be
> Mercy still reserved for me!
> Can my God his wrath forbear,
> Me, the chief of sinners, spare!

2.   I have long withstood his grace,
> Long provoked him to his face,
> Would not hearken to his calls,
> Grieved him by a thousand falls.

3.   I my Master have denied,
> I afresh have crucified,
> Oft profaned his hallowed name,
> Put him to an open shame.

4.   I have spilled his precious blood,
> Trampled on the Son of God,
> Filled with pains unspeakable,
> I—and yet *am not in Hell.*

8. *HSP* (1740) 82–84; original title.

5.   Lo! I cumber still the ground!
     Lo! an Advocate is found,
     "Hasten not to cut him down,
     Let this barren soul alone."

6.   Jesus speaks, and pleads his blood,
     He disarms the wrath of God,
     Now my Father's bowels move,
     Justice lingers into love.

7.   Kindled his relentings are,
     Me he now delights to spare,
     Cries, "*How shall I give thee up?*"
     Lets the lifted thunder drop.

8.   Whence to *me* this waste of love?
     Ask my Advocate above,
     See the cause in Jesu's face
     Now before the throne of grace.

9.   There for me the Saviour stands,
     Shows his wounds and spreads his hands,
     God is love! I know, I feel;
     Jesus weeps! but loves me still!

10. Jesus! answer from above,
     Is not all thy nature love!
     Wilt thou not the wrong forget,
     Suffer me to kiss thy feet?

11. If I rightly read thy heart,
     If thou all compassion art,
     Bow thine ear, in mercy bow,
     Pardon, and accept me now.

12. Pity from thine eye let fall;
     By a look my soul recall,
     Now the stone to flesh convert,
     Cast a look and break my heart.

13.   Now incline me to repent,
      Let me now my sins lament;
      Now my foul revolt deplore,
      Weep, believe, and sin no more!

Justifying Grace (49–53)

PARDON (49)

49. Free Grace[9]

1.   And can it be that I should gain
        An interest in the Savior's blood!
     Died he for me?—who caused his pain!
        For me?—who him to death pursued.
     Amazing love! How can it be
     That thou, my God, shouldst die for me?

2.   'Tis mystery all! th'Immortal dies!
        Who can explore his strange design?
     In vain the firstborn seraph tries
        To sound the depths of Love Divine.
     'Tis mercy all! Let earth adore;
     Let angel minds enquire no more.

3.   He left his Father's throne above
        (So free, so infinite his grace!),
     Emptied himself of all but love,
        And bled for Adam's helpless race:
     'Tis mercy all, immense and free!
     For O my God! it found out me!

4.   Long my imprisoned spirit lay,
        Fast bound in sin and nature's night;
     Thine eye diffused a quickening ray;
        I woke, the dungeon flamed with light;
     My chains fell off, my heart was free,
     I rose, went forth, and followed thee.

9. *HSP* (1739) 117–19; original title.

5. Still the small inward voice I hear,
        That whispers all my sins forgiv'n;
    Still the atoning blood is near,
        That quenched the wrath of hostile heav'n;
    I feel the life his wounds impart;
    I feel my Savior in my heart.

6. No condemnation now I dread;
        Jesus, and all in him, is mine;
    Alive in him, my living Head,
        And clothed in righteousness divine,
    Bold I approach th'eternal throne,
    And claim the crown through Christ my own.

ASSURANCE (50–53)

50. *The Marks of Faith*[10]

1. How can a sinner know
        His sins on earth forgiven?
    How can my Saviour show
        My name inscribed in heaven?
    What we ourselves have felt and seen,
        With confidence we tell,
    And publish to the sons of men
        The signs infallible.

2. We who in Christ believe
        That he for us hath died,
    His unknown peace receive
        And feel his blood applied.
    Exults for joy our rising soul,
        Disburdened of her load,
    And swells, unutterably full
        Of glory, and of God.

10. *HSP* (1749) 2:220–22, No. 161 [Hymn 1]; original title. The original opening two lines of stanza 1 read: "How can a sinner know / His sins on earth forgiven?" In most hymn books lines 1–4 of each stanza have been altered to conform to the meter of lines 5–8.

3.
  His love, surpassing far
    The love of all beneath
  We find within, and dare
    The pointless darts of death.
Stronger than death, or sin, or hell
  The mystic power we prove,
And conquerors of the world we dwell
  In heaven, who dwell in love.

4.
  The *pledge* of future bliss
    He now to us imparts,
  His gracious Spirit is
    The *earnest* in our hearts.
We antedate the joys above,
  We taste th'eternal powers,
And *know* that all those heights of love,
  And all those heavens are ours.

5.
  'Till he our life reveal,
    We rest in Christ secure;
  His Spirit is the *seal,*
    Which made our pardon sure.
Our sins his blood hath blotted out,
  And signed our soul's release;
And can we of his favour doubt,
  Whose blood declares us his?

6.
  We by his Spirit prove
    And know the things of God,
  The things which of his love
    He hath on us bestowed.
Our God to us his Spirit gave,
  And dwells in us, we *know,*
The witness in ourselves we have,
  And all his fruits we show.

7.   The meek and lowly heart
          Which in our Saviour was,
       He doth to us impart,
          And signs us with his cross.
   Our nature's course is turned, our mind
     Transformed in all its powers,
   And both the witnesses are joined,
    The Spirit of God with ours.

8.   Whate'er our pard'ning Lord
          Commands, we gladly do,
       And guided by his Word,
          We all his steps pursue.
   His glory is our sole design,
     We live our God to please,
   And rise with filial fear divine
    To perfect holiness.

51. All glory and praise[11]

1.   All glory and praise
         To the Ancient of Days,
   Who was born, and was slain to redeem a lost race.

2.   Salvation to God,
         Who carried our load,
   And purchased our lives with the price of his blood.

3.   And shall he not have
         The lives which he gave
   Such an infinite ransom for ever to save.

4.   Yes, Lord, we are thine,
         And gladly resign
   Our souls to be filled with the fullness divine.

---

11. *HLS* (1745) 130–31, Hymn 156.

5.   We yield thee thine own,
            We serve thee alone,
    Thy will upon earth as in heaven be done.

6.   How, when it shall be
            We cannot foresee;
    But Oh! Let us live, let us die unto thee!

52. *Blow ye the trumpet, blow*[12]

1.   Blow ye the trumpet, blow!
            The gladly solemn sound
    Let all the nations know,
            To earth's remotest bound:
The year of jubilee is come;
Return, ye ransomed sinners, home!

2.   Jesus, our great high priest,
            Hath full atonement made;
    Ye weary spirits, rest;
            Ye mournful souls, be glad:
The year of jubilee is come;
Return, ye ransomed sinners, home!

3.   Extol the Lamb of God,
            The all-atoning Lamb!
    Redemption in his blood
            Throughout the world proclaim:
The year of jubilee is come;
Return, ye ransomed sinners, home!

4.   Ye slaves of sin and hell,
            Your liberty receive,
    And safe in Jesus dwell,
            And blest in Jesus live:
The year of jubilee is come;
Return, ye ransomed sinners, home!

12. *New Year's Day Hymns*, 6–7, Hymn 3.

5.   Ye who have sold for nought
　　　　　　Your heritage above
　　　　Shall have it back unbought,
　　　　　　The gift of Jesu's love:
　　　　The year of jubilee is come;
　　　　Return, ye ransomed sinners, home!

6.   The gospel-trumpet hear,
　　　　　　The news of heavenly grace;
　　　　And saved from earth, appear
　　　　　　Before your Saviour's face:
　　　　The year of jubilee is come;
　　　　Return to your eternal home!

53. "Behold the Man"[13]

1.   Arise, my soul, arise,
　　　　　　Shake off thy guilty fears;
　　　　The bleeding sacrifice
　　　　　　In my behalf appears;
　　　　Before the throne my surety stands;
　　　　My name is written on his hands.

2.   He ever lives above
　　　　　　For me to intercede,
　　　　His all-redeeming love,
　　　　　　His precious blood, to plead;
　　　　His blood atoned for all our race,
　　　　And sprinkles now the throne of grace.

3.   Five bleeding wounds he bears,
　　　　　　Received on Calvary;
　　　　They pour effectual prayers,
　　　　　　They strongly speak for me;
　　　　Forgive him, O forgive, they cry,
　　　　Nor let that ransomed sinner die!

13. *HSP* (1742) 261–62; original title. The poem is based on John 19:5: "Behold the man!"

4.   The Father hears him pray,
       His dear Anointed One,
    He cannot turn away
       The presence of his Son;
His Spirit answers to the blood,
And tells me I am born of God.

5.   My God is reconciled,
       His pardoning voice I hear,
    He owns me for his child,
       I can no longer fear;
With confidence I now draw nigh,
And Father, Abba, Father, cry!

Sanctifying and Perfecting Grace (54–85)

NEW BIRTH AND THE NEW CREATURE (54–61)

54. Be born again[14]

1.   Thou Son of God, whose flaming eyes
       Our inmost thoughts perceive,
    Accept our evening sacrifice,
       Which now to thee we give:
We bow before thy gracious throne,
       And think ourselves sincere;
But show us, Lord, is every one
       Thy real worshipper?

2.   Is here a soul that knows thee not,
       Nor feels his want of thee,
    A stranger to the blood which bought
       His pardon on the tree?
Convince him now of unbelief,
       His desperate state explain,
And fill his careless heart with grief,
       And penitential pain.

14. *Family Hymns* (1767) 26–27, Hymn 25.

3. Speak with that voice which wakes the dead,
　　And bid the sleeper rise,
　And bid his guilty conscience dread
　　The death that never dies;
　Extort the cry, What must be done
　　To save a wretch like me?
　How shall a trembling sinner shun
　　That endless misery?

4. I must this instant now begin
　　Out of my sleep to wake,
　And turn to God, and every sin
　　Continually forsake.
　I must for faith incessant cry,
　　And wrestle, Lord, with thee,
　I must be born again, or die
　　To all eternity.

55. *'Till our souls are born again*[15]

1. The witnesses in heaven adored,
　The Father, Holy Ghost, and Word,
　One God with all his church we own,
　In persons three for ever one.

2. But 'till our souls are born again,
　We to the truth assent in vain,
　By notions right ourselves deceive,
　And only fancy we believe.

3. The Triune God we cannot know,
　Unless he doth the faith bestow,
　Faith which removes our mountain-load,
　And brings us to a pard'ning God.

15. *Trinity Hymns* (1767) 101–2, Hymn 18.

4. Sure evidence of things unseen,
    Which swallows up the gulf between,
    The light of life divine imparts,
    And forms Jehovah in our hearts.

5. O that we all might thus believe,
    The truth in humble love receive,
    Author of faith our Saviour find
    In God the Father of mankind;

6. In both the Holy Spirit know
    (Who doth where'er he listeth blow)
    And the whole Trinity receive
    For ever in our hearts to live!

56. Unless ye all are born again[16]

1. Sons of the church, yourselves who deem
    The temple of the Lord,
    Awake out of your fatal dream,
    And tremble at the word;
    Howe'er your privileges ye boast,
    On outward helps rely,
    Ye all must finally be lost,
    Who unconverted die.

2. Long as the things of earth ye love,
    Nor will from sin depart,
    Your own pretensions ye disprove,
    Poor heathens still in heart;
    Members of the true church in vain,
    Unchanged and unforgiven,
    Unless ye all are born again,
    Ye cannot enter heaven.

16. MS Matthew, 10; *Arminian Magazine* (1789) 501–2. See *Poet. Works*, 10:145–46.

57. *Who are not born again*[17]

1. For names the Christian world contend,
       For modes and forms, in vain,
    Who do not, Lord, on thee depend,
       Who are not born again:
    'Till thou redeem us from our fall,
       'Till thou thy Spirit impart,
    Baptized, or unbaptized, we all
       Are *Heathens* still in heart.

2. To save my soul from endless woe
       No outward things avail,
    Unless thy pardoning love I know
       I sink unchanged to hell;
    O might I feel th'atoning blood,
       And call the Saviour mine,
    Created after God, renewed
       In holiness divine.

3. Now, Saviour, now the work begin
       Of thy creating grace,
    Forgive, and make the sinner clean
       From all unrighteousness;
    Pronounce us perfected in love,
       Completely sanctified,
    And to our place prepared above
       Receive thy happy bride.

58. *Justification*[18]

1. Let us join; ('tis God commands)
    Let us join our hearts and hands;
    Help to gain our calling's hope,
    Build we each the other up.

17. *Scripture Hymns* (1762) 2:310–11, based on Gal 6:15, "In Christ Jesus neither circumcision availeth any thing, nor uncircumcision, but a new creation."
18. *HSP* (1740) 183–84, Part 3 of a five-part poem titled "The Love-Feast."

God his blessing shall dispense,
God shall crown his ordinance,
Meet in his appointed ways,
Nourish us with social grace.

2.   Let us then as brethren love,
Faithfully his gifts improve,
Carry on the earnest strife,
Walk in holiness of life.

Still forget the things behind,
Follow Christ in heart and mind,
Toward the mark unwearied press,
Seize the crown of righteousness.

3.   Plead we thus for faith *alone*,
Faith which by our works is shown;
God it is who justifies,
Only faith the grace *applies*,

Active faith that lives within,
Conquers hell, and death, and sin,
Hallows whom it first made whole,
Forms the Saviour in the soul.

4.   Let us for this faith contend,
Sure salvation, is its end;
Heaven already is begun,
Everlasting life is won:

Only let us persevere
Till we see our Lord appear,
Never from the Rock remove,
Saved by faith which works by love.

59. *Wrestling Jacob*[19]

1.   Come, O thou Traveler unknown,
         Whom still I hold, but cannot see,
       My company before is gone,
         And I am left alone with thee;
       With thee all night I mean to stay
       And wrestle till the break of day.

2.   I need not tell thee who I am,
         My misery, or sin declare;
       Thyself hast called me by my name,
         Look on thy hands and read it there.
       But who, I ask thee, who art thou?
       Tell me thy name, and tell me now.

3.   In vain thou strugglest to get free,
         I never will unloose my hold;
       Art thou the man that died for me?
         The secret of thy love unfold;
       Wrestling, I will not let thee go
       Till I thy name, thy nature know.

4.   Wilt thou not yet to me reveal
         Thy new, unutterable name?
       Tell me, I still beseech thee, tell,
         To know it now resolved I am;
       Wrestling, I will not let thee go,
       Till I thy name, thy nature know.

5.   'Tis all in vain to hold thy tongue
         Or touch the hollow of my thigh;
       Though every sinew be unstrung,
         Out of my arms thou shalt not fly;
       Wrestling, I will not let thee go
       Till I thy name, thy nature know.

19. *HSP* (1742) 115–18; original title.

6.   What though my shrinking flesh complain
        And murmur to contend so long?
    I rise superior to my pain,
        When I am weak then I am strong,
    And when my all of strength shall fail
    I shall with the God-man prevail.

7.   My strength is gone, my nature dies,
        I sink beneath thy weighty hand,
    Faint to revive, and fall to rise;
        I fall, and yet by faith I stand;
    I stand and will not let thee go
    Till I thy name, thy nature know.

8.   Yield to me now—for I am weak
        But confident in self-despair!
    Speak to my heart, in blessings speak,
        Be conquered by my instant prayer;
    Speak, or thou never hence shalt move,
    And tell me if thy name is Love.

9.   'Tis Love! 'tis Love! thou diedst for me,
        I hear thy whisper in my heart;
    The morning breaks, the shadows flee,
        Pure Universal Love thou art:
    To me, to all thy bowels move—
    Thy nature, and thy name is Love.

10.   My prayer hath power with God; the grace
        Unspeakable I now receive;
    Through faith I see thee face to face,
        I see thee face to face and live!
    In vain I have not wept and strove—
    Thy nature, and thy name is Love.

11.   I know thee, Saviour, who thou art,
        Jesus, the feeble sinner's friend;
    Nor wilt thou with the night depart,
        But stay and love me to the end;

> Thy mercies never shall remove,
> Thy nature, and thy name is Love.

12. The Sun of Righteousness on me
>   Hath risen with healing in his wings;
> Withered my nature's strength; from thee
>   My soul its life and succour brings;
> My help is all laid up above;
> Thy nature, and thy name is Love.

13. Contented now upon my thigh
>   I halt, till life's short journey end;
> All helplessness, all weakness I
>   On thee alone for strength depend;
> Nor have I power from thee to move;
> Thy nature, and thy name is Love.

14. Lame as I am, I take the prey,
>   Hell, earth, and sin with ease o'ercome;
> I leap for joy, pursue my way,
>   And as a bounding hart fly home,
> Through all eternity to prove
> Thy nature, and thy name is Love.

60. *Making me anew*[20]

> Thrice acceptable word,
> I long to prove it true!
> Take me into thyself, O Lord,
> By making me anew;
> Me for thy mercy sake
> Out of myself remove,
> Partaker of thy nature make,
> Thy holiness and love.

20. *Scripture Hymns* (1762) 2:300, Hymn 577, based on 2 Cor 5:17: "If any man be in Christ, he is a new creature."

61. *All things new become*[21]

Hasten the joyful day
Which shall my sins consume,
When old things shall be past away,
And all things new become;
Th' original offence
Out of my heart erase,
Enter thyself and drive it hence,
And take up all the place.

HOLINESS OF HEART (61–70)
(Personal transformation)

62. *Pleading for the Promise of Sanctification*[22]
Ezekiel 36:23, etc.

1. God of all power, and truth, and grace,
    Which shall from age to age endure,
    Whose word, when heaven and earth shall pass,
    Remains, and stands for ever sure:

2. Calmly to thee my soul looks up,
    And waits thy promises to prove,
    The object of my steadfast hope,
    The seal of thine eternal love.

3. That I thy mercy may proclaim,
    That all mankind thy truth may see,
    Hallow thy great and glorious name,
    And perfect holiness in me.

21. *Scripture Hymns* (1762) 2:301, Hymn 578, based on 2 Cor 5:17: "Old things are passed away; behold, all things are become new."

22. *HSP* (1742) 261–64; original title. The poem is based on Ezekiel 36:23, "And I will sanctify my great name, which was profaned among the heathen, which ye have profaned in the midst of them; and the heathen shall know that I am the Lord, saith the Lord God, when I hall be sanctified in you before their eyes."

4.   Chose from the world if now I stand
        Adorned in righteousness divine,
    If brought into the promised land,
        I justly call the Saviour mine:

5.   Perform the work thou hast begun,
        My inmost soul to thee convert;
    Love me, for ever love thine own,
        And sprinkle with thy blood my heart.

6.   Thy sanctifying Spirit pour,
        To quench my thirst and wash me clean;
    Now, Father, let the gracious shower
        Descend, and make me pure from sin.

7.   Purge me from every sinful blot,
        My idols all be cast aside;
    Cleanse me from every evil thought,
        From all the filth of self and pride.

8.   Give me a new, a perfect heart,
        From doubt, and fear, and sorrow free;
    The mind which was in Christ impart,
        And let my spirit cleave to thee.

9.   O take this heart of stone away,
        (Thy sway it doth not, cannot own)
    In me no longer let it stay,
        O take away this heart of stone.

10.   The hatred of the carnal mind
        Out of my flesh at once remove;
    Give me a tender heart, resigned,
        And pure, and full of faith and love.

11.   Within me thy good Spirit place,
        Spirit of health, and love, and power;
    Plant in me thy victorious grace,
        And sin shall never enter more.

12. Cause me to walk in Christ my way,
    And I thy statutes shall fulfill,
    In every point thy law obey,
    And perfectly perform thy will.

13. Hast thou not said, who canst not lie,
    That I thy law shall keep and do?
    Lord, I believe, though men deny;
    They all are false, but thou art true.

14. O that I now from sin released,
    Thy word might to the utmost prove!
    Enter into the promised rest,
    The Canaan of thy perfect love.

15. There let me ever, ever dwell;
    Be thou my God, and I will be
    Thy servant; O set to thy seal,
    Give me eternal life in thee.

16. From all remaining filth within
    Let me in thee salvation have;
    From actual and from inbred sin
    My ransomed soul persist to save.

17. Wash out my deep original stain,—
    Tell me no more it cannot be,
    Demons or men! The Lamb was slain,
    His blood was all poured out for me.

18. Sprinkle it, Jesu, on my heart!
    One drop of thine[23] all-cleansing blood
    Shall make my sinfulness depart,
    And fill me with the life of God.

23. "Thy" in the first edition is changed to "thine" in the second edition (1745).

19.   Father, supply my every need;
        Sustain the life thyself hast given:
    Call for the never-failing bread,
        The manna that comes down from heaven.

20.   The gracious fruits of righteousness,
        Thy blessings' unexhausted store,
    In me abundantly increase,
        Nor let me ever hunger more.

21.   Let me no more, in deep complaint,
        "My leanness, O my leanness!" cry;
    Alone consumed with pining want,
        Of all my Father's children, I!

22.   The painful thirst, the fond desire,
        Thy joyous presence shall remove,
    While my full soul doth still require
        Thy whole eternity of love.

23.   Holy, and true, and righteous Lord,
        I wait to prove thy perfect will;
    Be mindful of thy gracious word,
        And stamp me with thy Spirit's seal.

24.   Thy faithful mercies let me find,
        In which thou causest me to trust;
    Give me the meek and lowly mind,
        And lay my spirit in the dust.

25.   Show me how foul my heart hath been,
        When all renewed by grace I am;
    When thou hast emptied me of sin,
        Show me the fullness of my shame.

26.   Open my faith's interior eye;
        Display thy glory from above,
    And all I am shall sink and die,
        Lost in astonishment and love.

27.   Confound, o'erpower me with thy grace!
      I would be by myself abhorred.
   (All might, all majesty, all praise,
      All glory be to Christ my Lord!)

28.   Now let me gain perfection's height!
      Now let me into nothing fall!
   Be less than nothing in thy sight,
      And feel that Christ is all in all.

63. *Come then, and dwell in me*[24]

1.   Come then, and dwell in me,
      Spirit of power within,
   And bring the glorious liberty
      From sorrow, fear, and sin.

2.   Hasten the joyful day
      Which shall my sins consume,
   When old things shall be done away,
      And all things new become.

3.   I want the witness, Lord,
      That all I do is right,
   According to thy mind and word,
      Well-pleasing in thy sight.

4.   I seek no higher state;
      Indulge me but in this,
   And soon or later then translate
      To thine eternal bliss.

24. *Scripture Hymns* (1762) 2:298, based on 2 Cor 3:17: "Now the Lord is that Spirit: and where the Spirit of the Lord is, there is liberty"); 2:301 (stanza 2 [first four lines of Hymn 578], based on 2 Cor 5:17: "Therefore, if any man be in Christ, he is a new creature: old things are passed away; behold, all things are become new"); 2:367 (stanzas 3 and 4 [Hymn 713], based on Heb 11:5: "Before his translation, he had this testimony, that he pleased God").

64. Desiring to Love[25]

1. Love divine, all loves excelling,
    Joy of heaven, to earth come down;
    Fix in us thy humble dwelling;
    All thy faithful mercies crown.
    Jesu, thou art all compassion,
    Pure, unbounded love thou art;
    Visit us with thy salvation,
    Enter every trembling heart.

2. Breathe, O breathe thy loving Spirit
    Into every troubled breast.
    Let us all in thee inherit;
    Let us find that second rest.
    Take away our *power*[26] of sinning;
    Alpha and Omega be;
    End of faith as its beginning,
    Set our hearts at liberty.

3. Come, Almighty to deliver,
    Let us all thy life receive;
    Suddenly return and never,
    Nevermore thy temples leave.
    Thee we would be always blessing,
    Serve thee as thy hosts above,
    Pray and praise thee without ceasing,
    Glory in thy perfect love.

4. Finish, then, thy new creation;
    Pure and sinless let us be.
    Let us see thy great salvation
    Perfectly restored in thee;

25. *Redemption Hymns* (1747) 11–12, Hymn 9.

26. The word "power" is changed from plain text in the first edition to italics in the second edition (1747) and following printings.

Changed from glory into glory,
    Till in heaven we take our place,
Till we cast our crowns before thee,
    Lost in wonder, love, and praise!

65. For a Tender Conscience[27]

1.   Almighty God of truth and love,
    In me thy power exert,
The mountain from my soul remove,
    The hardness from my heart:
My most obdurate heart subdue,
    In honour of thy Son,
And now the gracious wonder show,
    And take away the stone.

2.   I want a principle within
    Of jealous, godly fear,
A sensibility of sin,
    A pain to feel it near.
I want the first approach to feel
    Of pride, or wrong desire,
To catch the wand'rings of my will,
    And quench the kindling fire.

3.   From thee that I no more may part,
    No more thy goodness grieve,
The filial awe, the fleshly heart,
    The tender conscience give.
Quick as the apple of an eye,
    O God, my conscience make;
Awake my soul, when sin is nigh,
    And keep it still awake.

4.   If to the right, or left I stray,
    That moment, Lord, reprove,
And let me weep my life away
    For having grieved thy love:

27. *HSP* (1749) 2:230–31, Hymn 167; original title.

> Give me to feel an idle thought
>   As actual wickedness,
> And mourn for the minutest fault
>   In exquisite distress.

5. O may the least omission pain
>   My well-instructed soul,
> And drive me to the blood again,
>   Which makes the wounded whole:
> More of this tender spirit, more
>   Of this affliction send,
> And spread the *moral sense* all o'er,
>   'Till pain with life shall end.

66. *A charge to keep I have*[28]

1.   A charge to keep I have,
>   A God to glorify,
> A never-dying soul to save,
>   And fit it for the sky.
> To serve the present age,
>   My calling to fulfill;
> O may it all my powers engage
>   To do my Master's will!

2.   Arm me with jealous care,
>   As in thy sight to live,
> And O! thy servant, Lord, prepare
>   A strict account to give.
> Help me to watch and pray,
>   And on thyself rely,
> Assured, if I my trust betray,
>   I shall forever die.

---

28. *Scripture Hymns* (1762) 1:58–59, based on Lev 8:35: "Keep the charge of the Lord, that ye die not."

67. *Psalm 2:10* [BCP][29]

"Make me a clean heart, O God,
and renew a right spirit within me."

1.   O for an heart to praise my God,
        An heart from sin set free!
    An heart that always feels thy blood
        So freely spilt for me!

2.   An heart resigned, submissive, meek,
        My dear Redeemer's throne,
    Where only Christ is heard to speak,
        Where Jesus reigns alone.

3.   An humble, lowly, contrite heart,
        Believing, true, and clean,
    Which neither life nor death can part
        From him that dwells within.

4.   An heart in every thought renewed,
        And full of love divine,
    Perfect, and right, and pure, and good,
        A copy, Lord, of thine.

5.   Thy tender heart is still the same,
        And melts at human woe:
    Jesu, for thee distressed I am,
        I want thy love to know.

6.   My heart, thou know'st, can never rest,
        Till thou create my peace;
    Till of my Eden repossessed,
        From self and sin I cease.

29. *HSP* (1742) 30–31; original title.

7.   Fruit of thy gracious lips, on me
            Bestow that peace unknown,
       The hidden manna, and the tree
            Of life, and the white stone.

8.   Thy nature, dearest Lord, impart;
            Come quickly from above;
       Write thy new name upon my heart,
            Thy new, best name of Love.

68. *Against Hope, Believing in Hope*[30]

1.   My God! I know, I feel thee mine,
            And will not quit my claim,
       Till all I have be lost in thine,
            And all renewed I am.

2.   I hold thee with a trembling hand,
            I will not let thee go,
       Till steadfastly by faith I stand,
            And all thy goodness know.

3.   When shall I see the welcome hour
            That plants my God in me!
       Spirit of health, and life, and power,
            And perfect liberty!

4.   Jesu, thy all-victorious love
            Shed in my heart abroad;
       Then shall my feet no longer rove,
            Rooted and fixed in God.

5.   Love only can the conquest win,
            The strength of sin subdue,
       (Mine own unconquerable sin)
            And form my soul anew.

30. *HSP* (1740) 156–58; original title.

6.   Love can bow down the stubborn neck,
        The stone to flesh convert,
    Soften, and melt, and pierce, and break
        An adamantine heart.

7.   O! that in me the sacred fire
        Might now begin to glow;
    Burn up the dross of base desire
        And make the mountains flow!

8.   O that it now from heaven might fall,
        And all my sins consume!
    Come, Holy Ghost, for thee I call,
        Spirit of burning, come!

9.   Refining fire, go through my heart,
        Illuminate my soul,
    Scatter thy life through every part
        And sanctify the whole.

10.   Sorrow and self shall then expire,
        While entered into rest,
    I only live my God t'admire,
        My God for ever blest.

11.   No longer then my heart shall mourn,
        While purified by grace,
    I only for his glory burn,
        And always see his face.

12.   My steadfast soul, from falling free,
        Can now no longer move;
    Jesus is all the world to me,
        And all my heart is love.

II: Poetical Selections

(Participation in the divine nature / *theosis*)

69. *An inward baptism, Lord, of fire*[31]

1. An inward baptism, Lord, of fire,
      Wherewith to be baptized I have;
    'Tis all my longing soul's desire;
      This, only this, my soul can save.

2. Straitened I am till this be done:
      Kindle in me the living flame,
    Father, in me reveal thy Son,
      Baptize me into Jesu's name.

3. Transform my nature into thine,
      Let all my powers thine impress feel,
    Let all my soul become divine,
      And stamp me with thy Spirit's seal.

4. Deferred my hope, and sick my heart,
      O when shall I thy promise prove,
    Set to my seal that true thou art,
      Thy nature, and thy name is Love!

5. Love, mighty Love, my heart o'erpower;
      Ah! Why dost thou so long delay?
    Cut short the work, bring near the hour,
      And let me see thy perfect day.

6. Behold, for thee I ever wait,
      Now let in me thy image shine;
    Now the new heavens and earth create,
      And plant with righteousness divine.

---

31. *HSP* (1742) 136–37. The poem is preceded by Luke 12:50: "I have a baptism to be baptized with; and how am I straitened till it be accomplished!"

7. If with the wretched sons of men
    It still be thy delight to live,
  Come, Lord, beget my soul again,
    Thyself, thy quickening Spirit give.

8. With me he dwells, and bids thee come;
    Answer thine own effectual prayer,
  Enter my heart, and fix thine[32] home,
    Thine everlasting presence there.

70. Partakers of the Life Divine[33]

1. O thou, whose eyes run to and fro
    Through earth, and every creature see,
  What is it which thou dost not know?
    All things are manifest to thee.

2. Thou hast the spirits, seven and one,
    Thou hast the stars in thy right hand,
  And all our works to thee are known:
    How shall we in thy judgment stand?

3. Thou know'st we take in vain thy name,
    While dead in trespasses we live,
  Thee for our Lord we falsely claim,
    While to the world our hearts we give.

4. A powerless form, a lifeless sound,
    Our works as vanity are light,
  Wanting, alas! They all are found,
    And worse than nothing in thy sight.

32. "Thy" appears here and at the beginning of the next line in the first edition, but both occurrences are changed to "thine" in the second edition (1745) and following printings.

33. *HSP* (1742) 292–94. The poem is preceded by Rev 3:1–2, etc.: "To the angel of the church in Sardis."

5.   O that we now might turn again,
      And cherish the last spark of grace,
Strengthen the things that yet remain,
      And call to mind the ancient days.

6.   Surely did we thy faith receive,
      We heard with joy the gospel-word;
O let us now repent and live,
      And watch to apprehend our Lord;

7.   Stir ourselves up, renounce our ease,
      Before thy sudden judgments come,
And watch, and pray, and never cease,
      Till thou repeal our threat'ning doom.

8.   A few thou still hast left, who stand
      And deprecate th'impending blow,
Protectors of a guilty land,
      And guardian angels here below.

9.   They, by thy mercy reconciled,
      For our unhappy Sardis[34] plead,
Harmless, and pure, and undefiled,
      They ever in thy footsteps tread.

10.   Before they see the realms of light,
      Deserving here through thy desert,
Worthy they walk with thee in white,
      In spotless purity of heart.

11.   Partakers of the life divine,
      Who in the fight of faith o'ercome,
They all shall in thine[35] image shine,
      Made ready for their heavenly home.

34. An ancient city in Asia Minor whose ruins lie near the western coast of modern Turkey, to the northeast of Syria; the capital of Lydia.

35. "Thy" appears in the first edition but is changed to "thine" in the second edition (1745) and following printings.

12. They *here* shall be redeemed from sin,
        Shall *here* put on their glorious dress,
     Fine linen, pure, and white, and clean,
        The saints' inherent righteousness.

13. Love, perfect love, expels all doubt,
        Love makes them to the end endure;
     Their names thou never wilt blot out;
        Their life is hid, their heart is pure.

14. Their names thou wilt vouchsafe to own
        Before thy Father's majesty,
     Pronounce them good, and say "Well done,
        Enter, and ever reign with me!"

HOLINESS OF LIFE (71–74)

71. *Hymns for Believers—Before Work*[36]

1. Forth in thy name, O Lord, I go,
        My daily labour to pursue;
     Thee, only thee, resolved to know
        In all I think, or speak, or do.

2. The task thy wisdom hath assigned,
        O let me cheerfully fulfill;
     In all my works thy presence find,
        And prove thine acceptable will.

3. Preserve me from my calling's snare,
        And hide my simple heart above,
     Above the thorns of choking care,
        The gilded baits of worldly love.

---

36. *HSP* (1749) 1:246–47, Hymn 144 (Hymn 32 of Hymns for Believers); original title. Though the printed number of the hymn is 144, it should be 145. See footnote number 1 on page 124.

4.   Thee may I set at my right hand,
           Whose eyes mine inmost substance see,
       And labour on at thy command,
           And offer all my works to thee.

5.   Give me to bear thy easy yoke,
           And every moment watch and pray,
       And still to things eternal look,
           And hasten to thy glorious day.

6.   For thee delightfully employ
           Whate'er thy bounteous grace hath given;
       And run my course with even joy,
           And closely walk with thee to heaven.

72. Ministry With and Among the Poor[37]

1.   The poor as Jesus' bosom-friends,
           The poor he makes his latest care,
       To all his successors commends,
           And wills us on our hands to bear;
       The poor our dearest care we make,
       And love them for our Saviour's sake.

2.   Whate'er thou dost to us entrust,
           With thy peculiar blessing blessed;
       O make us diligent and just,
           As stewards faithful to the least,
       Endowed with wisdom to possess
       The mammon of unrighteousness.

37. *Unpub. Poetry*, 2:404, alt., based on Acts 20:36: "And when he had thus spoken, he kneeled down, and prayed with them all." Original sources: stanza 1: MS Acts, 421; stanzas 2 and 3: MS Luke, 232–33; in *Unpub. Poetry*, 2:157. Stanza 1 as printed here combines lines 1–5 of the original with a sixth line structured from original lines 7 and 8. This forms a stanza in 8.8.8.8.88 meter to match the two following stanzas from MS Luke.

3.   Help us to make the poor our friends
       By that which paves the way to hell,
That when our loving labour ends,
       And dying from this earth we fail,
Our friends may greet us in the skies
Born to a life that never dies.

73. Your duty let the apostle show[38]

1.   Your duty let the apostle show:
Ye ought, ye ought to labour so,
       In Jesus' cause employed,
Your calling's works at times pursue,
And keep the Tentmaker[39] in view,
       And use your hands for God.

2.   Work for the weak, and sick, and poor,
Raiment and food for them procure,
       And mindful of his Word,
Enjoy the blessedness to give,
Lay out your gettings to relieve
       The members of your Lord.

3.   Your labour which proceeds from love,
Jesus shall graciously approve,
       With full felicity,
With brightest crowns your loan repay,
And tell you in that joyful day,
       "Ye did it unto Me."

---

38. *Unpub. Poetry*, 2:403–4, based on Acts 20:35: "I have showed you all things, how that so labouring ye ought to support the weak, and to remember the words of the Lord Jesus, how he said, It is more blessed to give than to receive." Original source: MS Acts, 420.

39. The Apostle Paul.

74. For Peace[40]

1.   Our earth we now lament to see
         With floods of wickedness o'erflowed,
       With violence, wrong, and cruelty,
         One wide-extended field of blood,
       Where men, like fiends, each other tear,
       In all the hellish rage of war.

2.   As listed on Abaddon's side,
         They mangle their own flesh, and slay;
       Tophet is moved, and opens wide
         Its mouth for its enormous prey;
       And myriads sink beneath the grave,
       And plunge into the flaming wave.

3.   O might the universal Friend
         This havoc of his creatures see!
       Bid our unnatural discord end,
         Declare us reconciled in thee!
       Write kindness on our inward parts,
       And chase the murderer from our hearts!

4.   Who *now* against each other rise,
         Then nations of the earth constrain
       To follow after peace, and prize
         The blessings of thy righteous reign,
       The joys of unity to prove,
       The paradise of perfect love!

---

40. *Intercession Hymns* (1758) 4, Hymn 2; original title.

GRADUAL HOLINESS (75–80)

75. *In gradual holiness complete*[41]

Who madest thus the earth and skies,
The world, a six days' work of thine,
Thou bidst the new creation rise,
Nobler effect of grace divine!
We might spring up at thy command,
For glory in an instant meet;
But by thy will at last we stand
In gradual holiness complete.

76. And *after that* full holiness[42]

Thou dost not say, the seed springs up
Into an instantaneous crop;
But waiting long for its return,
We see the blade; the ear; the corn:
The weak; and *then* the stronger grace,
And *after that* full holiness.

77. *'Till we gain the height of grace*[43]

1.   No, not after twenty years
Of labouring in the word!
After all his fights, and fears,
And sufferings for his Lord,
Paul hath not attained the prize,
Though caught up to the heavenly hill;
Daily still the apostle dies,
And lives imperfect still!

---

41. *Scripture Hymns* (1762) 1:5, Hymn 7, based on Gen 2:1: "Thus the heavens and earth were finished."

42. *Scripture Hymns* (1762) 2:201, Hymn 286, based on Mark 4:28: "The earth bringeth forth first the blade; then the ear; then the full corn in the ear."

43. *Scripture Hymns* (1762) 2:317, Hymn 621, based on Phil 3:13: "I count not myself to have apprehended."

2.   "But we now, the prize t'attain,
    An easier method see,
   Save ourselves the toil and pain,
    And ling'ring agony,
   Reach at once the ladder's top,
  While standing on its lowest round,
   Instantaneously spring up,
    With pure perfection crowned."

3.   *Such* the credulous dotard's dream,
    And *such* his shorter road,
   Thus he makes the world blaspheme,
    And shames the church of God,
   Staggers thus the most sincere,
  'Till from the gospel hope they move,
   Holiness as error fear,
    And start at perfect love.

4.   Lord, thy real work revive,
    The counterfeit to end,
   That we lawfully may strive,
    And truly apprehend,
   Humbly still thy servant trace,
  Who least of saints himself did call,
   'Till we gain the height of grace,
    And into nothing fall.

78. Lord, give us wisdom to suspect[44]

   Lord, give us wisdom to suspect
    The sudden growths of seeming grace,
  To prove them first, and then reject,
    Whose haste their shallowness betrays;
  Who instantaneously spring up,
    Their own great imperfection prove:
  They want the toil of patient hope,
    They want the root of humble love.

44. *Scripture Hymns* (1762) 2:165, Hymn 155, based on Matt 13:5: "Forthwith they sprung up, because they had no deepness of earth."

79. *A grain of grace may we not see*[45]

A grain of grace may we not see
This moment, and the next a tree?
Or *must* we patiently attend
To find the precious seed ascend?
Our Lord declares it *must* be so;
And striking deep our root, we grow,
And lower sink, and higher rise,
Till Christ transplant us to the skies.

80. *And seal us, perfectly restored*[46]

1.   May we not 'scape the killing pain,
        And perfected this moment be?
This moment, Lord, if thou ordain,
        We can the final victory
O'er hell, the world, and death, and sin,
With everlasting glory win.

2.   But if thou bidst us mortify
        Our lusts and passions here below,
Take up our cross, and daily die,
        And in thy gracious knowledge grow,
Who shall thine oracles gainsay,
Or dare prescribe a shorter way?

3.   We, Jesus, will on thee attend,
        To thee the times and seasons leave,
Labouring, and suffering to the end,
        'Till thou the long-sought blessing give,

45. *Scripture Hymns* (1762) 2:167, Hymn 161, based on Matt 13:31: "The kingdom of heaven is like to a grain of mustard seed."

46. *Scripture Hymns* (1762) 2:322–23, Hymn 629, based on Col 3:5: "Mortify therefore your members which are upon the earth; fornication, uncleanness, inordinate affection."

Like many of Charles Wesley's hymns and poems from *Scripture Hymns* (1762), this text was omitted from the second edition of the work. Whoever edited the second edition after Charles's death eliminated numerous texts in which he severely attacked the idea of instantaneous holiness.

And seal us, perfectly restored,
True followers of our *silent* Lord.

PRAYER, TRUST, HOPE (81–82)

81. *In Temptation*[47]

1.   Jesu, Lover of my soul,
    Let me to thy bosom fly,
While the nearer waters roll,
    While the tempest still is high.
Hide me, O my Savior, hide,
    Till the storm of life is past;
Safe into the haven guide;
    O receive my soul at last.

2.   Other refuge have I none,
    Hangs my helpless soul on thee;
Leave, ah! leave me not alone,
    Still support and comfort me.
All my trust on thee is stayed,
    All my help from thee I bring;
Cover my defenseless head
    With the shadow of thy wing.

3.   Wilt thou not regard my call?
    Wilt thou not accept my prayer?
Lo! I sink, I faint, I fall—
    Lo! On thee I cast my care.
Reach me out thy gracious hand!
    While I of thy strength receive,
Hoping against hope I stand,
    Dying, and behold I live!

4.   Thou, O Christ, art all I want,
    More than all in thee I find;
Raise the fallen, cheer the faint,
    Heal the sick, and lead the blind.

47. *HSP* (1740) 67–68; original title.

Just and holy is thy name,
    I am all unrighteousness;
False and full of sin I am;
    Thou art full of truth and grace.

5.   Plenteous grace with thee is found,
    Grace to cover all my sin;
Let the healing streams abound,
    Make and keep me pure within.
Thou of life the fountain art,
    Freely let me take of thee;
Spring thou up within my heart;
    Rise to all eternity!

82. O Thou who camest from above[48]

1.   O thou who camest from above,
    The pure celestial fire t'impart,
Kindle a flame of sacred love
    On the mean altar of my heart.
There let it for thy glory burn
    With inextinguishable blaze,
And trembling to its source return,
    In humble prayer, and fervent praise.

2.   Jesus, confirm my heart's desire
    To work, and speak, and think for thee
Still let me guard the holy fire,
    And still stir up thy gift in me,
Ready for all thy perfect will,
    My acts of faith and love repeat,
'Till death thy endless mercies seal,
    And make my sacrifice complete.

---

48. *Scripture Hymns* (1762) 1:57, Hymn 183, based on Lev 6:13: "The fire shall ever be burning upon the altar; it shall never go out."

STRENGTH IN TRIALS (83–85)

83. *Jesus weeps, our tears to see*[49]

> Jesus weeps, our tears to see!
> Feels the soft infirmity;
> Feels, whene'er a friend we mourn,
> From our bleeding bosom torn:
> Let him still in spirit groan,
> Make our every grief his own,
> Till we all triumphant rise,
> Called to meet him in the skies.

84. *Of blessings infinite I read*[50]

> Of blessings infinite I read,
> The foremost, that my heart hath bled
> And thank thee for a moment's pain,
> Whose fruit shall evermore remain;
> How good for me the suffering given!
> 'Tis grace, 'tis holiness, 'tis heaven!

85. *"The Whole Armour of God"*[51]
Ephesians 6

> 1.   Soldiers of Christ, arise,
>   And put your armour on,
> Strong in the strength which God supplies
> Through his eternal Son;

---

49. *Scripture Hymns* (1762) 2:254, Hymn 444, based on John 11:35: "Jesus wept."

50. *Scripture Hymns* (1762), 1:275, Hymn 866, based on Psalm 119:71: "It is good for me that I have been in trouble." (The English translation is from BCP.)

51. *HSP* (1749) 1:236–39, Hymn 141 (Hymn 28 of Hymns for Believers); original title. The poem is based on Ephesians 6. Charles Wesley first published this hymn as a broadsheet in 1742, and the same year it was included at the end of John Wesley's *The Character of a Methodist*.

Strong in the Lord of Hosts,
And in his mighty power,
Who in the strength of Jesus trusts
Is more than conqueror.

2.   Stand then in his great might,
With all his strength endued,
But take to arm you for the fight
The panoply of God;
That having all things done,
And all your conflicts passed,
Ye may o'ercome through Christ alone
And stand entire at last.

3.   Stand then against your foes,
In close and firm array:
Legions of wily fiends oppose
Throughout the evil day;
But meet the sons of night,
But mock their vain design,
Armed in the arms of heavenly light
Of righteousness divine.

4.   Leave no unguarded place,
No weakness of the soul,
Take every virtue, every grace,
And fortify the whole;
Indissolubly joined,
To battle all proceed;
But arm yourselves with all the mind
That was in Christ your Head.

5.   Let truth the girdle be,
That binds your armour on,
In faithful, firm sincerity
To Jesus cleave alone,

Let faith and love combine
To guard your valiant breast:
The plate of righteousness divine,
Imputed, and impressed.

6.   Still let your feet be shod,
Ready his will to do,
Ready in all the ways of God
His glory to pursue;
Ruin is spread beneath,
The gospel greaves[52] put on,
And safe through all the snares of death
To life eternal run.

7.   But above all, lay hold
Of faith's victorious shield,
Armed with that adamant, and gold,
Be sure to win the field;
If faith surround your heart,
Satan shall be subdued;
Repelled his every fiery dart,
And quenched with Jesu's blood.

8.   Jesus hath died for you!
What can his love withstand?
Believe, hold fast your shield, and who
Shall pluck you from his hand?
Believe, that Jesus reigns,
All power to him is given;
Believe, 'till freed from sin's remains,
Believe yourselves to heaven.

9.   Your Rock can never shake:
Hither, he saith, come up!
The helmet of salvation take,
The confidence of hope;

52. "Greave" comes from old French "greve" and indicates a piece of armor that provides shin protection.

Hope for his perfect love,
Hope for his people's rest,
Hope to sit down with Christ above,
And share the marriage feast.

10.   Brandish in faith 'till then
        The Spirit's two-edged sword,
Hew all the snares of fiends and men
        In pieces with the Word;
        'Tis written; this applied
        Baffles their strength, and art;
Spirit and soul with this divide,
        And joints and marrow part.

11.   To keep your armour bright,
        Attend with constant care,
Still walking in your Captain's sight,
        And watching unto prayer;
        Ready for all alarms,
        Steadfastly set your face,
And always exercise your arms,
        And use your every grace.

12.   Pray without ceasing, pray,
        (Your Captain gives the word)
His summons cheerfully obey
        And call upon the Lord;
        To God your every want
        In instant prayer display,
Pray always, pray and never faint,
        Pray, without ceasing, pray.

13.   In fellowship, alone,
        To God with faith draw near,
Approach his courts, besiege his throne
        With all the powers of prayer:

> Go to his temple, go,
> Nor from his altar move;
> Let every house his worship know,
> And every heart his love.

14.   To God your spirits dart,
> Your souls in words declare,
> Or groan, to him who reads the heart,
> Th' unutterable prayer.
> His mercy now implore,
> And now show forth his praise,
> In shouts, or silent awe, adore
> His miracles of grace.

15.   Pour out your souls to God,
> And bow them with your knees,
> And spread your hearts and hands abroad,
> And pray for Zion's peace;
> Your guides, and brethren, bear
> For ever on your mind;
> Extend the arms of mighty prayer,
> Ingrasping all mankind.

16.   From strength to strength go on,
> Wrestle, and fight, and pray,
> Tread all the powers of darkness down,
> And win the well fought day;
> Still let the Spirit cry,
> In all his soldiers, "Come,"
> 'Till Christ the Lord descends from high,
> And takes the conquerors home.

Part 4:

The Community of Faith

The Nature of the Church (86–103)

86. *The gift of elders' hands bestowed*[1]

1.   Impowered through Moses' hallowing hands,
       Aaron before the altar stands,
           The consecrated priest of God!
       Jesus *his* officers ordains:
       And thus the *Christian* priest obtains
           The gift of elders' hands bestowed.

2.   Ye that uncalled the power assume,
       Expect the rebels' fearful doom;
           The pit its mouth hath opened wide
       For Jesu's sacrilegious foes!
       Repent before its mouth it close
           On all the hardened sons of pride.

87. *A church which may remain*[2]

1.   Jesus, we wait to see
       That spotless church of thine,
       The heaven-appointed ministry,
       The hierarchy divine:

1. *Scripture Hymns* (1762) 2:351, Hymn 685, based on Heb 5:4: "No man taketh this honour unto himself, but he that is called of God, as was Aaron."

2. *Scripture Hymns* (1762) 1:392, Hymn 1160, based on Isa 66:21–23: "And I will also

> Command her now to rise
> With perfect beauty pure,
> Long as the new-made earth and skies
> To flourish and endure;

> 2.   A church which may remain
> With all thy works restored,
> Commensurate with time, obtain
> The nature of her Lord;
> A church to comprehend
> The whole of human race,
> And live in joys that never end
> Before thy glorious face.

88. The church, O God, shall find fulfilled[3]

> The church, O God, shall find fulfilled
> Thy sure prophetic word,
> The Branch, the Man divine, shall build
> The temple of the Lord:
> The temple of the Lord are these
> Who still in Christ abide,
> Till raised to perfect righteousness,
> And wholly sanctified.

89. See here the miracle renewed[4]

> See here the miracle renewed,
> A bush that doth the fire abide,
> A burning bush, bedewed with blood,
> A church, preserved in Jesu's side!

---

take of them for priests and for Levites, saith the Lord. For as the new heavens and the new earth, which I will make, shall remain before me, saith the Lord, so shall your seed and your name remain. And it shall come to pass, that from one new moon to another, and from one sabbath to another, shall all flesh come to worship before me, saith the Lord."

3. *Scripture Hymns* (1762) 2:106, Hymn 1422, based on Zech 6:12: "Behold the man whose name is The Branch; and he shall build the temple of the Lord."

4. *Scripture Hymns* (1762) 1:35, Hymn 105, based on Exod 3:2: "Behold, the bush

90. *Lo, the church with gradual light*[5]

1.
    Lo, the church with gradual light
      Her opening charms displays,
    After a long dreary night
      Looks forth with glimmering rays,
    Scarce perceptible appears,
Until the Day-spring from on high
    All the face of nature cheers,
      And gladdens earth and sky.

2.
    Fair as the unclouded moon,
      With borrowed rays she shines,
    Shines, but ah! she changes soon,
      And when at full declines,
    Frequent, long eclipses feels,
'Till Jesus drives the shades away,
    All her doubts and sins dispels,
      And brings the perfect day.

3.
    Now she without spot appears,
      For Christ appears again,
    Sun of righteousness, he clears
      His church from every stain,
    Rising in full majesty
He blazes with meridian light:
    All th'horizon laughs to see
      The joyous heavenly sight.

4.
    Bright with lustre not her own
      The woman now admire,
    Clothed with that eternal Sun
      Which sets the worlds on fire!

burned with fire, and the bush was not consumed."

5. *Scripture Hymns* (1762) 1:298, Hymn 944, based on the Song of Solomon 6:10: "Who is she that looketh forth as the morning, fair as the moon, clear as the sun, and terrible as an army with banners?"

Bright she shall for ever shine,

Enjoying, like the church above,

All the light of truth divine,

And all the fire of love.

91. *Bought with the blood*[6]

1.   Bought with the blood

Of very God,

The church in every nation,

Publishes through earth abroad,

The God of their salvation.

2.   The God made man

For sinners slain,

The life of each believer,

Did from everlasting reign,

And reigns in us for ever.

BORN OF THE SPIRIT (92)

92. *[After Preaching to the Newcastle Colliers]*[7]

1.   See how great a flame aspires,

Kindled by a spark of grace!

Jesu's love the nations fires,

Sets the kingdoms on a blaze.

To bring fire on earth he came,

Kindled in some hearts it is;

O that all might catch the flame,

All partake the glorious bliss!

---

6. *Scripture Hymns* (1762) 2:274, based on Acts 20:28: "The church of God, which he hath purchased with his own blood."

7. *HSP* (1749) 1:315–16, Hymn 200 (Hymn 4 in a series of poems titled "After Preaching to the Newcastle Colliers"). Though the printed number of the hymn is 199, it should be 200. See footnote number 1 on page 124.

2.   When he first the work begun,
       Small and feeble was his day;
    Now the Word doth swiftly run,
       Now it wins its widening way;
    More and more it spreads and grows,
       Ever mighty to prevail;
    Sin's strongholds it now o'erthrows,
       Shakes the trembling gates of hell.

3.   Sons of God, your Saviour praise,
       Who the door hath opened wide;
    He hath given the word of grace,
       Jesu's word is glorified;
    Jesus mighty to redeem,
       Who alone the work hath wrought;
    Worthy is the work of him,
       Him who spake a world from nought.

4.   Saw ye not the cloud arise,
       Little as a human hand?
    Now it spreads along the skies,
       Hangs o'er all the thirsty land!
    Lo! The promise of a shower
       Drops already from above,
    But the Lord will shortly pour
       All the Spirit of his love.

UNITED IN CHRIST (93–100)

93. *How happy are thy servants, Lord*[8]

1.   How happy are thy servants, Lord,
       Who thus remember thee!
    What tongue can tell our sweet accord,
       Our perfect harmony!

8. *HLS* (1745) 138–39, Hymn 165.

2. Who thy mysterious Supper share,
   Here at thy table fed,
   Many, and yet but one we are,
   One undivided bread.

3. One with the Living Bread Divine,
   Which now by faith we eat,
   Our hearts, and minds, and spirits join,
   And all in Jesus meet.

4. So dear the tie where souls agree
   In Jesu's dying love;
   Then only can it closer be,
   When all are joined above.

94. *His body mystical and One*[9]

Myself begotten from above,
I must my Father's children love:
Born of the Spirit and the word,
Are we not brethren in the Lord,
Flesh of his flesh, bone of his bone,
His body mystical and One!

95. *The Communion of Saints*[10]

1. Christ, from whom all blessings flow,
   Perfecting the saints below,
   Hear us, who thy nature share,
   Who thy mystic body are:

   Join us, in one spirit join,
   Let us still receive of thine;
   Still for more on thee we call,
   Thee, who fillest all in all.

9. *Scripture Hymns* (1762) 2:392, based on 1 Pet 2:17: "Love the brotherhood."

10. *HSP* (1740) 194–95; original title. These stanzas are Part 4 of a six-part poem titled "The Communion of Saints."

2.   Closer knit to thee our Head,
Nourish us, O Christ, and feed,
Let us daily growth receive,
More and more in Jesus live:

Jesu! we thy members are,
Cherish us with kindest care,
Of thy flesh, and of thy bone:
Love, for ever love thine own.

3.   Move, and actuate, and guide,
Diverse gifts to each divide;
Placed according to thy will,
Let us all our work fulfill.

Never from our office move,
Needful to the others prove;
Use the grace on each bestowed,
Tempered by the art of God.

4.   Sweetly now we all agree,
Touched with softest sympathy,
Kindly for each other care;
Every member feels its share:

Wounded by the grief of One,
All the suffering members groan;
Honoured if one member is
All partake the common bliss.

5.   Many are we now, and one,
We who Jesus have put on;
There is neither bond nor free,
Male nor female, Lord, in thee.

Love, like death, hath all destroyed,
Rendered all distinctions void:
Names and sects and parties fall;
Thou, O CHRIST, art ALL in ALL!

96. At the meeting of friends[11]

1. And are we yet alive,
    And see each other's face?
  Glory and thanks to Jesus give
    For his almighty grace.
    Preserved by power divine
    To full salvation here,
  Again in Jesu's praise we join,
    And in his sight appear.

2. What troubles have we seen,
    What mighty conflicts past,
  Fightings without, and fears within,
    Since we assembled last!
    Yet out of all the Lord
    Hath brought us by his love,
  And still he doth his help afford,
    And hides our life above.

3. Then let us make our boast
    Of his redeeming power,
  Which saves us to the uttermost,
    'Till we can sin no more.
    Let us take up the cross
    'Till we the crown obtain,
  And gladly reckon all things loss
    So we may Jesus gain.

4. Jesus, to thee we bow,
    And for thy coming wait:
  Give us for good some token now
    In our imperfect state;

11. *HSP* (1749) 2:321–22, Hymn 46 in a series of poems titled "Hymns for Christian Friends."

Apply the hallowing word,
Tell each who looks for thee,
Thou shalt be perfect as thy Lord,
Thou shalt be all like me!

97. *At Meeting of Friends*[12]

1.   All praise to our redeeming Lord,
    Who joins us by his grace,
And bids us, each to each restored,
    Together seek his face.
He bids us build each other up,
    And, gathered into one,
To our high calling's glorious hope
    We hand in hand go on.

2.   The gift which he on one bestows,
    We all delight to prove,
The grace through every vessel flows
    In purest streams of love
E'en now we think and speak the same,
    And cordially agree,
Concentered all, through Jesus' name,
    In perfect harmony.

3.   We all partake the joy of one;
    The common peace we feel,
A peace to sensual minds unknown,
    A joy unspeakable.
And if our fellowship below
    In Jesus be so sweet,
What height of rapture shall we know
    When round his throne we meet!

12. *Redemption Hymns* (1747) 43, Hymn 32; original title.

98. A Prayer for Persons Joined in Fellowship[13]

Part 1

1.   Try us, O God, and search the ground
      Of every sinful heart;
Whate'er of sin in us is found,
      O bid it all depart.

2.   When to the right or left we stray,
      Leave us not comfortless,
But guide our feet into the way
      Of everlasting peace.

3.   Help us to help each other, Lord,
      Each other's cross to bear;
Let each his friendly aid afford,
      And feel his brother's care.

4.   Help us to build each other up,
      Our little stock improve;
Increase our faith, confirm our hope,
      And perfect us in love.

5.   Up into thee, our living Head,
      Let us in all things grow,
Till thou hast made us free indeed
      And sinless here below.

6.   Then, when the mighty work is wrought,
      Receive thy ready bride,
Give us in heaven an happy lot
      With all the sanctified.

---

13. *HSP* (1742) 83; original title. Parts 1 and 4 of a four-part poem appear here.

Part 4

1.   Jesu, united by thy grace[14]
          And each to each endeared,
      With confidence we seek thy face
          And know our prayer is heard.

2.   Still let us own our common Lord,
          And bear thy[15] easy yoke—
      A band of love, a threefold cord
          Which never can be broke.

3.   Make us into one spirit drink,
          Baptise into thy name,
      And let us always kindly think,
          And sweetly speak the same.

4.   Touched by the lodestone of thy love,
          Let all our hearts agree,
      And ever towards each other move,
          And ever move[16] towards thee.

5.   To thee, inseparably joined,
          Let all our spirits cleave;
      O may we all the loving mind
          That was in thee receive.

6.   This is the bond of perfectness,
          Thy spotless charity;
      O let us (still we pray) possess
          The mind that was in thee.

---

14. *HSP* (1742) 86–87.
15. In the second edition (1745) "thy" was changed to "thine."
16. The original "more" was corrected in the errata.

7.   Grant this, and then from all below
          Insensibly remove;
      Our souls their change shall scarcely know,
          Made perfect first in love.

8.   With ease our souls through death shall glide
          Into their paradise,
      And thence on wings of angels ride
          Triumphant through the skies.

9.   Yet when the fullest joy is given
          The same delight we prove;
      In earth, in paradise, in heaven
          Our all in all is love.

99. For a Family[17]

1.   Jesu, Lord, we look to thee;
      Let us in thy name agree;
      Show thyself the Prince of Peace,
      Bid our jars for ever cease.

2.   By thy reconciling love
      Every stumbling block remove,
      Each to each unite, endear;
      Come, and spread thy banner here.

3.   Make us of one heart and mind,
      Courteous, pitiful, and kind,
      Lowly, meek in thought and word,
      Altogether like our Lord.

4.   Let us for each other care,
      Each his brother's burden bear;
      To thy church the pattern give,
      Show how true believers live.

17. *HSP* (1749) 1:248, Hymn 146 (Hymn 34 in a series of poems titled "Hymns for Believers"); original title. Though the printed number of the hymn is 146, it should be 147. See footnote number 1 on page 124.

5. Free from anger and from pride,
    Let us thus in God abide;
    All the depths of love express,
    All the height of holiness.

6. Let us then with joy remove
    To the family above;
    On the wings of angels fly,
    Show how true believers die.

100. He that believeth shall not make haste.[18]

[Isaiah 28:16]

1. Unchangeable Almighty Lord,
    Our souls upon thy truth we stay;
    Accomplish now thy faithful word,
    And give, O give us all one way.

2. O let us all join hand in hand
    Who seek redemption in thy blood,
    Fast in one mind and spirit stand,
    And build the temple of our God.

3. Thou only canst our wills control,
    Our wild unruly passions bind,
    Take the old Adam in our soul,
    And make us of one heart and mind.

4. Speak but the reconciling word,
    The winds shall cease, the waves subside;
    We all shall praise our common Lord,
    Our Jesus, and him crucified.

18. *HSP* (1742) 273–74; original title. This is Part 3 of a four-part poem based on Isa 28:16.

5.   Giver of peace and unity,
          Send down thy mind pacific Dove;
      We all shall then in one agree,
          And breathe the Spirit of thy love.

6.   We all shall think and speak the same
          Delightful lesson of thy grace,
      One undivided Christ proclaim,
          And jointly glory in thy praise.

7.   O let us take a softer mould;
          Blended and gathered into thee,
      Under one Shepherd make one fold,
          Where all is love and harmony.

8.   Regard thine own eternal prayer,
          And send a peaceful answer down;
      To us thy Father's name declare,
          Unite, and perfect us in one.

9.   So shall the world believe and know
          That God hath sent thee from above,
      When thou art seen in us below,
          And every soul displays thy love.

CALLED TO GOD'S MISSION (101–3)

101. Fully on these my mission prove[19]

I would the precious time redeem,
    And longer live for this alone,
To spend and to be spent for them
    Who have not yet my Saviour known;
Fully on these my *mission* prove,
And only breathe, to breathe thy love.

19. From "O that I was as heretofore," *HSP* (1749) 1:300, Hymn 149 (stanza 3 of Hymn 12 in the series titled "Hymns for a Preacher of the Gospel"). See No. 129 below for the complete poem.

102. On us, O Christ, thy mission prove[20]

On us, O Christ, thy mission prove,
    Thy full authority to heal,
The blindness of our hearts remove,
    The lameness of our feeble will,
Open our faith's obedient ear,
    Our filthy, leprous nature cure,
Call us out of the sepulchre,
    And preach perfection to the poor.

103. A Prayer for Labourers[21]

1.   Lord of the harvest, hear
        Thy needy servants cry;
    Answer our faith's effectual prayer,
        And all our wants supply.

2.   On thee we humbly wait,
        Our wants are in thy view,
    The harvest, truly, Lord, is great,
        The labourers are few.

3.   Convert, and send forth more
        Into thy church abroad,
    And let them speak thy word of power,
        As workers with their God.

4.   Give the pure gospel-word,
        The word of general grace,
    Thee let them preach, the common Lord,
        Saviour of human race.

20. *Unpub. Poetry*, 2:100, based on Luke 7:22: "The blind see, the lame walk . . ." Original source: MS Luke, 99.

21. *HSP* (1742) 282–83; original title.

5.   O let them spread thy name,
       Their mission fully prove,
     Thy universal grace proclaim,
       Thy all-redeeming love.

6.   On all mankind forgiven
       Empower them still to call,
     And tell each creature under heaven
       That thou hast died for all.

The Book of the Church: Holy Scripture (104–12)

104. Another [Before Reading the Scriptures][22]

1.   Come, Holy Ghost, our hearts inspire,
       Let us thy influence prove;
     Source of the old prophetic fire,
       Fountain of life and love.

2.   Come, Holy Ghost, (for moved by thee
       The prophets wrote and spoke)
     Unlock the truth, thyself the key,
       Unseal the sacred book.

3.   Expand thy wings, prolific Dove,
       Brood o'er our nature's night;
     On our disordered spirits move,
       And let there now be light.

4.   God, through himself we then shall know
       If thou *within* us shine,
     And sound, with all thy saints below,
       The depths of love divine.

22. *HSP* (1740) 42–43; original title.

105. *Come, divine Interpreter*[23]

1. Come, divine Interpreter,
       Bring me eyes thy book to read,
   Ears the mystic words to hear,
       Words which did from thee proceed,
   Words that endless bliss impart,
   Kept in an obedient heart.

2. All who read, or hear, are blessed,
       If thy plain command we do;
   Of thy kingdom here possessed,
       Thee we shall in glory view
   (When thou com'st on earth t'abide)
   Reign triumphant at thy side.

106. *The sacred instrument*[24]

1. If faith in our dear dying Lord
       The sacred instrument applies,
   The virtue of his hallowing word
       Shall make us to salvation wise,
   Wise our high calling's prize t'attain,
   And everlasting glory gain.

2. Jesus, the Spirit of faith bestow,
       Who only can thy book unseal,
   And give me all thy will to know,
       And give me all thy mind to feel,
   Filled with the wisdom from above,
   The purity of heavenly love.

---

23. *Scripture Hymns* (1762) 2:412, Hymn 821; based on Rev 1:3: "Blessed is he that readeth, and they that hear the words of this prophecy, and keep those things which are written therein."

24. *Scripture Hymns* (1762) 2:337, Hymn 664, based on 2 Tim 3:15: "The scriptures are able to make thee wise unto salvation, through faith which is in Christ Jesus."

107. *All thy word without addition*[25]

Self thy word would fain diminish,
   Pride thy word would fain increase,
But what thou art pleased to finish,
   Never can be more or less;
All thy word without addition
   Renders us for glory meet,
Fits us for the blissful vision,
   Makes the man of God complete.

108. *The sacred standard*[26]

1.   Doctrines, experiences to try,
    We to the sacred standard fly,
    Assur'd the Spirit of our Lord
    Can never contradict his word:
    Whate'er his Spirit speaks in me,
    Must with the written word agree;
    If not: I cast it all aside,
    As Satan's voice, or nature's pride.

2.   The text of truth and righteousness,
    O God, thy records we confess,
    And who thine oracles gainsay,
    Have missed the right celestial way;
    Their pardon sure they vainly boast
    In nature sunk, in darkness lost;
    Or if they of perfection dream,
    The light of grace is not in them.

---

25. *Scripture Hymns* (1762) 1:89, Hymn 278, based on Deut 4:2: "Ye shall not add unto the word which I command you, neither shall ye diminish ought from it."

26. *Scripture Hymns* (1762) 1:310, Hymn 973, based on Isa 8:20: "To the law and to the testimony! if they speak not according to this word, it is because there is no light in them."

109. *Can these dry bones perceive*[27]

1. Can these dry bones perceive
    The quickening power of grace,
  Or Christian infidels retrieve
    The life of righteousness?
    All-good, almighty Lord,
     Thou know'st thine own design,
  The virtue of thine own great word,
    The energy divine.

2. Now for thy mercy's sake
    Let thy great word proceed,
  Dispensed by whom thou wilt, to wake
    The spiritually dead;
    Send forth to prophesy
     Thy chosen messenger,
  And thou the gospel-word apply,
    And force the world to hear.

110. *Thy word in the bare literal sense*[28]

1. Thy word in the bare *literal* sense,
    Though heard ten thousand times, and read,
  Can never of itself dispense
    The saving power which wakes the dead;
    The meaning *spiritual* and true
     The learned expositor may give,
  But cannot give the virtue too,
    Or bid his own dead spirit live.

---

27. *Scripture Hymns* (1762) 2:51, Hymn 1273, based on Ezek 37:3–4: "And he said unto me, Son of Man, can these dry bones live?" etc. Though this poem appears above on p. 120, it is included here for the emphasis of stanza two on the power of the word of God.

28. *Scripture Hymns* (1762) 2:249, Hymn 429, based on John 6:63: "It is the Spirit that quickeneth; the flesh profiteth nothing."

2.   But breathing in the sacred leaves
         If on the soul thy Spirit move,
      The re-begotten soul receives
         The quickening power of faith and love;
      Transmitted through the gospel-word
         Whene'er the Holy Ghost is given,
      The sinner hears, and feels restored
         The life of holiness and heaven.

111. *Whether the word be preached or read*[29]

1.   Whether the word be preached or read,
         No saving benefit I gain
      From empty sounds or letters dead;
         Unprofitable all and vain,
      Unless by faith thy word I hear
      And see its heavenly character.

2.   Unmixed with faith, the Scripture gives
         No comfort, life, or light to me,
      But darker still the dark it leaves,
         Implunged in deeper misery,
      O'erwhelmed with nature's sorest ills.
      The Spirit saves, the letter kills.

3.   Most wretched comforters are they
         Who bid "On the bare word rely!"
      Physicians of no price, they say
         I must the promises apply;
      And destitute of inward sense,
      Draw all my consolations hence.

4.   Their counsels aggravate my grief,
         (But never move the heart of stone,)
      Insult my helpless unbelief
         Who cannot find a God unknown,

29. *MS Scriptural Hymns* (1783) 90–91; see *Poet. Works*, 13:123–25.

While without eyes they bid me look,
And read the sealed, unfolded book.

5.   If God enlighten through his Word,
    I shall my kind Enlightener bless,
But void and naked of my Lord,
    What are all verbal promises?
Nothing to me, till faith divine
Inspire, inspeak, and make them mine.

6.   Jesus, th'appropriating grace
    'Tis thine on sinners to bestow;
Open mine eyes to see thy face,
    Open my heart thyself to know.
And then I through thy Word obtain
Sure, present, and eternal gain.

112. *Thy book be my companion still*[30]

1.   The table of my heart prepare,
    (Such power belongs to thee alone)
And write, O God, thy precepts there,
    To show thou still canst write in stone,
So shall my pure obedience prove
All things are possible to love.

2.   Father, instruct my docile heart,
    Apt to instruct I then shall be,
I then shall all thy words impart,
    And teach (as taught myself by thee)
My children in their earliest days,
To know, and live the life of grace.

---

30. *Scripture Hymns* (1762) 1:91–93, based on Deut 6:6–7: "And these words, which I command thee, shall be in thine heart: And thou shalt teach them diligently unto thy children, and shalt talk of them this day when thou sittest in thine house, and when thou walkest by the way, and when thou liest down, and when thou risest up."

3.   When quiet in my house I sit,
      Thy book be my companion still,
   My joy thy sayings to repeat,
      Talk o'er the records of thy will,
   And search the oracles divine,
   'Till every heart-felt word is mine.

4.   O might the gracious words divine
      Subject of all my converse be,
   So would the Lord his follower join,
      And walk and talk himself with me,
   So would my heart his presence prove,
   And burn with everlasting love.

5.   Oft as I lay me down to rest,
      O may the reconciling word
   Sweetly compose my weary breast,
      While on the bosom of my Lord
   I sink in blissful dreams away,
      And visions of eternal day.

6.   Rising to sing my Saviour's praise,
      Thee may I publish all day long,
   And let thy precious word of grace
      Flow from my heart, and fill my tongue,
   Fill all my life with purest love,
   And join me to thy church above.

The Sacraments and Rites of the Church (113–31)

BAPTISM (113–14)

113. Truly baptized into the name[31]

Truly baptized into the name
   Of Jesus I have been,
Who partner of his nature am,
   And saved indeed from sin;

---

31. *Unpub. Poetry,* 2:389–90, based on Acts 19:5: "They were baptized in the name of the Lord Jesus." Original source: MS Acts, 379.

Thy nature, Lord, through faith I feel,
Thy love revealed in me;
In me my full salvation, dwell
To all eternity.

114. *At the Baptism of Adults*[32]

1.   Come, Father, Son, and Holy Ghost,
Honour the means injoined by Thee,
Make good our apostolic boast,
And own thy glorious ministry.

2.   We now thy promised presence claim,
Sent to disciple all mankind,
Sent to baptize into thy name:
We now thy promised presence find.

3.   Father in these reveal thy Son,
In these for whom we seek thy face,
The hidden Mystery make known,
The inward, pure, baptizing grace.

4.   Jesu, with us thou always art,
Effectuate now the sacred sign,
The gift unspeakable impart,
And bless thine ordinance divine.

5.   Eternal Spirit, descend from high,
Baptizer of our spirits thou,
The sacramental seal apply,
And witness with the water now.

6.   O! that the souls baptized herein,
May now thy truth and mercy feel,
May rise, and wash away their sin—
Come, Holy Ghost, their pardon seal.

32. *HSP* (1749) 2:245, Hymn 181; original title.

EUCHARIST / HOLY COMMUNION / LORD'S SUPPER (115–25)

115. *Constant Communion*[33]

1.   Happy the saints of former days
         Who first continued in the Word,
       A simple lowly loving race,
         True followers of their Lamb-like Lord.

2.   In holy fellowship they lived,
         Nor would from the commandment move,
       But every joyful day received
         The tokens of expiring love.

3.   Not then above their Master wise,
         They simply in his paths remained,
       And called to mind his sacrifice
         With steadfast faith and love unfeigned.

4.   From house to house they broke the bread
         Impregnated with Life divine,
       And drank the Spirit of their Head
         Transmitted in the sacred wine.

5.   With Jesu's constant presence blest,
         While duteous to his dying word,
       They kept the Eucharistic feast,
         And supped in Eden with their Lord.

6.   Throughout their spotless lives was seen
         The virtue of this heavenly food,
       Superior to the sons of men
         They soared aloft, and walked with God.

7.   O what a flame of sacred love
         Was kindled by the altar's fire!
       They lived on earth like those above,
         Glad rivals of the heavenly choir.

33. *HLS* (1745) 139–41, Hymn 166.

8.   Strong in the strength herewith received,
          And mindful of the Crucified;
      His confessors for him they lived,
          For him his faithful martyrs died.

9.   Their souls from chains of flesh released,
          By torture from their bodies driven
      With violent faith the kingdom seized,
          And fought and forced their way to heaven.

10.   Where is the pure primeval flame,
          Which in their faithful bosom glowed?
      Where are the followers of the Lamb,
          The dying witnesses for God?

11.   Why is the faithful seed decreased,
          The life of God extinct and dead?
      The daily sacrifice is ceased,
          And charity to heaven is fled.

12.   Sad mutual causes of decay,
          Slackness and vice together move,
      Grown cold we cast the means away,
          And quenched our latest spark of love.

13.   The sacred signs thou didst ordain,
          Our pleasant things are all laid waste;
      To men of lips and hearts profane,
          To dogs and swine, and heathen cast.

14.   Thine holy ordinance contemned
          Hath let the flood of evil in,
      And those who by thy name are named,
          The sinners unbaptized out-sin.

15.   But canst thou not thy work revive
          Once more in our degenerate years?
      O wouldst thou with thy rebels strive,
          And melt them into gracious tears!

16. O wouldst thou to thy church return!
　　　For which the faithful remnant sighs,
　For which the drooping nations mourn,
　　　Restore the daily sacrifice.

17. Return, and with thy servants sit,
　　　Lord, of the sacramental feast,
　And satiate us with heavenly meat,
　　　And make the *world* thy happy guest.

18. Now let the spouse, reclined on thee,
　　　Come up out of the wilderness,
　From every spot and wrinkle free,
　　　And washed and perfected in grace.

19. Thou hear'st the pleading Spirit's groan,
　　　Thou know'st the groaning Spirit's will:
　Come in thy gracious kingdom down,
　　　And all thy ransomed servants seal.

20. Come quickly, Lord, the Spirit cries,
　　　The number of thy saints complete,
　Come quickly, Lord, the Bride replies,
　　　And make us all for glory meet.

21. Erect thy tabernacle here,
　　　The *New Jerusalem* send down,
　Thyself amidst thy saints appear,
　　　And seat us on thy dazzling throne.

22. Begin the great millennial day,
　　　Now, Saviour, with a shout descend,
　Thy standard in the heavens display,
　　　And bring thy joy which ne'er shall end!

116. How the means transmit the power[34]

1.   God incomprehensible,
      Shall man presume to know,
Fully search him out, or tell
      His wondrous ways below?
Him in all his ways we find;
      How the means transmit the power
Here he leaves our thought behind,
      And faith inquires no more.

2.   How he did these creatures raise
      And make this bread and wine
Organs to convey his grace
      To this poor soul of mine,
I cannot the way decry,
      Need not know the mystery,
Only this I know that I
      Was blind, but now I see.

3.   Now mine eyes are opened wide
      To see his pard'ning love,
Here I view the God that died
      My ruin to remove;
Clay upon mine eyes he laid
      (I at once my sight received)
Blessed and bid me eat the bread,
      And lo! My soul believed.

117. Father, Son, and Holy Spirit[35]

1.   Father, Son, and Holy Spirit
      Saved by Thee
      Happy we
      Shall thy throne inherit:

34. *HLS* (1745) 43, Hymn 59.
35. *Trinity Hymns* (1767) 121–22, Hymn 37.

Here our heavenly banquet tasting.
In thy love
Joy we prove
Ever, ever lasting.

2.   Rapturous anticipation!
Who believe
We receive
Sensible salvation;
Silent bliss and full of glory
In thine eye
While we lie
Prostrated before Thee.

3.   Manna spiritual and hidden,
Perfect peace
We possess,
Our recovered Eden:
'Till we find the fullness given
In that sight
Mercy's height,
Love's sublimest heaven!

118. Come, thou everlasting Spirit[36]

1.   Come, thou everlasting Spirit,
Bring to every thankful mind
All the Saviour's dying merit
All his suffering for mankind:
True recorder of his Passion,
Now the living faith impart,
Now reveal his great salvation,
Preach his gospel to our heart.

36. *HLS* (1745) 13, Hymn 16.

2. Come, thou witness of his dying,
    Come, Remembrancer Divine,
Let us feel thy power applying
    Christ to every soul and mine;
Let us groan thine inward groaning,
    Look on him we pierced, and grieve,
All receive the grace atoning,
    All the sprinkled blood receive.

119. *Come, Holy Ghost, thine influence shed*[37]

1. Come, Holy Ghost, thine influence shed,
        And realize the sign,
    Thy life infuse into the bread,
        Thy power into the wine.

2. Effectual let the tokens prove,
        And made by heavenly art
    Fit channels to convey thy love
        To every faithful heart.

120. *Isaiah 64:5,*
"Thou meetest those that remember thee in thy ways."[38]

1. Come, Lord, to a soul
        That waits in thy ways,
    That stays at the pool
        Expecting thy grace:
    To see thy salvation,
        And prove all thy will,
    With sure expectation
        I calmly stand still.

---

37. *HLS* (1745) 51, Hymn 72.

38. *A Short View of the Difference Between the Moravian Brethren, Lately in England, And the Rev. Mr. John and Charles Wesley* (1745), 19; original title.

2.   With fasting and prayer
      My Saviour I seek,
And listen to hear
      The Comforter speak;
In searching and hearing
      The life-giving Word
I wait thy appearing,
      I look for my Lord.

3.   Because thou hast said:
      "Do this for my sake,"
The mystical bread
      I gladly partake;
I thirst for the Spirit
      That flows from above,
And long to inherit
      Thy fullness of love.

4.   'Tis *here* I look up
      And grasp at thy mind,
Here *only* I hope
      Thine image to find;
The means of bestowing
      Thy gifts I embrace;
But all things are owing
      To Jesus's grace.

121. *Come to the feast, for Christ invites*[39]

1.   Come to the feast, for Christ invites,
      And promises to feed,
'Tis here his closest love unites
      The members to their Head.

39. *HLS* (1745) 43–44, Hymn 60.

2.   'Tis here he nourishes his own
       With living bread from heaven,
  Or makes himself to mourners known,
       And shows their sins forgiven.

3.   Still in his instituted ways
       He bids us ask the power,
  The pard'ning or the hallowing grace,
       And wait th'appointed hour.

4.   'Tis not for us to set our God
       A time his grace to give,
  The benefit whene'er bestowed,
       We gladly should receive.

5.   Who seek redemption through his love
       His love shall them redeem;
  He came self-emptied from above
       That we might live through him.

6.   Expect we then the quick'ning Word
       Who at his altar bow:
  But if it be thy pleasure, Lord,
       O let us find thee now.

122. *The sacred true effectual sign*[40]

1.   Author of our salvation, thee
       With lowly thankful hearts we praise
  Author of this great mystery,
       Figure and means of saving grace.

2.   The sacred true effectual sign
       Thy body and thy blood it shows,
  The glorious instrument divine
       Thy mercy and thy strength bestows.

40. *HLS* (1745) 22, Hymn 28.

3.   We see the blood that seals our peace,
        Thy pard'ning mercy we receive:
    The bread doth visibly express
        The strength through which our spirits live.

4.   Our spirits drink a fresh supply,
        And eat the bread so freely given,
    Till borne on eagles' wings we fly,
        And banquet with our Lord in heaven.

123. *Author of life divine*[41]

1.   Author of life divine,
        Who hast a table spread,
    Furnished with mystic wine
        And everlasting bread,
    Preserve the life thyself hast given,
    And feed, and train us up for heaven.

2.   Our needy souls sustain
        With fresh supplies of love,
    Till all thy life we gain,
        And all thy fullness prove,
    And strengthened by thy perfect grace,
    Behold without a veil thy face.

124. *O thou who this mysterious bread*[42]

1.   O thou who this mysterious bread
        Didst in Emmaus break,
    Return herewith our souls to feed,
        And to thy followers speak.

41. *HLS* (1745) 30, Hymn 40.
42. *HLS* (1745) 22–23, Hymn 29.

2.   Unseal the volume of thy grace,
        Apply the gospel-word;
    Open our eyes to see thy face,
        Our hearts to know the Lord.

3.   Of thee we commune still, and mourn
        Till thou the veil remove;
    Talk with us, and our hearts shall burn
        With flames of fervent love.

4.   Enkindle now the heavenly zeal,
        And make thy mercy known,
    And give our pardoned souls to feel
        That God and love are one.

125. *Sure and real is the grace*[43]

1.   O the depth of love divine,
        Th'unfathomable grace!
    Who shall say how bread and wine
        God into man conveys?
    How the bread his flesh imparts,
        How the wine transmits his blood,
    Fills his faithful people's hearts
        With all the life of God!

2.   Let the wisest mortal show
        How we the grace receive;
    Feeble elements bestow
        A power not theirs to give.
    Who explains the wondrous way?
        How through these the virtue came?
    These the virtue did convey,
        Yet still remain the same.

43. *HLS* (1745) 41, Hymn 57.

3.   How can heavenly spirits rise,
          By earthly matter fed,
       Drink herewith divine supplies
          And eat immortal bread?
       Ask the Father's wisdom *how;*
          Him that did the means ordain
       Angels round our altars bow
          To search it out in vain.

4.   Sure and real is the grace,
          The manner be unknown;
       Only meet us in thy ways
          And perfect us in one.
       Let us taste the heavenly powers,
          Lord, we ask for nothing more;
       Thine to bless, 'tis only ours
          To wonder and adore.

MARRIAGE (126–28)

126. *Thou, Lord, direct my ways*[44]

1.   And is there hope for me
          In life's distracting maze,
       And shall I live on earth to see
          A few unruffled days?
       A man of sorrows I,
          A sufferer from the Womb,
       'Twas all my hope in peace to die,
          And rest within my tomb.

2.   How then can I conceive
          A good for me designed
       The greatest God himself could give,
          The Parent of mankind?

44. *Unpub. Poetry,* 1:231–33. These are stanzas of an intended eight-stanza poem written by Charles Wesley to Sally Gwynne, his wife-to-be, during their courtship. Particularly stanzas 6 and 7 convey a strong sense of Christian partnership in marriage. Original source: MS Wesley Family Letters, IV, 48.

A good by sovereign love
 To sinless Adam given
His joyous paradise t'improve,
 And turn his earth to heaven.

3. God of unbounded grace,
   If yet thou wilt bestow
On me the vilest of the race
  Thy choicest gift below;
  My drooping heart prepare
  The blessing to receive
And bid the child of sad despair
  With confidence believe.

4. My new and strange distress
   To thee I simply own,
Inured to pain I start from peace
  And dread a *Good* unknown:
  My heart thou seest it ache
  Its dearest wish t'obtain
And know'st my fear of measuring back
  My steps to earth again.

5. Assure my trembling soul
   Of thy decisive will
My endless doubts and fears control,
  And bid my heart be still:
  Regard thy servant's call
  And shed thy love abroad,
The sign infallible that all
  My works are wrought in God.

6. Thou, Lord, direct my ways,
   On all my counsels shine
And lead by thine unerring grace
  This feeble soul of mine;

Thy pard'ning love reveal
In proof of thy decree,
And stamp her with thy Spirit's seal,
The friend *designed* for me.

7.   With steadfast faith and love
Let me thy creature take
As a good angel from above,
Sent down for Jesus' sake.
Not to enthrall my will,
Not to put out my eyes,
But fix my heart and fire my zeal
And lift me to the skies.

8.   *I have not time to finish: Your heart will say Amen to a prayer
in which yourself are so nearly concerned. L[ondo]n. Tues. N[igh]t.*

127. *Another*[45] [i.e. Wedding Song]

1.   O thou, who didst an help ordain
To bless the pure primaeval man,
And crown the joys of paradise,
See at thy feet a simple pair,
Bound in the closest bond to bear
Each other's burden to the skies.
Met in the mighty Jesus' name
We come, great God, the grace to claim
For all designed by thy decree,
For us, whose prostrate souls adore
Thy wisdom, truth and love, and power
And grasp to find their all in thee.

45. *Unpub. Poetry,* 1:255–56. This is a poem written during Charles's courtship of Sally Gwynne; original title. Original source: MS Richmond, 6–7.

2.   Throughout our lives to vindicate
       The reverend, pure, and high estate,
          For this our hearts and hands we join,
       Resolved, if thou thy blessing give,
       Its sacred honour to retrieve,
          And prove its dignity divine:
       So worthy of thyself t'ordain,
       So suited to the state of man,
          So *like* the fellowship above,
       Type of that awful mystery
       That union of the church with thee,
          That glorious league of nuptial love.

3.   But who sufficient is to *show*
       Thy marriage with thy church below,
          So dearly each to each allied?
       Who shall the spotless pattern give,
       And represent the second Eve,
          That issued from her husband's side?
       Jesu, to thee we humbly pray,
       Thou only canst the grace convey,
          The mystic power of love unknown,
       Pure heavenly love that flows from thee,
       From all the dross of nature free,
          And perfects both our souls in one.

128. So teach us, Lord, to count our days[46]

1.   Being of Beings, Lord of all,
       On thee with trembling hearts we call,
       Thy favour seek, thy grace implore,
       Till life's uneasy dream is o'er
       And both obtain the lasting rest,
       And meet in God for ever blest.

---

46. *Unpub. Poetry,* 1:273–74. This is one of Charles's courtship poems to Sally Gwynne. Titled "Another." Original source: MS Wesley Family Letters I, 50, fo. 2.

2.   Thou know'st the state of short-lived man,
   His longest life is but a span,
   A thousand years are as one day,
   So soon with thee they pass away,
   So soon we all from earth are gone,
   And stand arraigned before thy throne.

3.   How needless then our anxious fear
   Of momentary evils here,
   How fondly we our pains employ
   T'insure a momentary joy,
   As life would last for ages sure,
   Or time eternally endure.

4.   So teach us, Lord, to count our days,
   That both may live but to thy praise,
   In mutual league of purest love
   Our short uncertain time improve,
   To heavenly things our hearts apply,
   And wisely live, and calmly die.

5.   With that celestial prize in view,
   And guided by thy Spirit's clue,
   Still may we walk before thy sight,
   Unblameable in spotless white,
   And keep our wedding garments pure
   And faithful unto death endure.

6.   Our work performed, when she or I
   Obtain the glorious grace to die,
   Let neither, long condemned to stay,
   Expect our second Bridal-Day,
   But call us both in heaven to join,
   To meet within the arms divine.

ORDINATION (129)

129. *Hymns for a Preacher of the Gospel*[47]

1.   O that I was as heretofore
        When first sent forth in Jesu's name
    I rushed thro' every open door,
        And cried to all, "Behold the Lamb!"
    Seized the poor trembling slaves of sin,
    And forc'd the outcasts to come in.

2.   The God who kills, and makes alive,
        To me the quick'ning power impart,
    Thy grace restore, thy work revive,
        Retouch my lips, renew my heart,
    Forth with a fresh commission send,
    And all thy servant's steps attend.

3.   Give me the faith which can remove
        And sink the mountain to a plain;
    Give me the childlike praying love,
        That longs to build thy house again;
    Thy love which once my heart o'erpowered,
    And all my simple soul devoured.

4.   I want an even strong desire,
        I want a calmly-fervent zeal,
    To save poor souls out of the fire,
        To snatch them from the verge of hell,
    And turn them to the pardning God,
    And quench the brands in Jesu's blood.

5.   I would the precious time redeem,
        And longer live for this alone,
    To spend and to be spent for them
        Who have not yet my Saviour known;

47. *HSP* (1749) 1:300–301, Hymn 189 (Hymn 12 in a series of poems titled "Hymns for a Preacher of the Gospel"). Though the printed number of the hymn is 188, it should be 189. See footnote number 1 on page 124.

Fully on these my mission prove,
And only breathe, to breathe thy love.

6. My talents, gifts, and graces, Lord,
      Into thy blessed hands receive;
    And let me live to preach thy word,
      And let me to thy glory live;
    My every sacred moment spend
    In publishing the sinner's Friend.

7. Enlarge, inflame, and fill my heart
      With boundless charity divine,
    So shall I all my strength exert,
      And love them with a zeal like thine,
    And lead them to thine open side,
    The sheep, for whom the Shepherd died.

8. Or if, to serve thy church and thee
      Myself be offered up at last,
    My soul brought thro' the purple sea
      With those beneath the altar cast
    Shall claim the palm to martyrs given,
    And mount the highest throne in heaven.

FUNERAL AND SERVICE OF DEATH AND RESURRECTION[48] (130–31)

130. *The golden rule she has pursued*[49]

1. The golden rule she has pursued,
    And did to others as she would
      Others should do to her:
    Justice composed her upright soul,
    Justice did all her thoughts control,
      And formed her character.

48. See below also selection #146, "Come, let us join our friends above" from the second series of *Funeral Hymns* (1759).

49. *Funeral Hymns.* London: [Strahan], 1759; stanza 1 = Hymn 31, Part II, stanza 3 on page 51; stanzas 2–4 = Hymn 32, Part IV, stanzas 2–4 on page 53; stanza 5 = Hymn 30, [Part I] on pages 49–50. See also Jackson, *The Journal of the Rev. Charles Wesley, M.A.,*

2.   Affliction, poverty, disease,
Drew out her soul in soft distress,
    The wretched to relieve:
In all the works of love employed,
Her sympathizing soul enjoyed
    The blessedness to give.

3.   Her Saviour in his members seen,
A stranger she received him in,
    An hungry Jesus fed,
Tended her sick, imprisoned Lord,
And flew in all his wants t'afford
    Her ministerial aid.

4.   A nursing-mother to the poor,
For them she husbanded her store,
    Her life, her all, bestowed;
For them she laboured day and night,
In doing good her whole delight,
    In copying after God.

5.   Away, my tears and selfish sighs!
The happy saint in paradise
    Requires us not to mourn;
But rather keep her life in view,
And still her shining steps pursue,
    Till all to God return.

131. *If death my friend and me divide*[50]

1.   If death my friend and me divide,
    Thou dost not, Lord, my sorrow chide,

2:338, 339, 341. The constellation of five stanzas printed here was first published in *Songs for the Poor*, No. 12.

50. *Scripture Hymns* (1762) 2:324–25, based on 1 Thess 4:13: "Sorrow not, even as others which have no hope."

Or frown my tears to see;
Restrained from passionate excess,
Thou bidst me mourn in calm distress
For them that rest in thee.

2.   I feel a strong immortal hope,
Which bears my mournful spirit up
Beneath its mountain load;
Redeemed from death, and grief, and pain,
I soon shall gain my friend again
Within the arms of God.

3.   Pass a few fleeting moments more
And death the blessing shall restore
Which death has snatched away;
For me thou wilt the summons send,
And give me back my parted friend
In that eternal day.

Particular Times of Worship (132–39)

OPENING OF WORSHIP (132–33)

132. On the Same [For the Lord's Day][51]

1.   Come, let us join with one accord
In hymns around the throne!
This is the day our rising Lord
Hath made and called his own.

2.   This is the day which God hath blessed,
The brightest of the seven;
Type of that everlasting rest
The saints enjoy in heaven.

51. *Hymns for Children* (1763) 56, Hymn 62.

3.   Then let us in his name sing on,
        And hasten to that day,
When our Redeemer shall come down,
        And shadows pass away.

4.   Not one, but all our days below,
        Let us in hymns employ;
And in our Lord rejoicing, go
        To his eternal joy.

133. Glory to God on high[52]

Glory to God on high!
    The God of love and power,
Who made both earth and sky,
    Let all his works adore.
Praise to the great Three-One be given
By all on earth, and all in heaven.

CLOSING OF WORSHIP (134)

134. At Parting[53]

1.   Blest be the dear uniting love
        That will not let us part;
Our bodies may far off remove,
        We still are joined in heart.

2.   Joined in one Spirit to our Head,
        Where he appoints we go,
And still in Jesu's footsteps tread,
        And do *his* work below.

3.   O let us ever walk in him,
        And nothing know beside,
Nothing desire, nothing esteem,
        But Jesus crucified.

52. *Gloria Patri* (1746) 6, Hymn 9.
53. *HSP* (1742) 159–60; original title.

4.   Closer and closer let us cleave
        To his beloved embrace;
    Expect his fullness to receive,
        And grace to answer grace.

5.   While thus we walk with Christ in light,
        Who shall our souls disjoin,
    Souls, which himself vouchsafes t' unite
        In fellowship divine!

6.   We all are one who him receive,
        And each with each agree,
    In him the one, the truth, we live;
        Blest point of unity!

7.   Partakers of the Saviour's grace,
        The same in mind and heart,
    Nor joy, nor grief, nor time, nor *place*,
        Nor life, nor death can part:

8.   But let us hasten to the day
        Which shall our flesh restore,
    When death shall all be done away,
        And bodies part no more.

MORNING (135–37)

135. *Morning Hymn*[54]

1.   Christ, whose glory fills the skies,
        Christ, the true, the only light,
    Sun of Righteousness, arise,
        Triumph o'er the shades of night;
    Day-spring from on high, be near;
    Day-star, in my heart appear.

54. *HSP* (1740) 24–25; original title.

2.   Dark and cheerless is the morn
            Unaccompanied by thee;
        Joyless is the day's return,
            Till thy mercy's beams I see;
        Till they inward light impart,
        Glad my eyes and warm my heart.

3.   Visit then this soul of mine;
            Pierce the gloom of sin and grief;
        Fill me, Radiancy divine,
            Scatter all my unbelief;
        More and more thyself display,
        Shining to the perfect day.

136. A Morning Hymn[55]

1.   We lift our hearts to thee
            O day-star from on high!
        The sun itself is but thy shade,
            Yet cheers both earth and sky.

2.   O let thy orient beams
            The night of sin disperse!
        Those[56] mists of error and of vice
            Which shade the universe!

3.   How beauteous nature now!
            How dark and sad before!
        With joy we view the pleasing change,
            And nature's God adore.

---

55. *CPH* (1741/1743) 50–51; original title. Some have attributed this hymn to John Wesley.

56. "Those" was changed to "The" in the second edition (1743) and thereafter.

4. O may no gloomy crime
    Pollute the rising day!
  Or Jesu's blood,[57] like evening dew,
    Wash all the stains away.

5. May we this life improve,
    To mourn for errors past,
  And live this short-revolving day
    As if it were our last.

6. To God the Father, Son,
    And Spirit, One and Three,
  Be glory, as it was, is now,
    And shall for ever be.

137. For the Morning[58]

1. Where is my God, my joy, my hope,
    The dear desire of nations, where?
  Jesus, to thee my soul looks up,
    To thee directs her morning prayer,
  And spreads her arms of faith abroad,
  T' embrace my hope, my joy, my God.

2. Mine eyes prevent the morning ray,
    Looking, and longing for thy word:
  Come, O my Jesus, come away,
    And let my heart receive its Lord;
  Which pants, and struggles to be free,
  And breaks to be detained from thee.

3. Appear in me, bright Morning Star,
    And scatter all the shades of night;
  I saw thee once, and came from far;
    But quickly lost thy transient light;

57. "Or kindly tears" of the first edition is changed to "Or Jesu's blood" in the second edition (1743), which Charles co-edited, and in succeeding editions.

58. *HSP* (1749) 1:202–3, Hymn 117; original title. It is numbered as Hymn 4 in the section "Hymns for Believers."

And now again in darkness pine,
Till thou throughout my nature shine.

4. In patient hope I now give heed
      To the sure word of promised grace,
   Whose rays a feeble luster shed,
      Faint glimmering through the darksome place,
   Till thou thy glorious light impart,
   And rise, the Day-Star, in my heart.

5. Come, Lord, be manifested here,
      And all the devil's work destroy,
   Now without sin in me appear,
      And fill with everlasting joy;
   The beatific face display;
   Thy presence is the perfect day.

EVENING (138–39)

138. An Evening Hymn[59]

1. All praise to him who dwells in bliss,
      Who made both day and night;
   Whose throne is darkness, in th'abyss
      Of uncreated light.

2. Each thought and deed his piercing eyes
      With strictest search survey:
   The deepest shades no more disguise
      Than the full blaze of day.

3. Whom thou dost guard, O King of kings,
      No evil shall molest;
   Under the shadow of thy wings
      Shall they securely rest.

59. *CPH* (1741/1743) 51; original title.

4. Thy angels shall around their beds
      Their constant stations keep:
    Thy faith and truth shall shield their heads,
      For thou dost never sleep.

5. May we with calm and sleep repose,
      And heavenly thoughts refreshed
    Our eyelids with the morn's unclose,
      And bless the Ever-blessed.

139. *For the Evening*[60]

1. Thou, Lord, art rich in grace to all,
      Attend my earnest cry,
    With lifted hands and heart I call,
      And look to feel thee nigh.

2. O that my prayers might now to thee
      As clouds of incense rise,
    And let my thanks accepted be,
      My evening sacrifice.

3. Not unto me, O Lord, the praise,
      But to thy name I give,
    If kept by thine almighty grace,
      Still unconsumed I live.

4. Through thee, my God, through thee alone
      I incorrupt have been,
    Thou hast thy power in weakness shown
      Withholding me from sin.

5. Restrained from my own wickedness,
      Thy outstretched arm I see,
    And bless thee for my faith's increase,
      And closer cleave to thee.

60. *HSP* (1749) 1:203–4, Hymn 118 (Hymn 5 in a series of poems titled "Hymns for Believers"); original title.

6.   With humble thankfulness I own,
        Sufficient is thy grace,
     Thou who from sin hast kept me one,
        Canst keep me all my days.

Christian Year and Special Observances: (ADVENT [19], CHRISTMAS [20–25], PASSION [29–35], EASTER [36–39], ASCENSION [40], PENTECOST [28, 41], TRANSFIGURATION [140–141], ALL SAINTS' DAY [146–148]), LOVE FEAST (142), COVENANT SERVICE (143)

TRANSFIGURATION (140–41)

140. *When six great days of God are passed*[61]

1.   When six great days of God are passed
        (Which man computes six thousand years)
     Th'eternal rest begins at last,
        And Christ with all his saints appears!
     The members in pure light arrayed
        On that celestial mountain meet,
     And fashioned like their dazzling head
        Make the triumphant church complete.

2.   Thou city of the living God,
        Mother and church of the first-born,
     Jerusalem the saints' abode,
        To thee we languish to return,
     To put our glorious Saviour on,
        Illustrious with his lustre shine,
     Clear as the everlasting Sun,
        And pure as purity divine.

---

61. MS Mark, 94–95; see Osborn, *Poet. Works*, 11:20–21; based on Mark 9:2: "And after six days Jesus taketh with him Peter, and James, and John, and leadeth them up into an high mountain apart by themselves: and he was transfigured before them."

141. *Surrounded with the golden blaze*[62]

1. Surrounded with the golden blaze,
   Hid in the secret of his face,
   Received within the lucid cloud,
   Caught to the bosom of our God,
   A voice shall bless us from the throne,
   "This is my well-beloved Son,
   Th' essential Truth and Life Divine,
   Through everlasting ages thine."

2. Faithful and good, thy Saviour hear,
   And seeing live, all eye, all ear.
   Hear him, and let thy joys abound,
   And fall transported at the sound,
   The utmost powers of music prove,
   Be fed, be feasted with his love;
   And while eternity glides on
   Thy banquet is but just begun.

LOVE-FEAST (142)

142. *The Love-Feast*[63]

Part 1

1. Come, and let us sweetly join,
   Christ to praise in hymns divine;
   Give we all with one accord
   Glory to our common Lord:

   Hands and hearts and voices raise,
   Sing as in the ancient days,
   Antedate the joys above,
   Celebrate the feast of love.

---

62. MS Mark, 97; see Osborn, *Poet. Works*, 11:22; based on Mark 9:7: "And there was a cloud that overshadowed them: and a voice came out of the cloud, saying, This is my beloved Son: hear him."

63. *HSP* (1740), 181–85; original title. Parts 1–3 of a five-part poem are included here. Though Part 3 of this poem appears above on pages 180–81, it is repeated here with Parts 1 and 2 for continuity in reading.

2. Strive we, in affection strive:
    Let the purer flame revive,
    Such as in the martyrs glowed,
    Dying champions for their God.

    We, like them, may live and love,
    Called we are their joys to prove;
    Saved with them from future wrath,
    Partners of like precious faith.

3. Sing we then in Jesu's name,
    Now, as yesterday the same,
    One in every age and place,
    Full for all of truth and grace.

    We for Christ our Master stand
    Lights in a benighted land;
    We our dying Lord confess,
    We are Jesu's witnesses.

4. Witnesses that Christ hath died,
    We with him are crucified;
    Christ hath burst the bands of death,
    We his quick'ning Spirit breathe.

    Christ is now gone up on high,
    (Thither all our wishes fly):
    Sits at God's right-hand above,
    There with him we reign in love!

Part 2

1. Come, thou high and lofty Lord,
    Lowly, meek, incarnate Word;
    Humbly stoop to earth again,
    Come, and visit abject man.

    Jesu, dear expected guest,
    Thou art bidden to the feast;
    For thyself our hearts prepare;
    Come, and sit, and banquet there.

2.   Jesu, we the promise claim,
We are met in thy great name:
In the midst do thou appear,
Manifest thy presence here;

Sanctify us, Lord, and bless,
Breathe thy Spirit, give thy peace;
Thou thyself within us move,
Make our feast a feast of love.

3.   Let the fruits of grace abound,
Let in us thy bowels sound;
Faith, and love, and joy increase,
Temperance, and gentleness.

Plant in us thy humble mind:
Patient, pitiful, and kind,
Meek, and lowly let us be,
Full of goodness, full of thee.

4.   Make us all in thee complete,
Make us all for glory meet,
Meet t'appear before thy sight,
Partners with the saints in light.

Call, O call us each by name
To the marriage of the Lamb,
Let us lean upon thy breast,
Love be there our endless feast.

Part 3

1.   Let us join ('tis God commands)
Let us join our hearts and hands;
Help to gain our calling's hope,
Build we each the other up.

God his blessing shall dispense,
God shall crown his ordinance,
Meet in his appointed ways,
Nourish us with social grace.

2. Let us then as brethren love,
    Faithfully his gifts improve,
    Carry on the earnest strife,
    Walk in holiness of life.

    Still forget the things behind,
    Follow Christ in heart and mind,
    Toward the mark unwearied press,
    Seize the crown of righteousness.

3. Plead we thus for faith *alone,*
    Faith which by our works is shown;
    God it is who justifies,
    Only faith the grace *applies,*

    Active faith that lives within,
    Conquers hell, and death, and sin,
    Hallows whom it first made whole,
    Forms the Saviour in the soul.

4. Let us for this faith contend,
    Sure salvation, is its end;
    Heaven already is begun,
    Everlasting life is won.

    Only let us persevere
    Till we see our Lord appear,
    Never from the Rock remove,
    Sav'd by faith which works by love.

COVENANT SERVICE (143)

143. *Come, let us use the grace divine*[64]

1. Come, let us use the grace divine,
    And all with one accord,
    In a perpetual covenant join
    Ourselves to Christ the Lord.

64. *Scripture Hymns* (1762) 2:36–37, based on Jer 50:5: "Come, and let us join our-selves to the Lord in a perpetual covenant that shall not be forgotten." (May be used also for service of baptism.)

Give up ourselves, through Jesu's power,
  His name to glorify,
And promise in this sacred hour,
  For God to live, and die.

2.   The covenant we this moment make
  Be ever kept in mind!
We will no more our God forsake,
  Or cast his words behind;
We never will throw off his fear,
  Who hears our solemn vow:
And if thou art well-pleased to hear,
  Come down, and meet us now!

3.   Thee, Father, Son, and Holy Ghost,
  Let all our hearts receive,
Present with thy celestial host
  The peaceful answer give;
To each the covenant-blood apply
  Which takes our sins away,
And register our names on high,
  And keep us to that day!

Part 5:

A New Heaven and a New Earth (144–50)

Death and Eternal Life (144–45)

144. Death with Christ[1]

Determined after thee I bear
My cross to Calvary,
And come thy bitterest cup to share,
And with my Saviour die.
The place where once thy body lay,
The place it did perfume,
There will I drop my breathless clay,
And rest within thy tomb.

145. Another [Desiring Death][2]

1. On thee, Omnipotent to save,
Thy creatures tottering o'er the grave,
Thy dear-bought creature, I
For mercy and salvation call,
Jesus, redeem me from my fall,
And suffer me to die.

---

1. *Scripture Hymns* (1762) 1:138, Hymn 430, based on Ruth 1:17: "Where thou diest will I die, and there will I be buried."

2. *Unpub. Poetry*, 3:355–56; original title "Another"; original source: *MS Misc. Hymns*, 25–27.

2.   Warned to put off this mold'ring clay
     I bless thee for my strength's decay
        And sink into the tomb;
     Welcome infirmities and pains,
     Welcome whate'er my God ordains
        To bring his servant home.

3.   My days are as a shadow fled;
     And let me bow my weary head,
        Thine open face to see:
     I ask no temporal reprieve,
     I only long in thee to live,
        And then to die in thee.

4.   O wouldst thou, Lord, thy blood apply,
     My heart to calm and purify,
        My poor, unhallowed heart:
     Thou knowst, I only wait for this,
     To gain the reconciling kiss,
        And then with joy depart.

5.   O might my useless warfare end,
     O might my struggling spirit ascend
        And spurn the earth I leave!
     Regard my struggling spirit's groan,
     Pleading in me regard thy own,
        And now my soul receive.

6.   A wretched, weak, entangled thing,
     To thee my last distress I bring,
        Grace, only grace implore:
     Plunge in the fountain of thy blood,
     And bear me through the purple flood
        To that eternal shore.

7. Appear, and chase these endless sighs,
   Appear before my streaming eyes,
    And wipe these tears away;
   Thy presence is my heavenly light,
   Thy presence swallows up my night
    In everlasting day.

Communion of the Saints (146–48)

146. *Come, let us join our friends above*[3]

1. Come, let us join our friends above
   That have obtained the prize,
   And on the eagle-wings of love
    To joy celestial rise.
   Let all the saints terrestrial sing
    With those to glory gone,
   For all the servants of our King
    In earth and heaven are one.

2. One family we dwell in him,
   One church above, beneath,
   Though now divided by the stream,
    The narrow stream of death;
   One army of the living God,
    To his command we bow;
   Part of his host have crossed the flood,
    And part is crossing *now*.

3. Ten thousand to their endless home
   This solemn moment fly,
   And we are to the margin come,
    And we expect to die.
   His militant, embodied host,
    With wishful looks we stand,
   And long to see that happy coast,
    And reach that heavenly land.

3. *Funeral Hymns* (1759) 1–2, Hymn 1.

4.   Our old companions in distress
         We haste again to see,
And eager long for *our* release
         And full felicity;
Ev'n now by faith we join our hands
         With those that went before,
And greet the blood-besprinkled bands
         On the eternal shore.

5.   Our spirits too shall quickly join,
         Like theirs with glory crowned,
And shout to see our Captain's sign,
         To hear his trumpet sound.
O that we now might grasp our guide,
         O that the word were given!
Come, Lord of Hosts, the waves divide,
         And land us all in heaven.

147. *Lift up your eyes of faith and see*[4]

1.   Lift your eyes[5] of faith and see
         Saints and angels joined in One,
What a countless company
         Stands before yon dazzling throne!
Each before his Saviour stands,
         All in milk-white robes arrayed,
Palms they carry in their hands,
         Crowns of glory on their head.

2.   Saints begin the endless song,
         Cry aloud in heavenly lays
Glory doth to God belong,
         God the glorious Saviour praise,

---

4. *HLS* (1745) 89–90, Hymn 105.

5. Wesley originally wrote "Lift up your eyes of faith and see," but in a later version (1765) he corrected the line to "Lift your eyes of faith and see" because the meter was in 7s.

All from him salvation came,
 Him who reigns enthroned on high,
Glory to the bleeding Lamb
 Let the morning stars reply.

3. Angel-powers the throne surround,
 Next the saints in glory they,
Lulled with the transporting sound
 They their silent homage pay,
Prostrate on their face before
 God and his Messiah fall,
Then in hymns of praise adore,
 Shout the Lamb that died for all.

4. Be it so, they all reply,
 Him let all our orders praise,
Him that did for sinners die,
 Saviour of the favored race,
Render we our God his right,
 Glory, wisdom, thanks and power,
Honour, majesty and might,
 Praise him, praise him evermore!

148. *The Communion of Saints*[6]

Part 1

1. Father, Son, and Spirit, hear
Faith's effectual, fervent prayer,
Hear, and our petitions seal;
Let us now the answer feel.

Mystically one with thee,
Transcript of the Trinity,
Thee let all our nature own
One in Three, and Three in One.

---

6. *HSP* (1740) 188–90; original title. This is Part 1 of a six-part poem titled "The Communion of Saints."

2.   If we now begin to be
Partners with thy saints and thee,
If we have our sins forgiven,
Fellow-citizens of heaven,

Still the fellowship increase,
Knit us in the bond of peace,
Join, our new-born spirits join
Each to each, and all to thine.

3.   Build us in one body up,
Called in one high calling's hope;
One the Spirit whom we claim,
One the pure baptismal flame,

One the faith, and common Lord,
One the Father lives, adored
Over, through, and in us all,
God incomprehensible.

4.   One with God, the source of bliss,
Ground of our communion this;
Life of all that live below,
Let thy emanations flow,

Rise eternal in our heart:
Thou our only Eden art;
Father, Son, and Holy Ghost,
Be to us what Adam lost.

5.   Bold we ask through Christ the Son,
Thou, O Christ, art all our own;
Our exalted flesh we see
To the Godhead joined in thee.

Glorious now thy heaven we share,
Thou art here, and we are there,
We participate of thine,
Human nature of divine.

6. Live we now in Christ our Head,
   Quickened by thy life, and fed;
   Christ, from whom the Spirit flows,
   Into thee thy body grows;

   While we feel the vital blood,
   While the circulating flood,
   Christ, through every member rolls,
   Soul of all believing souls.

7. Daily growth the members find,
   Fitly each with other joined;
   Closely all compacted rise;
   Every joint its strength supplies,

   Life to every part conveys,
   Till the whole receive increase,
   All complete the body prove,
   Perfectly built up in love.

Return and Reign of the Lord (149)

149. *The Same [Thy Kingdom Come]*[7]

1. Lo! he comes with clouds descending,
   Once for favoured sinners slain!
   Thousand, thousand saints attending
   Swell the triumph of his train:
   Hallelujah,
   God appears on earth to reign!

2. Every eye shall now behold him,
   Robed in dreadful majesty,
   Those who set at nought and sold him,
   Pierced and nailed him to the tree,
   Deeply wailing
   Shall the true Messiah see.

7. *Intercession Hymns* (1758) 32–33, Hymn 39; original title.

3. The dear tokens of his passion
   Still his dazzling body bears,
   Cause of endless exaltation
   To his ransomed worshipers;
   With what rapture
   Gaze we on those glorious scars!

4. Yea, Amen! Let all adore thee,
   High on thine eternal throne!
   Saviour, take the power and glory,
   Claim the kingdom for thine own.
   Jah, Jehovah,
   Everlasting God, come down.

The Completion of Creation / The City of God (150)

150. The heavenly new Jerusalem[8]

1. Saviour, on me the grace bestow
   To trample on my mortal foe,
   Conqueror of death with thee to rise,
   And claim my station in the skies,
   Fixed as the throne which ne'er can move,
   A pillar in thy church above.

2. As beautiful, as useful there
   May I that weight of glory bear,
   With all who finally o'ercome,
   Supporters of the heavenly dome,
   Of perfect holiness possessed,
   For ever in thy presence blessed.

---

8. *Scripture Hymns* (1762) 2: 420–21, Hymn 843, based on Rev 3:12: "Him that over-cometh will I make a pillar in the temple of my God, and he shall go no more out: and I will write upon him the name of my God, and the name of the city of my God, which is new Jerusalem, which cometh down out of heaven from God: and I will write upon him my new name."

3. Write upon me the name divine,
   And let thy Father's nature shine,
   His image visibly expressed,
   His glory pouring from my breast
   O'er all my bright humanity,
   Transformed into the God I SEE!

4. Inscribing with the city's name
   The heavenly new Jerusalem,
   To me the victor's title give
   Among thy glorious saints to live,
   And all their happiness to know,
   A citizen of heaven below.

5. When thou hadst all thy foes o'ercome,
   Returning to thy glorious home,
   Thou didst receive the full reward,
   That I might share it with the Lord,
   And thus thine own new name obtain,
   And one with thee for ever reign.

Bibliography

Allchin, A. M. *Participation in God: A Forgotten Strand in Anglican Tradition*. London: Darton Longman & Todd, 1988.

Andrewes, Lancelot. *Preces Privatae*. Edited and translated by F. E. Brightman. New York: Living Age, 1961.

Alter, Robert. *The Art of Biblical Poetry*. New York: Basic, 1985.

Augustine. *The Confessions of St. Augustine*. Translated by E. B. Pusey. London: Dent, 1920.

Baker, Frank. *Charles Wesley's Verse*. London: Epworth, 1988.

———, editor. *Representative Verse of Charles Wesley*. London: Epworth, 1962.

Bell, John. *Many and Great: Songs of the World Church*. Vol. 1. Chicago: GIA, 1990.

Berger, Teresa. *Theology in Hymns?* Translated by Timothy E. Kimbrough. Nashville: Abingdon, 1995; originally published in German as *Theologie in Hymnen? Zum Verhältnis der Theologie und Doxologie um Beispiel der "Collection of Hymns for the use of the People called Methodists" (1780)*. Altenberge: Telos, 1989.

Berthier, Jacques. *Cantos de Taizé*. Chicago: GIA, 1986.

———. *Music from Taizé*. Vol. 1. Chicago: GIA, 1978.

Bett, Henry. *The Hymns of Methodism*. London: Epworth, 1945.

Bouteneff, Peter. "All Creation in United Thanksgiving: Gregory of Nyssa and the Wesleys on Salvation." In *Orthodox and Wesleyan Spirituality*, edited by S T Kimbrough, Jr., 189–201. Crestwood, NY: St. Vladimir's Seminary Press, 2002.

Brevint, Daniel. *On the Christian Sacrament and Sacrifice, By way of Discourse, Meditation, & Prayer Upon The Nature, Parts, and Blessings Of The Holy Communion*. London: Hatchard, 1672.

Brueggemann, Walter. *Israel's Praise: Doxology Against Idolatry and Ideology*. Philadelphia: Fortress, 1988.

Coleridge, Samuel T. *Biographia Literaria*. Oxford: Oxford University Press, 1907, 1967.

Colvin, Tom. *Fill Us with Your Love and Other Hymns from Africa*. Carol Stream, IL: Hope, 1983.

Dale, James. "Charles Wesley and the Line of Piety: Antecedents of the Hymns in English Devotional Verse." *PCWS* 8 (2002) 55–64.

———. "Holy Larceny? Elizabeth Rowe's Poetry in Charles Wesley's Hymns." *PCWS* 3 (1996) 5–20.

Davie, Donald. *A Gathered Church: The Literature of the English Dissenting Interest, 1700–1930*. The Clark Lectures 1976. New York: Oxford University Press, 1978.

Dawn, Marva J. *Reaching Out without Dumbing Down: A Theology of Worship for This Urgent Time*. Grand Rapids: Eerdmans, 1995.

Bibliography

Deer, Alvin, and Carlton R. Young. *Singing the Sacred: Musical Gifts from Native American Communities.* New York: GBGMusik, 2009.

Drew, Elizabeth A. *Poetry: A Modern Guide to its Understanding and Enjoyment.* The Laurel Poetry Series. New York: Dell, 1959.

Edwards, Michael. *Towards a Christian Poetics.* Grand Rapids: Eerdmans, 1984.

Eliot, T. S. *Essays Ancient and Modern.* New York: Harcourt Brace, 1936.

———. *Selected Essays 1917–1932.* New York: Harcourt Brace, 1936.

England, Martha Winburn, and John Sparrow. *Hymns Unbidden: Donne, Herbert, Blake, Emily Dickinson, and the Hymnographers.* New York: New York Public Library, 1966.

Frost, Francis. "The Christ-Mysticism of Charles Wesley: The Eucharist and the Heavenly Jerusalem." *PCWS* 9 (2003–2004) 11–26.

Frost, Robert. "The Constant Symbol." Introductory essay to *The Poems of Robert Frost.* New York: Modern Library, 1946.

———. "The Figure a Poem Makes." Introduction to *Collected Poems.* New York: Holt, 1949.

Garbuzova, Ludmila, S T Kimbrough, Jr., and Mark McGurty. *Russian Praise.* New York: GBGMusik, 1999.

Hawn, C. Michael. *Gather into One: Praying and Singing Globally.* Grand Rapids: Eerdmans, 2003.

———. *Halle, Halle: We Sing the World Round.* Dallas: Choristers Guild, 1999.

———. *One Bread, One Body: Exploring Cultural Diversity in Worship.* Herndon, VA: Alban Institute, 2003.

Heitzenrater, Richard P. *Wesley and the People Called Methodists.* Nashville: Abingdon, 1995.

Hesla, Bret, Mary Preus, and Tom Witt. *Global Songs—Local Voices: Songs of Faith and Liberation from Around the World.* Minneapolis: Bread for the Journey, 1995.

Hildebrandt, Franz, and Oliver A. Beckerlegge, editors. *A Collection of Hymns for the Use of the People Called Methodists.* The Works of John Wesley 7. New York: Oxford University Press, 1983.

Hofstra, Marilyn M. *Voices: Native American Hymns and Worship Resources.* Nashville: Discipleship Resources, 1992.

Hustad, Donald. *Jubilate II.* Carol Stream, IL: Hope, 1993.

Jackson, Thomas. *The Journal of the Rev. Charles Wesley, M.A.* 2 vols. Grand Rapids: Baker, 1980.

———. *The Life of the Rev. Charles Wesley, M.A.* 2 vols. London: John Mason, 1841. New York: Lane & Sanford, 1844.

Jones, Richard G., and Ivor H. Jones. *Hymns and Psalms.* London: Methodist, 1983.

Kimbrough, S T, Jr. "Charles Wesley and the Poor." In *The Portion of the Poor: Good News to the Poor in the Wesleyan Tradition,* edited by M. Douglas Meeks, 147–67. Nashville: Kingswood, 1995.

———. "Charles Wesley as a Biblical Interpreter." *Methodist History* 26:3 (1988) 139–53.

———, editor. *Charles Wesley: Poet and Theologian.* Nashville: Abingdon, 1990.

———. "Charles Wesley's Lyrical Commentary on the Holy Scriptures." In *Orthodox and Wesleyan Scriptural Understanding and Practice,* edited by S T Kimbrough, Jr., 171–206. Crestwood, NY: St. Vladimir's Seminary Press, 2005.

———. "Hymns Are Theology." *Theology Today* 42 (1985) 59–68.

———. "Hymnody of Charles Wesley." In *T. & T. Clark Companion to Methodism*, edited by Charles Yrigoyen, Jr., 36–60. New York: T. & T. Clark, 2010.

———. "John Wesley: Editor-Poet-Priest." *Methodist History* 43 (2005) 131–52.

———. "Lyrical Theology: Theology in Hymns." *Theology Today* 63 (2006) 22–37.

———. "Perfection Revisited: Charles Wesley's Theology of 'Gospel Poverty.'" In *The Poor and the People Called Methodists, 1729–1999*, edited by Richard P. Heitzenrater, 101–19. Nashville: Kingswood, 2002.

———. "Theosis in the Writings of Charles Wesley." *St. Vladimir's Theological Seminary Quarterly* 52:2 (2008) 199–212.

Kimbrough, S T, Jr., and Oliver A. Beckerlegge, editors. *The Unpublished Poetry of Charles Wesley*. 3 vols. Nashville: Abingdon, 1988, 1990, 1992.

Kimbrough, S T, Jr., Timothy E. Kimbrough, and Carlton R. Young, editors. *Songs for the Poor: Singer's Edition*. New York: General Board of Global Ministries, 1997.

Kimbrough, S T, Jr., and Kenneth G. C. Newport, editors. *The Manuscript Journal of The Reverend Charles Wesley, M.A.* 2 vols. Nashville: Abingdon, 2008.

Kimbrough, S T, Jr., and Carlton R. Young, editors. *Global Praise 1*. New York: GBGMusik, 1996, rev. 1999, 2000.

———. *Global Praise 2: Songs for Worship and Witness*. New York: GBGMusik, 2000.

———. *Global Praise 3: More Songs for Worship and Witness*. New York: GBGMusik, 2004.

Kimbrough, S T, Jr., Carlton R. Young, and Jorge Lockward, editors. *Put Your Arms Around the World*. New York: GBGMusik, 2009.

Lawson, John. *The Wesley Hymns: As a Guide to Scriptural Teaching*. Grand Rapids: Francis Asbury, 1987.

Leaver, Robin A. "Charles Wesley and Anglicanism." In *Charles Wesley: Poet and Theologian*, edited by S T Kimbrough, Jr., 157–75. Nashville: Abingdon, 1992.

Lockward, Jorge, editor. *Tenemos Esperanza*. New York: GBGMusik, 2002.

———, and Christopher Heckert, editors. *For Everyone Born*. New York: GBGMusik, 2008.

Loh, I-to, editor. *Hymns from the Four Winds: A Collection of Asian-American Hymns*. Nashville: Abingdon, 1983.

———. *Sound the Bamboo: CCA Hymnal 2000*. Hong Kong: Christian Conference of Asia, 2000.

Long, Thomas G. *Beyond the Worship Wars: Building Vital and Faithful Worship*. Washington, DC: Alban Institute, 2001.

Lossky, Nicholas. "Lancelot Andrewes: A Bridge Between Orthodoxy and the Wesley Brothers." In *Orthodox and Wesleyan Scriptural Understanding and Practice*, edited by S T Kimbrough, Jr., 149–56. Crestwood, NY: St. Vladimir's Seminary Press, 2005.

Martinez, Raquel, editor. *Mil Voces para Celebrar: Himnario Metodista*. Nashville: United Methodist, 1996.

Matsikenyiri, Patrick, compiler. *Africa Praise 1*. New York: GBGMusik, 1996.

Matthews, Rex D. *Timetables of History for Students of Methodism*. Nashville: Abingdon, 2007.

Moore, Henry. *Life of the Rev. John Wesley*. 2 vols. London: John Kershaw, 1824.

Mulrain, George. "The Theological Understanding of Rhythm and Music." Unpublished paper.

Mulrain, George, S T Kimbrough, Jr., and Carlton R. Young, editors. *Caribbean Praise*. New York: GBGMusik, 2000.

Newport, Kenneth G. C., editor. *The Sermons of Charles Wesley: A Critical Edition with Introduction and Notes.* Oxford: Oxford University Press, 2001.

Newport, Kenneth G. C., and Ted A. Campbell, editors. *Charles Wesley, Life, Literature and Legacy.* Peterborough: Epworth Press, 2007.

Nichols, Kathryn. "Charles Wesley's Eucharistic Hymns: Their Relationship to the Book of Common Prayer." *The Hymn* 39:2 (1988) 13–21.

Osborn, George, editor. *The Poetical Works of John and Charles Wesley,* 13 vols. London: Wesleyan-Methodist Conference Office, 1868–1872.

Peacock, David, and Geoff Weaver. *World Praise.* London: HarperCollins, 1993.

———. *World Praise 2: Songs and Hymns for a New Millennium.* Nashville: LifeWay, 2000.

Rattenbury, J. Ernest. *The Evangelical Doctrines of Charles Wesley's Hymns.* London: Epworth, 1941.

Ricoeur, Paul. *Essays in Biblical Imagination.* Edited by Lewis S. Mudge. Philadelphia: Fortress, 1980.

Robertson, Charles, editor. *Singing the Faith: Essays by Members of the Joint Liturgical Group on the Use of Hymns in Liturgy.* Norwich: Canterbury, 1990.

Robinson, Elaine. "A Single, Steady Aim: Images of Hope in Wesleyan Hymnody." *PCWS* 6 (1999–2000) 31–57.

Routley, Erik. *Cantate Domino: An Ecumenical Hymn Book.* Oxford: Oxford University Press, 1980.

Rowe, Elizabeth. *Miscellaneous Works in Prose and Verse of Mrs. Elizabeth Rowe.* 2 vols. London, 1739.

Shaw, George B. *Man and Superman.* New York: Penguin, 2001.

Schilling, Paul. *The Faith We Sing.* Philadelphia: Westminster, 1983.

Shields, Kenneth D. "Charles Wesley as a Poet." In *Charles Wesley: Poet and Theologian,* 45–71. Nashville: Abingdon, 1992.

Sosa, Pablo. "Rhythm: A Global Perspective." Unpublished paper.

Ware, Kallistos. *The Orthodox Way.* Crestwood, NY: St. Vladimir's Seminary Press, 1998.

Watson, J. R. "Charles Wesley and the Thirty-Nine Articles of Religion of the Church of England." *PCWS* 9 (2003–2004) 27–38.

——————— "Charles Wesley's Hymns and the Book of Common Prayer." In *Thomas Cranmer, Essays in Commemoration of the 500th Anniversary of His Birth.* Durham: Tumstone Ventures, 1990.

Waterhouse, John W. *The Bible in Charles Wesley's Hymns.* Peterborough: Epworth, 1954.

Wesley, Charles. *The Cause and Cure of Earthquakes.* London: [Strahan], 1750.

———. *An Elegy on the Late Reverend George Whitefield, M.A.* Bristol: Pine, 1771.

———. *An Epistle to the Reverend Mr George Whitefield.* London: J. & W. Oliver, 1771.

———. *An Epistle to the Reverend Mr John Wesley.* London: [Strahan] for J. Robinson, 1755.

———. *Funeral Hymns.* [London: Strahan, 1746].

[Charles Wesley]. *Funeral Hymns.* London: [Strahan], 1759.

———. *Gloria Patri &c., or Hymns on the Trinity.* London: Strahan, 1746.

———. *Hymns and Sacred Poems.* 2 vols. Bristol: Farley, 1749.

———. *Hymns for Ascension-Day.* Bristol: Farley, 1746.

———. *Hymns for Children.* Bristol: Farley, 1763.

———. *Hymns for Our Lord's Resurrection.* London: Strahan, 1746.

———. *Hymns for the Nation in 1782.* [np], 1781.

———. *Hymns for the National Fast, Feb. 8, 1782*. London: Paramore, [1782].

———. *Hymns for New Year's Day, 1750*. Bristol: Farley, [1749].

———. *Hymns for the Year 1756*. Bristol: Farley, 1756.

———. *Hymns for the Use of Families*. Bristol: Pine, 1767.

———. *Hymns for the Nativity of Our Lord*. London: Strahan, 1745.

———. *Hymns for the Public Thanksgiving Day, October 9, 1746*. London: Strahan, 1746.

———. *Hymns for those that seek and those that have Redemption in the Blood of Jesus Christ*. London: Strahan, 1747.

[John and Charles Wesley]. *Hymns for Times of Trouble*. [London: Strahan, 1744].

———. *Hymns for Times of Trouble and Persecution*. London: Strahan, 1744.

———. *Hymns occasioned by the Earthquake*. London, 1750. Second edition. Bristol: Farley, 1756.

———. *Hymns of Intercession for all mankind*. Bristol: Farley, 1758.

———. *Hymns of Intercession for the Kingdom of England*. [np], 1759.

———. *Hymns of Petition and Thanksgiving for the Promise of the Father*. Bristol: Farley, 1746.

———. *Hymns on the Expected Invasion*. London: Strahan, 1759.

———. *Hymns on God's Everlasting Love*. Bristol: Farley, 1741.

———. *Hymns on God's Everlasting Love*, 2nd series. London: Strahan, [1742].

[Charles Wesley?] *Hymns on the Great Festivals*. London: for M. Cooper, 1746.

———. *Hymns on the Trinity*. Bristol: Pine, 1767. A facsimile reprint of the first edition. Madison, NJ: Charles Wesley Society, 1998.

———. *Hymns to be used on the Thanksgiving-Day, Nov. 29, 1759*. London: Strahan, 1759.

———. *Short Hymns on Select Passages of the Holy Scriptures*. 2 vols. Bristol: Farley, 1762.

Wesley, John. *Select Hymns with Tunes Annext*. London, 1761.

[John Wesley, editor]. *A Collection of Psalms and Hymns*. Charlestown: Timothy, 1737.

[John Wesley, editor]. *A Collection of Psalms and Hymns*. London: [Bowyer for Hutton], 1738.

John Wesley, [editor]. *A Collection of Psalms and Hymns*. London: Strahan, 1741.

John Wesley, [editor]. *A Collection of Psalms and Hymns*. 2nd edition, enlarged. London: Strahan, 1743.

Wesley, John, and Charles Wesley. *A Short View of the Difference between the Moravian Brethren, Lately in England; And the Reverend Mr. John and Charles Wesley*. London: Strahan, 1745.

———. *Hymns and Sacred Poems*. London: Strahan, 1739.

———. *Hymns and Sacred Poems*. Bristol: Farley, 1742.

———. *Hymns on the Lord's Supper*. Bristol: Farley, 1745. A facsimile reprint of the first edition. Madison, NJ: Charles Wesley Society, 1995.

Wesley, Samuel. *An Epistle to a Friend concerning Poetry*. London: Charles Harper, 1700.

Wesley, Samuel. *Elegies on the Queen and Archbishop by Samuel Wesley*. London: Benjamin Motte, 1695.

———. *The Life of our Blessed Lord & Saviour Jesus Christ an Heroic Poem dedicated to Her Most Sacred Majesty: in ten books / attempted by Samuel Wesley*. London: Harper & Motte, 1693.

———. *Maggots: or, Poems on Several Subjects, Never Before Handled by a Scholar*. London: John Dunton, 1685

Bibliography

Wesley, Samuel [the Younger]. *Poems on Several Occasions.* London: Say, 1736.

Whitefield, George. *A Collection of Hymns for Social Worship.* London: Strahan, 1753.

Wren, Brian. *Praying Twice.* Louisville: Westminster John Knox, 2000.

Yeats, W. B. *The Autobiography of W. B. Yeats.* New York: Macmillan, 1953.

Young, Carlton R. *Companion to The United Methodist Hymnal.* Nashville: Abingdon, 1993.

Yrigoyen, Charles, Jr., editor. *T. & T. Clark Companion to Methodism.* New York: T. & T. Clark, 2010.

Index of Biblical References

Index of Names

Index of Names

Index of First Lines and Titles
of Poems in the Poetical Section[1]

1. First lines and titles are followed by page numbers. Poems marked with an asterisk
are not original first lines of poems but are first lines of known hymns.

Introduction to the Scriptural Index
to the Poetry of Charles Wesley

Charles Wesley's poetry is filled with the language of Holy Scripture, its metaphors, similes, phrases, and figures of speech. The Bible was the primary source of his lyrical inspiration. In his manuscripts and publications it was often his practice to cite a verse or passage of Scripture and then write his poetical response to it. The index provided here includes *only* specific passages of Scripture cited by Wesley at the beginning of poetical texts. Occasionally he included the words of the text or indicates the biblical content by thematic title without the scriptural reference, or he may note only part of the reference. Any such omissions have been enclosed in brackets in the index. For example, in *Hymns and Sacred Poems* (1742), on page 97, Wesley published a poem titled "The Woman of Canaan" but without the scriptural reference. It is based on the story found in the Gospel of Matthew, chapter 15:22 and following. Therefore, the index citation reads as follows: [15:22f.] HSP 1742, 96. The year of publication 1742, is followed by the page number.

Wesley often wrote more than one poem on the same passage of Scripture; therefore, it is not unusual to find duplications of verses of Scripture. For example, there are different poems based on Psalm 51:10 in *Hymns and Sacred Poems* (1742) and *Short Hymns on Select Passages of the Holy Scriptures* (1762); hence, 51:10 is repeated in the list of scriptural references with the appropriate source citations.

Hundreds of poems based on Holy Scripture were left in manuscript form at Wesley's death and these were published primarily in volume two of the series of three volumes *The Unpublished Poetry of Charles Wesley* (1988, 1990, 1992). These poems are cited by page number in the manuscript and in the volume(s) just mentioned. Some poems appeared for the first time in the *Arminian Magazine* and these are duly cited.

Introduction to the Scriptural Index to the Poetry of Charles Wesley

The index does not address biblical quotations and allusions within Wesley's poetry, but includes over 2,700 biblical references on which he wrote specific poems.

Abbreviations

1. Published Sources[1]

AM = *Arminian Magazine*

CPH 1741 = *Collection of Psalms and Hymns* (1741)

CPH 1743 = *Collection of Psalms and Hymns*, 2nd ed. (1743)

HEI = *Hymns on the Expected Invasion, 1759.* [1759]

HFF = *Hymns for the Use of Families* (1767)

HFN = *Hymns for the Nation in 1782* [1781]

HFY = *Hymns for the Year 1756* (1756)

HGEL 1741 = *Hymns on God's Everlasting Love* (1741)

HLE 1756 = *Hymns on the Lisbon Earthquake 1756*[2]

HNF 1782 = *Hymns for the National Fast, Feb. 8, 1782* [1782]

HOT 1767 = *Hymns on the Trinity* (1767)

HSP 1739 = *Hymns and Sacred Poems* (1739)

HSP 1740 = *Hymns and Sacred Poems* (1740)

HSP 1742 = *Hymns and Sacred Poems* (1742)

HSP 1749 = *Hymns and Sacred Poems* (1749)

HTTP = *Hymns for Times of Trouble and Persecution* (1744, 2nd ed. 1745)

MSP = *Collection of Moral and Sacred Poems* (1744)

PFD = *Preparation for Death, in Several Hymns* (1772)

Poet. Works = George Osborn. *The Poetical Works of John and Charles Wesley.* 13 vols. (London: 1868–72).

RH = *Hymns for those that seek and those that have Redemption in the Blood of Jesus Christ* (1747)

SH = *Short Hymns on Select Passages of the Holy Scriptures* (1762)

SV = *A Short View of the Difference between the Moravian Brethren, lately in England, and the Rev. Mr. John and Charles Wesley* (1745)

UP = S T Kimbrough, Jr., and Oliver A. Beckerlegge. *The Unpublished Poetry of Charles Wesley.* 3 vols. (1988, 1990, 1992)

WH = *Whitsunday Hymns* (1746) (subtitle); original full title is *Hymns of Petition and Thanksgiving for the Promise of Father*

1. All of the published sources of Charles Wesley may be accessed via the website of the Center for Studies in the Wesleyan Tradition of The Divinity School of Duke University: http://divinity.duke.edu/initiatives-centers/cswt/research-resources/wesley-studies-resources. The abbreviations used in this index have been shortened and put in block script due to the limited space of two columns.

2. [Charles Wesley.] *Hymns occasioned by the Earthquake, March 8, 1750. Pt. I: To which are added An Hymn upon the Pouring Out of the Seventh Vial, Rev. xvi, xvii, etc. Occasioned by the Destruction of Lisbon.* 2nd Bristol: Farley, 1756.

2. <u>Manuscript Sources</u>[3]   Accession numbers of the John
                                        Rylands Library, Manchester, UK

DDCW 6	DDCW 6
DDCW 7	DDCW 7
MSACTS = *Manuscript Acts*	MA 1977/555
MSCH = *Manuscript Cheshunt*	Westminster College, Cambridge
MSCL = *Manuscript Clarke*	MA 1977/561
MS CW III(a)	MA 1977/594
MS CW 1(q)	MA 1977/583/32
MSE = *Manuscript Epistles*	MA 1977/557
MSJN = *Manuscript John*	MA 1977/573
MSLK = *Manuscript Luke*	MA 1977/575
MSMK = *Manuscript Mark*	MA 1977/574
MSMT = *Manuscript Matthew*	MA 1977/577
MSMH = *Manuscript Miscellaneous Hymns*	MA 1977/556
MSPr = *MS Preachers*	MA 1977/583/32, #10
MSPAT = *Manuscript Patriotism*	MA 1977/559
MSPSS = *Manuscript Psalms*	MA 1977/553
MSR = *Manuscript Richmond*	MA 1977/551
MSSH = *Manuscript Scriptural Hymns*	MA 1977/576
MSSHD = *Manuscript Shorthand*	MA 1977/565

Selected Bibliography of Charles Wesley's Poetry in which are found poems based on specific passages of Holy Scripture, arranged chronologically by year of publication

John and Charles Wesley. *Hymns and Sacred Poems.* London: Strahan, 1739.

John and Charles Wesley. *Hymns and Sacred Poems.* London: Strahan, 1740.

[Charles Wesley.] *Hymns on God's Everlasting Love; To Which is Added the Cry of a Reprobate and the Horrible Decree.* Bristol: Farley, 1741.

John Wesley. *Collection of Psalms and Hymns.* London: Strahan, 1741; 2nd enlarged
    Edition, London: Strahan, 1743.

John and Charles Wesley. *Hymns and Sacred Poems.* Bristol: Farley, 1742.

3. See Frank Baker. *Representative Verse of Charles Wesley.* (Nashville: Abingdon, 1962), 387–94, for a description of the manuscript sources of Charles Wesley's poetry.

Introduction to the Scriptural Index to the Poetry of Charles Wesley

[John & Charles Wesley.] *Hymns for Times of Trouble.* [London: Strahan, 1744].

John Wesley. *Collection of Moral and Sacred Poems.* 3 vols. Bristol: Farley, 1744.

[John & Charles Wesley.] *Hymns for Times of Trouble and Persecution.* [London: Strahan, 1744]; 2nd edition Bristol: Farley, 1745. [adds "Hymns for 1745"]

[John and Charles Wesley.] *A Short View of the Difference between the Moravian Brethren, lately in England, and the Rev. Mr. John and Charles Wesley.* London: Strahan, 1745.

John and Charles Wesley. *Hymns of Petition and Thanksgiving for the Promise of Father.* Bristol: Farley, 1746.

[Charles Wesley.] *Hymns for those that seek and those that have Redemption in the Blood of Jesus Christ.* London: Strahan, 1747.

Charles Wesley. *Hymns and Sacred Poems.* 2 vols. Bristol: Farley, 1749.

[Charles Wesley.] *Hymns occasioned by the Earthquake, March 8, 1750, Pt. I; To which are added An Hymn upon the Pouring Out of the Seventh Vial, Rev. xvi, xvii, etc., Occasioned by the Destruction of Lisbon.* 2nd Bristol: Farley, 1756.

[Charles Wesley.] *Hymns for the Year 1756; Particularly for the Fast-Day, February 6.* Bristol: Farley, 1756.

[Charles Wesley.] *Hymns on the Expected Invasion, 1759.* [London: Strahan, 1759.] [Bristol: Farley, 1759.]

Charles Wesley. *Short Hymns on Select Passages of the Holy Scriptures.* 2 vols. Bristol: Farley, 1762.

Charles Wesley. *Hymns for the Use of Families.* Bristol: Pine, 1767.

[Charles Wesley.] *Hymns on the Trinity.* Bristol: Pine, 1767.

[Charles Wesley.] *Preparation for Death, in Several Hymns.* London, 1772.

[Charles Wesley.] *Hymns for the National Fast, Feb. 8, 1782.* London: Paramore, [1782].

[Charles Wesley.] *Hymns for the Nation in 1782.* [np, 1781.] (Hymns 1–9)
[Charles Wesley.] *Hymns for the Nation in 1782. Part II.* [np, 1781.] (Hymns 10–17)

S T Kimbrough, Jr., and Oliver A. Beckerlegge, *The Unpublished Poetry of Charles Wesley.* 3 vols. Nashville: Abingdon, 1988, 1990, 1992.

Sciptural Index to the Poetry of Charles Wesley

19:16	SH 1:21	3:8	SH 1:35
19:17	SH 1:22	3:14	SH 1:36
19:22	SH 1:22	4:10	SH 1:36
19:24	SH 1:22	4:11	SH 1:36
20:6	SH 1:23	5:17	SH 1:37
20:11	SH 1:23	5:23	SH 1:37
20:13	HOT 1767, 60	6:6	SH 1:37
22:2	SH 1:23	6:7	SH 1:38
22:9–10	SH 1:24	7:12	SH 1:38
22:10	SH 1:24	7:20	SH 1:38
22:12	SH 1:24	8:15	SH 1:39
22:16–18	SH 1:24	8:19	SH 1:39
22:18	SH 1:25	8:25	SH 1:39
22:20	SH 1:25	9:12	SH 1:39
23:20	SH 1:25	9:14	SH 1:40
25:8	SH 1:25	9:17	SH 1:40
27:15	SH 1:26	10:3	SH 1:40
27:27	SH 1:26	10:17	SH 1:40, 41
27:36	SH 1:26	10:23	SH 1:41
27:41	SH 1:26	12:7	SH 1:41
28:12–13	SH 1:27, 28	12:13	SH 1:42
28:17	SH 1:29	13:17	SH 1:42
30:1	SH 1:29	13:21	SH 1:42
[32]	HSP 1742, 115	13:22	SH 1:43
32:26	AM 1793, 54; UP 2:439	14:13	SH 1:43
35:6	HOT 1767, 60	14:15	SH 1:44
42:21	SH 1:29	14:19	SH 1:44
46:4	SH 1:30	14:20	SH 1:44, 45
47:29	SH 1:30	14:24–25	SH 1:45
48:16	SH 1:30, 31	15:1	SH 1:45
49:4	SH 1:31	15:2	SH 1:46
49:10	SH 1:31, 32	15:4	SH 1:46
49:18	SH 1:32	15:18	SH 1:46
49:19	SH 1:32	15:25	SH 1:46
49:33	SH 1:33	15:26	SH 1:47
		16:15	SH 1:47
		16:18	SH 1:47
Exodus		16:20	SH 1:47
		16:27	SH 1:48
1:10	SH 1:34	17:3	SH 1:48
1:13	SH 1:34	17:6	SH 1:49
3:2	SH 1:35	17:7	SH 1:48
3:6	SH 1:35	17:10	SH 1:49
3:7–8	SH 1:35		

Exodus (*continued*)

17:11	SH 1:49
17:12–13	SH 1:50
17:14	SH 1:50
19:4	SH 1:50
20:1	SH 1:50
20:24	SH 1:51
23:22	SH 1:51
32:10	SH 1:51
32:34	SH 1:52
33:12–34:9	HSP 1749, 1:286
33:18	SH 1:52
33:19	AM 1793, 54; UP 2:440
33:22	AM 1793, 56; UP 2:440
34:5	SH 1:52
34:6	SH 1:52, 53
34:7	SH 1:54
34:28	SH 1:54
34:29	SH 1: 55
34:33	SH 1: 55
34:34	SH 1: 55

Leviticus

2:11	SH 1:56
2:13	SH 1:56
6:13	SH 1:57
8:8	SH 1:57, 58
8:35	SH 1:58
9:22	SH 1:59
9:24	SH 1:59
10:2	SH 1:60
10:3	SH 1:60
11:45	SH 1:60
17:11	SH 1:60
26:11	SH 1:61
26:12	SH 1:61
26:13	SH 1:61
26:41–42	SH 1:61

Numbers

1:51	SH 1:62

6:24	SH 1:62
6:25	SH 1:62
6:24f.	HOT 1767, 66
6:26	SH 1:63
9:16	SH 1:63
9:18	SH 1:64
9:23	SH 1:64, 65
11:4	SH 1:66
11:15	SH 1:66
11:24	SH 1:66
11:23	SH 1:66
11:27	SH 1:67
11:28	SH 1:67
11:29	SH 1:68
11:33	SH 1:68
12:8	SH 1:69
13:28	SH 1:69
13:30	SH 1:70
13:31	SH 1:71
13:31–33	SH 1:70
14:2	SH 1:71
14:4	SH 1:71
14:8	SH 1:72
14:9	SH 1:72
14:10	SH 1:73
14:11	SH 1:73
14:17	SH 1:73
14:19	SH 1:74
14:20	SH 1:74
14:21	SH 1:74
14:24	SH 1:74, 75
14:29	SH 1:75
14:34	SH 1:75
14:44	SH 1:76
16:10	SH 1:76
16:21	SH 1:76
16:26	SH 1:76
16:41	SH 1:76
16:48	SH 1:77
20:28	SH 1:77
21:5	SH 1:77
21:9	SH 1:78
22:18	SH 1:78
23:8	SH 1:78

Joshua

1:2	SH 1:115
1:3	SH 1:115
1:5	SH 1:115
1:7	SH 1:115
1:9	SH 1:116
5:14	SH 1:116
6:15	SH 1:116
6:20	SH 1:117
7:9	SH 1:117
7:10	SH 1:118
7:11	SH 1:118
7:13	SH 1:118
7:18	SH 1:118
7:21	SH 1:118
9:15	SH 1:119
10:6	SH 1:119
10:12	SH 1:119
[10:12]	HSP 1749, 2:153
10:24	SH 1:120
10:26	SH 1:120
10:40	SH 1:120
11:18	SH 1:121
11:21	SH 1:121
11:23	SH 1:121
14:10	SH 1:122
18:3	SH 1:122
20:4	SH 1:122
20:7	SH 1:123[1]
20:8	SH 1:123, 124
23:10	SH 1:124
23:14	SH 1:124, 125
24:15	SH 1:125

Judges

2:23	SH 1:126
3:20	SH 1:126
5:20	SH 1:127

1. Note the printing error: this page is wrongly numbered 223 in the 1762 edition.

5:21	SH 1:127
5:31	SH 1:127
6:14	SH 1:128
6:31	SH 1:128
7:2	SH 1:129
7:18	SH 1:129
8:4	SH 1:129
10:13	SH 1:130
10:15	SH 1:130
10:16	SH 1:130
11:31	SH 1:131
11:39	SH 1:131
13:8	SH 1:131
13:12	SH 1:131
13:23	SH 1:132
15:14	SH 1:132
15:14	HOT 1767, 56
16:3	SH 1:132
16:16–17	SH 1:133
16:19	SH 1:133
16:20	SH 1:133
16:20	HOT 1767, 56
16:21	SH 1:134
16:22	SH 1:134
16:28	SH 1:135
16:29–30	SH 1:135
[16:30]	HSP 1742, 57

Ruth

1:5–6	SH 1:136
1:6	SH 1:136
1:15	SH 1:137
1:16	SH 1:137
1:17	SH 1:138
1:20	SH 1:138
1:21	SH 1:138
2:3	SH 1:139
2:4	SH 1:139
2:12	SH 1:140
2:19	SH 1:140
3:4	SH 1:140
3:9	SH 1:141
4:9–10	SH 1:141

Job (*continued*)

Psalm

2. Note the printing error: this page is wrongly numbered 239 in the 1762 edition.

3. Note the printing error: the verse reference is wrongly printed as "lviii. 12" in the 1762 edition.

4. Note the printing error: the verse reference is wrongly printed as "Ps. lxi.14" in the 1762 edition.

Psalm (*continued*)

89:46	SH 1:268
90:12	SH 1:269
91:15	SH 1:269
97:1	SH 1:269
97:10	SH 1:269
100:1	SH 1:270
100:3	HOT 1767, 79
101:2	SH 1:270
101:6	SH 1:270
102:15	SH 1:270
102:23	SH 1:271
103:1	HSP 1742, 154
103:3	SH 1:271
103:10	SH 1:271
106:4	SH 1:272
110:1	HSP 1742, 89
111:5	SH 1:272
113	MSPSS, 185; UP 2:449
114	CPH 1743, 109
116:8	SH 1:272
116:11–12	SH 1:272
118	CPH 1743, 81
118:13	SH 1:273
118:18	SH 1:273
119:8	SH 1:273
119:9	SH 1:274
119:32	SH 1:274
119:71	SH 1:275
119:81	SH 1:275
119:96	SH 1:275
119:121	SH 1:276
[119:126]	HSP 1742, 268
119:176	SH 1:276
120	CPH 1743, 85
121	CPH 1743, 86
121:7	SH 1:276
122	CPH 1743, 87
122:6	SH 1:276, 277
122:7	SH 1:277
122:8	SH 1:277
123	CPH 1743, 88
124	CPH 1743, 89

125	CPH 1743, 90
126	CPH 1743, 91
126:5	SH 1:277
127	CPH 1743, 92
127:1	SH 1:278
128	CPH 1743, 93
129	CPH 1743, 94
129:6	SH 1:278
130[5]	HSP 1740, 62
130	CPH 1741, 52[6]
130:3	SH 1:278
130:8	SH 1:279
131	CPH 1743, 95
132	CPH 1743, 96
133	CPH 1743, 97; HSP 1742, 174
134	CPH 1743, 99
136:1	SH 1:279
137	CPH 1743, 21
137:7	SH 1:279
138:8	SH 1:280
139:7	HOT 1767, 52
139:7–8	HOT 1767, 78
141:4	MS CW III(a), #2[7]
141:4	SH 1:280
141:9	SH 1:280
143:6	HSP 1740, 60
143:8	SH 1:280
143:10	SH 1:281
144:9	SH 1:281
144:10	SH 1:281
144:15	SH 1:282
145:9	SH 1:282
146:1	SH 1:282
146:7	SH 1:282

5. This poetical paraphrase of Psalm 130 was omitted from the fourth edition (1743) and thereafter, because it was moved to CPH 1743, 20.

6. Whether this poem is by Charles Wesley remains an open question.

7. The access number of the John Rylands Library for this manuscript reference is MA 1977/594/3.

Isaiah (*continued*)

5:4	SH 1:308
6	MSP 1744, 233
6:3	HOT 1767, 69
6:5	HOT 1767, 4
6:5[-8]	HOT 1767, 54
6:8	SH 1:308
6:8	HOT 1767, 60
6:13	SH 1:309
7:9	SH 1:309
8:13-14	HOT 1767, 3
8:17	SH 1:310
8:20	SH 1:310
9:2f.	MSP 1744, 238
9:2	SH 1:311
9:3	SH 1:311
9:4	SH 1:311
9:5	SH 1:312
9:6	SH 1:312
9:6	HOT 1767, 16
9:6-7	SH 1:312
9:7	SH 1:313
10:5	SH 1:314
10:24f.	MSP 1744, 241
11	MSP 1744, 243
11:1	SH 1:314
11:2-3	SH 1:314
11:3	SH 1:314
11:4	SH 1:315
11:5	SH 1:315
11:6-7	SH 1:316
11:8	SH 1:317
11:9	SH 1:317
11:10	SH 1:317
11:11-12	SH 1:318
11:13	SH 1:319
12	HSP 1742, 189
14 (Part 1)[8]	MSP 1744, 247
14 (Part 2)	MSP 1744, 252
14:5	SH 1:319

14:23	HOT 1767, 34
24:14-15	SH 1:319
24:23	SH 1:320
25	MSP 1744, 255
26 (Parts 1, 2, 3)	HSP 1749, 1:3, 6, 8
26:3	SH 1:321
26:9	SH 1:321
26:10	SH 1:321
26:13-14	HSP 1742, 191
26:16	SH 1:322
26:20-21	HTTP 1744, (2nd ed. 1745), 56
27:1-6f.	HSP 1749 1:11
27:3	SH 1:322
28:9	SH 1:322
28:12	SH 1:323
28:16	HSP 1742, 271
29:11	SH 1:324
30:18	SH 1:324, 325
30:19-21	SH 1:325
30:22	SH 1:326
30:25	SH 1:326
30:26	SH 1:327
31:5	SH 1:327
31:9	SH 1:328
32:2	SH 1:328, 329
32:2	HSP 1742, 145
32:11	SH 1:329
32:13-15	SH 1:329
32:16-17	SH 1:330
33:2	SH 1:331
33:5-6	SH 1:331
33:15-17	SH 1:332
33:17	SH 1:333
33:24	SH 1:333
34:16	HOT 1767, 66
35	HSP 1740, 107
35:4	SH 1:333
38:14	SH 1:334
38:17-18	HSP 1742, 155
38:20	SH 1:334
40	HSP 1742, 1
[40:8]	HSP 1742, 232

8. Part I of this poem was published separately as the *Fourteenth Chapter of Isaiah* (London: Strahan, 1742).

40:10	HOT 1767, 38	48:8	SH 1:349
40:13	HOT 1767, 72	48:9	SH 1:349
40:31	SH 1:335	48:10	SH 1:349
[40:31]	HSP 1742, 225	48:11	SH 1:350
41:10	SH 1:335	48:20	SH 1:350
41:11	SH 1:336	48:16	HOT 1767, 65
41:13–14	SH 1:336	48:17	HOT 1767, 84
41:15–16	SH 1:337	48:21	SH 1:351
41:17	SH 1:337	49:6	SH 1:351
41:18–19	SH 1:338	49:8	SH 1:352
41:20	SH 1:338	49:9–10	SH 1:353
42:1	SH 1:339	49:11	SH 1:353
42:2	SH 1:339	49:12	SH 1:354
42:3	SH 1:340	49:13	SH 1:354
42:4	SH 1:340	49:15	SH 1:355
42:6–7	SH 1:341	49:16	SH 1:355
42:10	SH 1:342	49:18	SH 1:355
42:11–12	SH 1:342	49:19	SH 1:356
42:16	SH 1:342	49:20	SH 1:356
42:24–25	MSPAT, 3–4, UP 1:59	49:22	SH 1:357
43:1, 2, 3	HSP 1739, 153	49:23	SH 1:357, 358
43:11	HOT 1767, 5	49:24–26	SH 1:359
43:13	SH 1:343	50:2	SH 1:359, 360
43:24–25	SH 1:343	50:10	SH 1:360
43:25	SH 1:344	51 (Parts 1, 2,[10] 3, 4)	HSP 1749, 1:18,
43:26	SH 1:345		20, 22, 23
44	HSP 1740, 200	51:9	HSP 1739, 222
44 (Parts 1, 2)	HSP 1749, 1:13, 15	51:12	SH 1:361
44:6	HOT 1767, 5	52	HSP 1742, 111
44:24[9]	HOT 1767, 71	52:3	SH 1:362
45:13	SH 1:345	52:14	SH 1:362
45:15	SH 1:346	52:15	SH 1:363
45:17	SH 1:346	53	HSP 1739, 87
45:19	SH 1:347	53:1–3	HSP 1739, 153
45:21–22	SH 1:347	53:5	SH 1:363
45:22	HSP 1740, 165	54:1–2	SH 1:364
45:23	HOT 1767, 34	54:3	SH 1:364
45:23–25	SH 1:348	54:4	SH 1:365
46:4	SH 1:349	54:5	SH 1:365
46:4	PFD 1772, 10	54:5	HOT 1767, 9
46:4	AM 1781, 511	54:6–8	SH 1:366

9. Note the misprint in the original "xliv.28."

10. Part 2 was published in HSP 1739, 222.

Isaiah (*continued*)

Jeremiah

11. This poem is printed also at the conclusion of John Wesley's extract of William Law's *A Serious Answer to Dr. Trapp's Four Sermons* (Cork: Harrison, 1748), 61–63.

12. Note the printing error: chapter 60 of Isaiah is cited in the 1762 edition for this reference, but it should be chapter 66.

3:16	SH 2:8	24:7	SH 2:25
3:17	SH 2:8	29:13	SH 2:25
3:18	SH 2:9	30:7	SH 2:25
3:19	SH 2:9, 10	30:8	SH 2:26
3:22	SH 2:10	30:9	SH 2:26
3:23	SH 2:10	30:10	SH 2:27
4, Parts 1, 2, 3, 4, 5, 6	HFY 1756, 11, 12,	30:11	SH 2:27
	13, 14, 15, 16	30:17	SH 2:28
4:1	SH 2:11	30:21	SH 2:28
4:14	SH 2:11	31:3	SH 2:28
[4:14]	DDCW 6/77; UP 2:455[13]	31:11	SH 2:29
6:8	SH 2:11	31:12	SH 2:29
6:14	SH 2:12	31:14	SH 2:30
6:16	SH 2:13	31:17	SH 2:30
7:4	SH 2:13	31:17	MSSH, 118; UP 2:456
8:9	SH 2:14	31:18	SH 2:30, 31
8:20	SH 2:14	31:19	SH 2:31
8:22	SH 2:15	31:20	SH 2:31
9:1	SH 2:15	31:22	SH 2:32
9:23	SH 2:16	31:33	SH 2:32
10:24	SH 2:17	31:34	SH 2:33
10:25	SH 2:17	32:39	SH 2:33
13:16	SH 2:17	32:40	SH 2:34
13:23	SH 2:18	33:6	SH 2:34
13:27	SH 2:18, 19	33:16	SH 2:35
14:8–9	SH 2:19	44:4	SH 2:35
15:6	SH 2:20	47:6–7	HEI 1759, 7
15:18	SH 2:20	49:11	SH 2:36
17:9	HSP 1742, 39	50:5	SH 2:36
17:9	SH 2:21, 22	50:20	SH 2:37
17:9–10	SH 2:21	50:33–34	SH 2:37
17:14	SH 2:23		
23:5	SH 2:23		
23:6	SH 2:23	**Lamentations**	
23:6	HOT 1767, 17, 72	1:12	SH 2:39
23:24	HOT 1767, 78	3:22	SH 2:40
23:28	SH 2:24	3:23	SH 2:40
23:29	SH 2:24	3:24	SH 2:40
		3:25	SH 2:41

13. The four lines of the third stanza of this poem based on Jeremiah 4:14 are transcribed from shorthand; however, the remaining four lines of the stanza have not been found.

3:26	SH 2:41
3:27–29	SH 2:41
3:31	SH 2:42
3:32	SH 2:42

Lamentations (*continued*)

3:33	SH 2:42
3:39	SH 2:43
5:16	SH 2:43

Ezekiel

8:1, 3	HOT 1767, 50, 72
9, Parts 1, 2, 3	HFY 1756, 7, 9, 10
16:62–63	SH 2:44
18:31	SH 2:45
18:31	HGEL 1742, 43
34:23	SH 2:46
34:25	SH 2:46
34:26	SH 2:47
34:27	SH 2:47
34:28	SH 2:48
34:29–30	SH 2:48
36:23f.[14]	HSP 1742, 261
36:26	SH 2:49[15]
36:36	SH 2:49
36:37	SH 2:50
37:1–2	SH 2:50
37:3–4	SH 2:51
37:4–5	SH 2:51
37:7–8	SH 2:52
37:9–10	SH 2:52
37:11–12	SH 2:53
37:13–14	SH 2:53
37:17	SH 2:54
37:21–22	SH 2:54
37:23	SH 2:55
37:24	SH 2:55
37:25	SH 2:56

14. The poem titled "Pleading the Promise of Sanctification. Ezek[iel] xxxvi. 23, &c." was first published at the conclusion of John Wesley's *Christian Perfection, a Sermon* (London: Strahan, 1741), 44–48.

15. Note the printing error: this page is incorrectly numbered 94 in the 1762 edition.

37:26	SH 2:56
37:27	SH 2:56
37:28	SH 2:57
39:29	SH 2:57

Daniel

2:35	SH 2:58
2:44	SH 2:58
[3]	HSP 1742, 213
3:16	SH 2:59
3:17	SH 2:59
3:18	SH 2:60
3:25	SH 2:60
4:26	HOT 1767, 64
4:30	SH 2:60
4:37	SH 2:61
5:17	SH 2:61
5:18, 20	HOT 1767, 64
5:25	SH 2:61
[6]	HSP 1742, 211
6:5	SH 2:62
6:10	SH 2:62
6:20	SH 2:63
7:18	SH 2:63
9	HTTP 1744, 3
9:24	SH 2:64
12:13	SH 2:64

Hosea

1:7	HOT 1767, 8
2:13	SH 2:67
2:14	SH 2:65, 66
2:15	SH 2:65, 66
4:17	SH 2:68
5:15	SH 2:68
6:1	SH 2:69
6:3	SH 2:69
6:4	SH 2:69
9:15	SH 2:69
10:2	SH 2:70
11:8	SH 2:70

16. Note the printing error: this verse is incorrectly numbered 23 in the 1762 edition.

Habakkuk (*continued*)

2:3	SH 2:92
2:4	SH 2:92
[2:4]	HSP 1740, 161
2:14	SH 2:92
3:2	SH 2:92, 93
3:17–19	HSP 1742, 138
3:19	SH 2:93

Zephaniah

1:12f.	HTTP 1745, 52 (2nd ed. 1744)
2:1–2	HTTP 1745, 52 (2nd ed. 1744)
2:3	SH 2:94
2:11	SH 2:94
3:8	SH 2:95
3:9	SH 2:95
3:10	SH 2:96
3:11–12	SH 2:96
3:13	SH 2:96
3:14–15	SH 2:97
3:17	SH 2:97
3:18	SH 2:98
3:19	SH 2:98
3:20	SH 2:98

Haggai

1:7	SH 2:99
2:4	SH 2:99
2:7	SH 2:100
2:19	SH 2:100
2:22	SH 2:100

Zechariah

1:3	SH 2:101
2:5	SH 2:101
2:8	SH 2:102
2:10	SH 2:102
2:12–13	SH 2:102
3:2	SH 2:102
3:4	SH 2:103

3:8	SH 2:103
4:6	SH 2:103
4:7f.	HSP 1742, 234, 236
4:7	SH 2:104
4:9	SH 2:104
4:10	SH 2:105, 106
6:12	SH 2:106
6:13	SH 2:106, 107
9:9	SH 2:108
9:10	SH 2:108
9:11	SH 2:109
9:12	SH 2:109
9:17	SH 2:109
12:4	HOT 1767, 36
12:7	SH 2:110
12:8	SH 2:110
12:10	SH 2:110, 111
12:10	HSP 1740, 34[17]
13:1	SH 2:112
13:6	SH 2:112
13:7	SH 2:112, 113
13:8	SH 2:113
13:9	SH 2:113, 114
14:5	SH 2:115
14:9	SH 2:115
14:21	SH 2:116

Malachi

1:6	HOT 1767, 62
1:8, 13	SH 2:116
1:11	SH 2:117
3:1	HOT 1767, 8
3:1	SH 2:117, 118
3:2	SH 2:118
3:3	SH 2:118, 119
3:4	SH 2:119
3:6	SH 2:119
3:16	SH 2:120
3:17	SH 2:120, 121

17. This poem is an English translation "from the German" and is more likely by John Wesley.

3:18	SH 2:121	5:3	HSP 1739, 97
4:1	SH 2:121	5:3–12	HSP 1749, 1:35
4:1	HNF 1782, 11	5:3–4, 6	HSP 1740, 65
4:2	SH 2:122	[5:4]	HSP 1740, 158
4:4	SH 2:122	5:4	SH 2:129
4:5	SH 2:122, 123	5:5	SH 2:130
4:6	SH 2:123	5:6	SH 2:130
		5:7	SH 2:130
		5:8	SH 2:130
	∽	5:9	SH 2:131
		5:10	SH 2:131

NEW TESTAMENT

Matthew

		5:11	SH 2:131
		5:12	SH 2:131
		5:13	SH 2:132
1:1	SH 2:125	5:14	SH 2:132, 133
[1:21]	HSP 1740, 68	5:15	SH 2:133
1:21	MSMT, 4; UP 2:17	5:16	SH 2:133
1:21	SH 2:126	5:17	SH 2:134
1:23	SH 2:126	5:18	SH 2:134
1:23	SH 2:126	5:19	SH 2:135
2:3	MSMT, 6; UP 2:17	5:20	SH 2:135
2:6	SH 2:126	5:22	SH 2:135, 136
2:13	SH 2:127	5:24	SH 2:136
3:11	HOT 1767, 7	5:26	SH 2:136
3:15	SH 2:127	5:27	SH 2:136
3:16	HOT 1767, 56	5:28	SH 2:137
3:17	SH 2:127	5:29	SH 2:137
4:1	HOT 1767, 45	5:39	SH 2:137
4:3	MSMT, 16,[18] UP 2:18	5:42	MSMT, 41; UP 2:19
4:4	SH 2:127	5:44	SH 2:138
4:7	SH 2:128	5:45	SH 2:138, 139
4:7	HOT 1767, 48	5:48	SH 2:139
4:10	MSMT, 22; UP 2:18	6:1	SH 2:140
4:10	SH 2:128	6:3	SH 2:140
4:11	SH 2:129	6:3	MSMT, 45; UP 2:20
4:17	SH 2:129	6:5	SH 2:140
4:16	MSMT, 23; UP 2:19	6:6	SV 1745, 18; also RH 1747, 48
4:19	SH 2:129	6:6	SH 2:141
5:3	SH 2:129	6:8	SH 2:141
		6:9	SH 2:141
		[6:10]	HSP 1742, 230
		6:10	SH 2:142
		6:11	SH 2:142

18. In MSMT there is another poem on this text numbered "I" that appears in *Poet. Works* 10:151.

Matthew (*continued*)

6:12	SH 2:142
6:13	SH 2:142, 143
6:18	SH 2:143
6:19	SH 2:143
6:20	SH 2:144
6:22	SH 2:144
6:24	SH 2:144
6:33	SH 2:145
6:33[19]	HSP 1749, 2:241
6:34	SH 2:145
7:1	SH 2:146
7:5	SH 2:146
7:6	SH 2:146
7:7	SH 2:147
7:7	SV 1745, 17; also HSP 1749, 1:42
7:8	SH 2:147, 148
7:11	SH 2:148
7:12	SH 2:148
7:14	SH 2:148
7:15	SH 2:149
7:16	SH 2:149
7:18	SH 2:149
7:20	SH 2:149
7:21	SH 2:150
7:25	SH 2:150
7:27	SH 2:150
8:2	HOT 1767, 23
8:2	SH 2:151
8:3	SH 2:151
8:4	SH 2:151
8:4	MSMT, 83; UP 2:20
8:7	SH 2:151
8:7	MSMT, 84; UP 2:21
8:10	SH 2:152
8:15	SH 2:152
8:20	SH 2:152
8:22	SH 2:152
8:25	SH 2:152
8:26	SH 2:153
8:27	SH 2:153

19. The chapter is misprinted "vii" in the 1762 and 1797 editions.

9:1	MSMT, 95; UP 2:21
9:2	SH 2:153
9:3	SH 2:153
9:5	MSMT, 96; UP 2:21
9:6	MSMT, 96; UP 2:22
9:11	SH 2:154
9:12	SH 2:154
9:13	SH 2:154
9:13	MSMT, 100; UP 2:22
9:15	MSMT, 101; UP 2:23
9:17	MSMT, 101–2; UP 2:23
9:28	SH 2:155
9:35	SH 2:155
9:37	SH 2:155
9:38	SH 2:155
9:38	HOT 1767, 40
10:4	MSMT, 112; UP 2:24
10:5	MSMT, 112; UP 2:25
10:8	SH 2:156
10:16	SH 2:156
10:17	SH 2:156
10:20	MSMT, 119; UP 2:25
10:21	MSMT, 119; UP 2:25
10:22	SH 2:157
10:23	HOT 1767, 24
10:25	SH 2:157
10:26	SH 2:157
10:27	SH 2:157
10:28	SH 2:158
10:30	SH 2:158
10:32	SH 2:158
10:33	SH 2:159
10:34	SH 2:159
10:34	MSMT, 123; UP 2:26
[10:39]	HSP 1742, 215
10:41	MSMT, 127; UP 2:26
10:42	SH 2:159
11:3	SH 2:160
11:4	MSMT, 129; UP 2:27
11:5	SH 2:160
11:6	SH 2:160
11:10	HOT 1767, 7
11:10	HOT 1767, 8

27:42	SH 2:195	8:23	SH 2:204
27:43	MSMT, 354; UP 2:47	8:26	MSMK, 90; UP 2:58
27:45	SH 2:195	8:30	MSMK, 91
27:46	SH 2:196, 233	8:36	SH 2:204
27:50	SH 2:196	9:10	MSMK, 98; UP 2:60
28:5	SH 2:196	9:23	SH 2:204
28:9	SH 2:196	[9:23]	HSP 1749, 2:158
28:10	SH 2:197	9:24	SH 2:205
28:18	SH 2:197	9:25	SH 2:205
28:19	SH 2:197	9:41	SH 2:205
28:19	HOT 1767, 67	9:44	SH 2:205
28:20	SH 2:197, 198	9:46	SH 2:206
		9:48	SH 2:206
		10:14	SH 2:206

Mark

		10:14	MSMK, 105; UP 2:60
1:3	MSMK, 1; UP 2:51	10:16	SH 2:207
1:8	SH 2:198	10:27	SH 2:207
1:13	SH 2:199	10:38	SH 2:207
2:9	SH 2:199	10:20	MSMK, 108; UP 2:60
2:19–20	MSMK, 18; UP 2:51	10:21	MSMK, 108; UP 2:60
2:19–20	MSMK, 19; UP 2:52	10:22	MSMK, 109; UP 2:61
2:23	MSMK, 20; UP 2:53	10:35	MSMK, 112; UP 2:61
3:5	SH 2:199	10:49	SH 2:208
3:7	MSMK, 26; UP 2:53	10:51	SH 2:208
3:8	MSMK, 27; UP 2:54	11:22–24	HSP 1742, 250
3:19	MSMK, 29; UP 2:54	11:22	SH 2:208
3:21	SH 2:200	11:24	SH 2:208, 209, 210, 211
4:24	SH 2:200	12:1	MSMK, 127; UP 2:62
4:25	SH 2:200	13:11	HOT 1767, 83
4:26–27	SH 2:200	13:21	MSMK, 145; UP 2:62
4:28	SH 2:201	13:27	MSMK, 148; UP 2:62
4:29	MSMK, 41; UP 2:55	13:31	SH 2:212
4:31–32	MSMK, 42; UP 2:55	13:37	SH 2:212, 213
4:38	SH 2:201	13:32	HOT 1767, 28
5:19	SH 2:202	14:12	MSMK, 154; UP 2:63
5:20	MSMK, 52; UP 2:56	14:13	MSMK, 155; UP 2:63
5:23–25	MSMK, 53; UP 2:56	14:21	SH 2:213
5:29	SH 2:203	14:34	MSMK, 161; UP 2:64
5:41	SH 2:203	14:35	MSMK, 162; UP 2:64
5:43	SH 2:203	14:49	MSMK, 165; UP 2:64
6:51	MSMK, 72; UP 2:57	14:50	MSMK, 165; UP 2:65
6:54–55	MSMK, 72; UP 2:57	15:13	MSMK, 172; UP 2:65
7:27	MSMK, 78; UP 2:58	15:17	MSMK, 172; UP 2:65

Luke (*continued*)

11:2, 4	HOT 1767, 45
11:3	SH 2:221
11:4	SH 2:221, 222
11:6	MSLK, 168; UP 2:127
11:7	MSLK, 168; UP 2:127
11:9	MSLK, 170; UP 2:128
11:10	MSLK, 170; UP 2:128
11:11–12	MSLK, 170; UP 2:128
11:13	SH 2:222
11:20	MSLK, 171; UP 2:129
11:20	HOT 1767, 50
11:21	MSLK, 171; UP 2:129
11:23	MSLK, 173; UP 2:130
11:24	MSLK, 173; UP 2:130
11:28	MSLK, 174; UP 2:131
11:33	MSLK, 175; UP 2:131
11:34	MSLK, 175; UP 2:132
11:35	MSLK, 176; UP 2:132
11:42	MSLK, 177; UP 2:133
11:46	MSLK, 178; UP 2:133
11:52	MSLK, 178; UP 2:133
11:53–54	MSLK, 179; UP 2:134
12:2	MSLK, 179; UP 2:134
12:4	MSLK, 180; UP 2:135
12:5	MSLK, 180; UP 2:135
12:8	MSLK, 181; UP 2:135
12:9	MSLK, 182; UP 2:136
12:12	MSLK, 182; UP 2:136
12:14	MSLK, 182; UP 2:136
12:15	MSLK, 183; UP 2:137
12:19	MSLK, 185; UP 2:138
12:19	SH 2:223
12:20	SH 2:223
12:22–23	MSLK, 186; UP 2:138
12:32	SH 2:223
12:35	MSLK, 189; UP 2:139
12:[36]	MSLK, 189; UP 2:139
12:37	MSLK, 190; UP 2:140
12:38	MSLK, 190; UP 2:140
12:40	MSLK, 190; UP 2:140
12:45	MSLK, 192; UP 2:141
12:46	MSLK, 193; UP 2:141
12:47	SH 2:224
12:48	MSLK, 193; UP 2:141
12:48	MSLK, 194; UP 2:142
12:50	HSP 1742, 136
12:50	HSP 1742, 136
12:56	SH 2:224
13:3	SH 2:224
13:5	MSLK, 197; UP 2:197
13:6	MSLK, 198; UP 2:143
13:7	MSLK, 198; UP 2:143
13:8–9	MSLK, 198; UP 2:144
13:13	MSLK, 200; UP 2:144
13:18	MSLK, 201[–19]; UP 2:145
13:21	MSLK, 202; UP 2:145
13:22	MSLK, 202; UP 2:146
13:23	MSLK, 202; UP 2:146
13:24	SH 2:225
13:25	MSLK, 204; UP 2:146
13:26	MSLK, 204; UP 2:147
13:27	MSLK, 205; UP 2:147
13:32	MSLK, 206; UP 2:148
13:35	MSLK, 208; UP 2:148
[14:7][20]	HSP 1749, 1:259
14:8	HSP 1739, 210; UP 2:149
14:9	MSLK, 367; UP 2:149
14:10	SH 2:225
14:11	SH 2:225
14:15	MSLK, 213; UP 2:149
14:16–24	RH 1747, 63
14:17	MSLK, 213; UP 2:150
14:18	MSLK, 214; UP 2:151
14:20	MSLK, 215; UP 2:151
14:21	MSLK, 216; UP 2:152
14:28	SH 2:226
14:34	MSLK, 220; UP 2:152
15:1	MSLK, 220; UP 2:152
15:2	SH 2:226
15:2	MSLK, 220; UP 2:153
15:6	MSLK, 221; UP 2:153
15:7	MSLK, 222; UP 2:153

20. The hymn in HSP 1749 based on this text was published previously in *Hymns on the Great Festivals* (1746).

15:8	MSLK, 222; UP 2:154	17:32		SH 2:229
15:10	HSP 1739, 103	17:33	MSLK, 256; UP 2:167	
15:12	MSLK, 223; UP 2:154	17:36	MSLK, 257; UP 2:168	
15:14	MSLK, 224; UP 2:155	17:37	MSLK, 257; UP 2:168	
15:17	MSLK, 226; UP 2:155	18:1	SV 1745, 20; also HSP 1749, 2:38	
[15:21]	HSP 1740, 147	18:1		SH 2:230
16:3	MSLK, 231; UP 2:156	18:[3]	HSP 1742, 202	
16:8	MSLK, 232; UP 2:156	18:9	MSLK, 261; UP 2:168	
16:9	MSLK, 232; UP 2:157	18:11–12	MSLK, 262; UP 2:169	
16:9[21]	SH 2:226	18:13		SH 2:230
16:10	MSLK, 233; UP 2:157	18:13	MSLK, 263; UP 2:169	
16:11	MSLK, 233; UP 2:158	18:14	MSLK, 264; UP 2:170	
16:14	MSLK, 235; UP 2:158	18:21	MSLK, 266; UP 2:171	
16:15	MSLK, 235; UP 2:158	18:22	MSLK, 266; UP 2:171	
16:16	MSLK, 236; UP 2:159	18:23	MSLK, 266; UP 2:171	
16:17	MSLK, 236; UP 2:159	18:24	MSLK, 266; UP 2:172	
16:21	SH 2:226	18:25	MSLK, 267; UP 2:172	
16:23	SH 2:226	18:26	MSLK, 267; UP 2:172	
16:25	MSLK, 240: UP 2:159	[18:27]	HSP 1742, 227	
16:25	MSLK, 241; UP 2:160	18:27	MSLK, 267; UP 2:173	
16:29	MSLK, 242; UP 2:160	18:28	MSLK, 268; UP 2:173	
17:4	MSLK, 245; UP 2:161	19:5		SH 2:230
17:4	SH 2:227	19:10	MSLK, 274; UP 2:173	
17:6	MSLK, 246; UP 2:161	19:11	MSLK, 275; UP 2:174	
17:7–8	SH 2:227	19:14	MSLK, 276; UP 2:174	
17:9–10	SH 2:228	19:15	MSLK, 277; UP 2:175	
17:12–13	MSLK, 248; UP 2:162	19:16		SH 2:230
17:14	MSLK, 249; UP 2:163	19:20	MSLK, 277; UP 2:175	
17:17	SH 2:229	19:24	MSLK, 278; UP 2:176	
17:18	SH 2:229	19:26	MSLK, 279; UP 2:177	
17:20	MSLK, 251; UP 2;163	19:27	MSLK, 279; UP 2:177	
17:21	MSLK, 252; UP 2:163	19:28	MSLK, 280; UP 2:178	
17:22	MSLK, 252; UP 2:164	19:36	MSLK, 281; UP 2:178	
17:23–24	MSLK, 253; UP 2:164	19:37–38	MSLK, 282; UP 2:179	
17:25	MSLK, 253; UP 2:165	19:39	MSLK, 282; UP 2:180	
17:26	MSLK, 253; UP 2:165	19:41		SH 2:231
17:27	MSLK, 254; UP 2:165	19:43–44	MSLK, 284; UP 2:180	
17:29	MSLK, 254; UP 2:166	19:46	MSLK, 285; UP 2:181	
17:30	MSLK, 255; UP 2:166	19:47	MSLK, 285; UP 2:181	
17:31	MSLK, 255; UP 2:167	20:1–2	MSLK, 286; UP 2:181	
		20:9	MSLK, 287; UP 2:182	

21. Note the printing error: the textual reference in the 1762 edition is "xv. 9," but it should be "xvi. 9."

20:14 — MSLK, 288; UP 2:183

20:15 — MSLK, 288; UP 2:183

13:27	MSJN, 269; UP 2:260	15:24	SH 2:261
13:30	MSJN, 271; UP 2:260	15:26	SH 2:261
13:32	MSJN, 273; UP 2:261	15:26–27	WH 1746, 16
13:33	MSJN, 274; UP 2:262	15:27	SH 2:262
13:34	SH 2:257	16:1–4	HSP 1749, 117
13:36	MSJN, 276; UP 2:262	16:3	SH 2:262
13:37	MSJN, 276; UP 2:262	16:6–7	WH 1746, 17
14:1	SH 2:257	16:7	SH 2:262
14:1–3	HAD 1746, 9	16:7	WH 1746, 19
14:1–4	WH 1746, 15	16:10	WH 1746, 22
14:3	SH 2:257	16:13–15	WH 1746, 25
14:6	SH 2:257	16:15	SH 2:263
14:8–9	HOT 1767, 29	16:18	WH 1746, 20
14:9	SH 2:257	16:20	SH 2:263
14:11	HOT 1767, 14	16:20–22	WH 1746, 27
14:14	SH 2:258	16:22	SH 2:263
14:15	SH 2:258	16:24	HSP 1739, 219
14:15	MSJN, 288; UP 2:263	16:33	SH 2:263
14:16	WH 1746, 10	16:33	MSJN, 349; UP 2:264
14:16–17	WH 1746, 12	17:20	HSP 1740, 192
14:17	HOT 1767, 41, 81	17:21	SH 2:264
14:18–21	WH 1746, 13	17:22	SH 2:264
14:19	SH 2:259	18:15	MSJN, 380; UP 2:265, 266
14:20	HOT 1767, 42	18:16	MSJN, 382; UP 2:266
14:21–23	WH 1746, 14	18:17	MSJN, 382; UP 2:267
14:25–27	WH 1746, 15	18:18	MSJN, 383; UP 2:267
14:26	SH 2:259	18:20	MSJN, 384; UP 2:268
14:26	HOT 1767, 80	18:20	SH 2:264
14:28	HOT 1767, 28	18:25	MSJN, 386; UP 2:268
14:28	MSJN, 298; UP 2:263	18:39	MSJN, 394; UP 2:269
14:30	MSJN, 299; UP 2:263	18:40	MSJN, 394; UP 2:270
15:2	SH 2:259	19:1	MSJN, 396; UP 2:271
15:3	SH 2:259	19:4	MSJN, 398; UP 2:272
15:4	SH 2:260	19:5	SH 2:264
15:5	SH 2:260	[19:5]	HSP 1742, 264
15:7	SH 2:260	19:6	MSJN, 399; UP 2:272
15:14	SH 2:260	19:9	MSJN, 401; UP 2:273, 274
15:15	SH 2:261	19:10	MSJN, 402; UP 2:274
15:16	SH 2:261	19:16	MSJN, 405; UP 2:275
15:16	MSJN, 313; UP 2:264		
15:18–19[22]	HSP 1739, 24		

22. While this poem bears the title "John xv. 18, 19" in HSP 1739, in the fourth edition (1743) and fifth edition (1756), it is titled James 4:4 ("Know ye not that the friendship of the world is enmity with God").

John (*continued*)

19:17	MSJN, 405; UP 2:275
19:26–27	SH 2:232
19:26–27	MSJN, 412; UP 2:276
19:28	SH 2:233
19:28	MS30, 190; UP 2:277
19:30	SH 2:234
19:30	MS30, 193; UP 2:279[23]
19:37	SH 2:265
19:37	HOT 1767, 36
20:16	SH 2:265
20:19	MSJN, 436; UP 2:279
20:22	SH 2:265
[20:28]	HSP 1742, 110
20:28	HOT 1767, 10, 25
21:1	HOT 1767, 21
21:4	MSJN, 442; UP 2:279
21:15	SH 2:265, 266
21:15–16	MSJN, 455; UP 2: 280
21:15–16	SH 2:266
21:18	MSJN, 461; UP 2: 281
21:19	SH 2:266
21:22	SH 2:266

Acts of the Apostles

1:4	HSP 1739, 106
1:4	MSACTS, 2; UP 2:285
1:8	MSACTS, 5; UP 2:285
1:16	HOT 1767, 51
1:17	MSACTS, 10; UP 2:286
1:19	MSACTS, 10, 11; UP 2:286
2:17	MSACTS, 21; UP 2:287
2:19–20	MSACTS, 23; UP 2:288
2:33	MSACTS, 27; UP 2:288
2:33–35	MSACTS, 28; UP 2:289
2:41	HSP 1739, 192
2:44–45	MSACTS, 34; UP 2:289
3:12	MSACTS, 44; UP 2:290
3:13	MSACTS, 44–45; UP 2:291

23. Verses 1, 5, 7, 10 appear with slight variations in *Short Hymns*, 2:234, and in MS John, 412–13.

3:14	HOT 1767, 77
3:14–15	MSACTS, 45; UP 2:291
3:25–26	MSACTS, 53; UP 2:292
4:8	MSACTS, 58; UP 2:293
4:11	MSACTS, 60; UP 2:293
4:16	MSACTS, 76; UP 2:294
4:17	MSACTS, 65; UP 2:294
4:24	HSP 1740, 114
4:24–25	HOT 1767, 51
4:29	SH 2:267
4:29	HSP 1739, 202
4:32	MSACTS, 71; UP 2:295
4:33	MSACTS, 72; UP 2:296, 297
4:34–35	MSACTS, 74; UP 2:297
4:36	MSACTS, 75; UP 2:298
5:3–4	HOT 1767, 44
5:8	MSACTS, 78; UP 2:299
5:9	HOT 1767, 48, 74
5:21	MSACTS, 86; UP 2:300
5:23	MSACTS, 86; UP 2:300
5:28	HOT 1767, 84
5:31	SH 2:267
5:31	MSACTS, 92a, 92c; UP 2:300, 301
5:31	MS CW III(a), 12; UP 2:302
5:34	MSACTS, 93; UP 2:303
5:35	MSACTS, 93; UP 2:303
5:40	MSACTS, 95; UP 2:304
5:41	MSACTS, 96; UP 2:304
6:1	MSACTS, 98; UP 2:305
6:3	MSACTS, 100; UP 2:306
6:4	MSACTS, 101; UP 2:307
6:6	MSACTS, 103; UP 2:308
6:7	MSACTS, 103; UP 2:308
6:11–12	MSACTS, 105; UP 2:309
7:8	MSACTS, 111; UP 2:310
7:14	MSACTS, 115; UP 2:310
7:32	MSACTS, 122; UP 2:311
7:35	MSACTS, 124; UP 2:312
7:40	MSACTS, 127; UP 2:312
7:42	MSACTS, 128; UP 2:313
7:44	MSACTS, 129; UP 2:313
7:51	MSACTS, 131, 132; UP 2:313, 214

Acts of the Apostles (*continued*)

13:2	HOT 1767, 39	15:9	MSACTS, 288; UP 2:367
13:2	MSACTS, 238; UP 2:349	15:11	MSACTS, 292; UP 2:367
13:3	MSACTS, 239; UP 2:350	15:14	MSACTS, 293; UP 2:368
13:4	HOT 1767, 40	15:19	MSACTS, 295; UP 2:368
13:6	MSACTS, 241; UP 2:350	15:22	MSACTS, 296; UP 2:368
13:7	MSACTS, 241; UP 2:351	15:33–34	MSACTS, 301; UP 2:369
13:9	MSACTS, 242; UP 2:351	15:35	MSACTS, 301; UP 2:370
13:17	MSACTS, 247; UP 2:352	16:1	MSACTS, 306; UP 2:370
13:24	MSACTS, 251; UP 2:353	16:2	MSACTS, 306; UP 2:370
13:26	MSACTS, 252; UP 2:354	16:5	MSACTS, 308; UP 2:371
13:27	MSACTS, 253; UP 2:354	16:7	MSACTS, 309; UP 2:372
13:28	MSACTS, 253; UP 2:354	16:9	MSACTS, 310: UP 2:372
13:31	MSACTS, 254; UP 2:355	16:10	MSACTS, 310; UP 2:372
13:32–33	MSACTS, 254; UP 2:355	16:14	SH 2:272
13:33	MSACTS, 254; UP 2:355	16:15	MSACTS, 314; UP 2:373
13:34	MSACTS, 255; UP 2:356	16:18	MSACTS, 316; UP 2:373
13:35	MSACTS, 255; UP 2:356	[16:30]	MSMH 37; UP 2:373
13:38–39	MSACTS, 256; UP 2:357	16:30	SH 2:272
13:39	MSACTS, 257; UP 2:357	16:31	SH 2:272
13:42	MSACTS, 259; UP 2:357	16:31	HSP 1742, 94
13:43	MSACTS, 259; UP 2:358	16:33	MSACTS, 325; UP 2:376
13:45	MSACTS, 260; UP 2:358	16:34	MSACTS, 325; UP 2:376
13:49	MSACTS, 264; UP 2:358	16:38	MSACTS, 328; UP 2:377
14:1	MSACTS, 267; UP 2:359	16:39	MSACTS, 328; UP 2:377
14:2	MSACTS, 268; UP 2:359	17:2–3	MSACTS, 330; UP 2:378
14:5	MSACTS, 270; UP 2:360	17:7	MSACTS, 334; UP 2:379
14:6	MSACTS, 271; UP 2:360	17:11–12	SH 2:272
14:8	MSACTS, 272; UP 2:360	17:18	MSACTS, 343; UP 2:379
14:9	MSACTS, 272; UP 2:361	17:30	MSACTS, 350; UP 2:380
14:10	MSACTS, 272, 273; UP 2:361	17:32	MSACTS, 354; UP 2:381
14:11	MSACTS, 273; UP 2:362	18:1	MSACTS, 356; UP 2:381
14:15	MSACTS, 275; UP 2:362	18:3	MSACTS, 356; UP 2:382
14:16	MSACTS, 275; UP 2:363	18:4	MSACTS, 357; UP 2:382
14:17	MSACTS, 276: UP 2:363	18:5	MSACTS, 357; UP 2:383
14:19	SH 2:270, 271	18:6	MSACTS, 358; UP 2:383
14:22	MSACTS, 278; UP 2:363	18:9	MSACTS, 360; UP 2:384
14:23	MSACTS, 280; UP 2:364	18:10	MSACTS, 360; UP 2:384
14:29–30	HOT 1767, 24	18:12	MSACTS, 361, 362; UP 2:385
15:3	MSACTS, 284; UP 2:365	18:19	MSACTS, 366; UP 2:385
15:5	MSACTS, 286; UP 2:366	18:20	MSACTS, 366; UP 2:386
15:8–9	MSACTS, 554; UP 2:366	18:21	MSACTS, 367; UP 2:386
15:8–9	SH 2:271	18:23	MSACTS, 368; UP 2:387
		18:28	MSACTS, 374; UP 2:388

2:13	HOT 1767, 43
2:16	HOT 1767, 74
3:13–14	MSSH, 35; UP 2:462
3:16	HOT 1767, 45
4:4	MSSH, 37; UP 2:463
4:8	SH 2:289
4:13	SH 2:290
4:19	SH 2:290
4:20	SH 2:291
5:6	MSSH, 38; UP 2:464
5:20	HOT 1767, 14
5:11	SH 2:291
6:10	SH 2:291
6:14	HOT 1767, 83
6:19	SH 2:291
6:19	HOT 1767, 45
6:20	SH 2:292
8:1	SH 2:292
8:6	HOT 1767, 25
9:27	SH 2:293
10:9	HOT 1767, 9, 74
[10:11]	HSP 1740, 71
10:12	SH 2:293
10:31	SH 2:294
11:3	HOT 1767, 28
12:3	MSSH, 41; UP 2:464
12:11	HOT 1767, 86
12:16	HOT 1767, 86
12:31	SH 2:294
13:13	SH 2:294
14:15	HSP 1749, 2:255
14:25	HOT 1767, 41, 81
15:10	SH 2:295
15:36	SH 2:295
15:42	SH 2:295
15:24	HOT 1767, 19
15:27	HOT 1767, 30
15:28	HOT 1767, 20
15:43	SH 2:206
15:44	SH 2:206
15:51–52	SH 2:206
16:14	SH 2:297
16:22	SH 2:297
16:22	MSCH, 209; UP 2:466

2 Corinthians

1:3	HOT 1767, 46
3:5–6	HOT 1767, 84
3:17	SH 2:298
4:11	SH 2:299
4:17	SH 2:299
5:4	SH 2:299
5:5	SH 2:300
5:7	SH 2:301
5:14	SH 2:301
[5:14]	HSP 1749, 1:198
5:17	SH 2:301, 302
5:19	HOT 1767, 12
5:20	SH 2:302
6:2	SH 2:301
6:10	SH 2:302
6:16	HOT 1767, 82
11:27	SH 2:302
11:29	MSSH, 54; UP 2:466
12:6	SH 2:302, 303
12:7	SH 2:303
12:8	SH 2:304
12:9	SH 2:304, 305
12:9	MSMH, 302; UP 2:467
12:9	HOT 1767, 76
12:11	SH 2:305
12:14	HOT 1767, 68
13:3	HOT 1767, 83
13:5	HOT 1767, 81
13:9	SH 2:305
13:11	SH 2:306
13:14	SH 2:306
13:14	HOT 1767, 68, 81
14:25	HOT 1767, 81

Galatians

1:12	HOT 1767, 32, 80, 82
3:22	HSP 1739, 92
2:20	SH 2:307
4:12	MSSH, 62; UP 2:468
5:16	SH 2:308
5:17	SH 2:308

Galatians (*continued*)

5:17	HSP 1749, 2:154
5:19–20	SH 2:308
5:22–23	SH 2:309
5:24	SH 2:309
6:2	HOT 1767, 73
6:3	MSSH, 66; UP 2:469
6:15	SH 2:310
6:16	SH 2:311
6:17	SH 2:311

Ephesians

1:7	SH 2:312
1:22	HOT 1767, 78
2:8	SH 2:312
3:2–3	HOT 1767, 32
3:7	HOT 1767, 75
3:17	HOT 1767, 82
4:8	HOT 1767, 34
4:8, 11f.	HSP 1749, 2:176
4:26	SH 2:313
4:32	HOT 1767, 22
5:5	SH 2:313
5:14	SH 2:313
5:22–24	SH 2:314
5:25	SH 2:314
5:25	HOT 1767, 22
5:27	HOT 1767, 31
5:30	SH 2:314
6[24]	HSP 1749, 1:236
6:13	SH 2:315

Philippians

1:10	HOT 1767, 37
1:21	SH 2:315
2:3	SH 2:316
2:27	SH 2:316
[2:5]	HSP 1742, 221
2:13	HSP 1749, 2:231, 232, 233
3:12	SH 2:316
3:12	HSP 1749, 2:172, 173
3:13	SH 2:317
3:13	HSP 1749, 2:175
3:15	HOT 1767, 82
3:20–21	HOT 1767, 30
4:6–7	DDCW 7/122a[25]; UP 3:432

Colossians

1:12	SH 2:318
1:23	SH 2:318
1:24	SH 2:319
1:27	SH 2:320
2:8–9	HOT 1767, 15
3:1–2	SH 2:320
3:3–4	SH 2:321
3:4	HOT 1767, 79
3:5	SH 2:321, 322
3:8–9	SH 2:322
3:11	HOT 1767, 86
3:13	HOT 1767, 22

1 Thessalonians

1:3	SH 2:323
4:3	HOT 1742, 75
4:3	SH 2:324
4:13	SH 2:324
4:13	HSP 1742, 127
5:10	SH 2:325
5:16	SH 2:325
5:17	SH 2:325

24. The hymn based on Ephesians 6 and titled "The Whole Armour of God" probably first appeared in 1742(?) as a broadsheet, and then was published later that year attached to John Wesley's tract *The Character of a Methodist.* Charles Wesley published the poem in HSP 1749, 1:236–39.

25. This is a fragmentary poem of one stanza of eight lines and a second stanza of four lines.

26. This is a fragmentary poem. There are parts of two stanzas probably intended for eight lines each. Stanza one includes only lines 1–4 and stanza two only lines 3–8. The access number of the John Rylands Library for this manuscript reference is MA 1977/583/32.

27. This poem was first published on May 24, 1740 by Charles Wesley as a pamphlet: *Life of Faith* (1740).

2:21	SH 2:383	1:14	SH 2:397
2:22	SH 2:383	1:21	HOT 1767, 42, 75
2:23	SH 2:384	3:9	SH 2:397
2:24	SH 2:384	3:12	HOT 1767, 37
2:25	SH 2:384	3:14	SH 2:398
2:26	SH 2:385	3:15	SH 2:398
3:2	SH 2:386	3:18	HOT 1767, 6
3:17	SH 2:386		
4:1	SH 2:387		
4:2–3	SH 2:387	**1 John**	
4:12	HOT 1767, 73	1:3	HOT 1767, 81
5:7	SH 2:387	1:8	MSSH, 120; UP 2:472
5:8	SH 2:388	1:9	HSP 1742, 224
5:13	MSSH, 109; UP 2:471	2:3[28]	HSP 1740, 123
5:13	SH 2:389	2:10	SH 2:399
5:15	SH 2:389	2:20	SH 2:399
5:17–18	SH 2:389	2:20	HOT 1767, 77
5:20	SH 2:390	3:3	SH 2:399
		3:5	MS CW III(a), 5.3[29];
			MSMH, 221; UP 2:473
1 Peter		3:5	SH 2:400
1:3	HSP 1740, 186	3:6	SH 2:400
1:5	SH 2:391	3:7	SH 2:400
2:7–8	HOT 1767, 3	3:8	SH 2:401
2:17	SH 2:392	[3:18]	HSP 1740, 118
2:21	SH 2:393	3:24	SH 2:401
[2:21]	HSP 1749, 2:3	3:29	HOT 1767, 9
3:8	SH 2:393, 394	4:1	MSSH, 135; UP 2:473
3:18	MSSH, 110; UP 2:471	4:1	SH 2:401, 402
3:18	HOT 1767, 83	4:18	SH 2:402
4:7	SH 2:394	4:19	SH 2:402
4:14	SH 2:394	5:3	SH 2:403
4:18	SH 2:395	[5:4]	HSP 1749, 160
5:5	SH 2:395	5:4	HOT 1767, 39
5:7	SH 2:396	5:6	MSSH, 136; UP 2:474
5:10	SH 2:396	5:6	HOT 1767, 77

2 Peter

1:1	HOT 1767, 11
1:4	HOT 1767, 33
1:10	SH 2:397
1:11	SH 2:397

28. The same poem appears in HGEL 1741, but with the biblical reference 1 John 2:1–2.

29. MS CW III(a) has a variant version in shorthand. The access number of the John Rylands Library for this manuscript reference is MA 1977/594/7.

1 John (*continued*)

5:7	HOT 1767, 69
5:13	SH 2:403
5:20	HOT 1767, 15
5:21	SH 2:403
5:24	HOT 1767, 44

2 John

v. 2	SH 2:405
v. 3	SH 2:405
v. 6	SH 2:406
v. 9	SH 2:406

3 John

v. 3	SH 2:407
v. 4	SH 2:407
v. 9	SH 2:407
v. 11	SH 2:407

Jude

v. 1	HOT 1767, 85
v. 4	HOT 1767, 31
vv. 14–15	SH 2:409
vv. 20–21	SH 2:410
vv. 21	SH 2:410
vv. 24	SH 2:410
vv. 24–25	HOT 1767, 31

Revelation of John

1:1	SH 2:411
1:3	SH 2:412
1:4–5	SH 2:412
1:5	SH 2:413
1:5–6	SH 2:413
1:4–6	HSP 1742, 278
1:7	HSP 1742, 279
1:8	HOT 1767, 18
1:10	SH 2:414
[1:]10–11f.	HSP 1742, 280

1:11	SH 2:414
1:17	SH 2:415
2:1	HSP 1742, 284
2:2, 7	SH 2:415
[2:]7	HSP 1742, 286
[2:]8–9f.	HSP 1742, 287
2:9	SH 2:416
2:10	SH 2:416
2:11	SH 2:416
2:17	SH 2:416
[2:]12–13f.	HSP 1742, 288
[2:]18–19f.	HSP 1742, 290
2:21	SH 2:417
2:23	HOT 1767, 33
2:25	SH 2:418
2:26–27	SH 2:418
3:1–2f.	HSP 1742, 292
3:2	SH 2:419
3:5	SH 2:419
3:7	HOT 1767, 77
[3:]7	HSP 1742, 294
3:10	SH 2:420
3:11	SH 2:420
3:12	SH 2:420
[3:]14	HSP 1742, 296
3:17	SH 2:421
3:17	HSP 1742, 42, 43
3:18	SH 2:422
3:19	MSPr (MS CW 1[q], #3a);[30] UP 3:432
3:19	SH 2:423
3:20	SH 2:423
3:21	SH 2:424
4:8	HOT 1767, 69
5:9	HOT 1767, 35
5:9–10	SH 2:424
5:12	SH 2:425
6:13	SH 2:426
8:1	SH 2:426

30. This is a fragmentary poem of only one stanza. The access number of the John Rylands Library for this manuscript reference is MA 1977/583/32.

12:10–12	SH 2:426
14:11	SH 2:427, 428
14:13	SH 2:428
15:3	SH 2:428
15:4	HOT 1767, 77
16	HLE 1756, 10
16:15	SH 2:429
17	HLE 1756, 10
19:6	SH 2:429
19:10	SH 2:429
19:11	HEI 1759, 11
22:4	SH 2:429
22:6, 16	HOT 1767, 6
22:12	HOT 1767, 38
22:13	HOT 1767, 5, 76
22:17	SH 2:430, 431
22:20	SH 2:431
22:21	SH 2:432
[22:17]	HSP 1742, 301